Transformations of the State

Series Editors: **Achim Hurrelmann**, Carleton University, Canada; **Stephan Leibfried**, University of Bremen, Germany; **Kerstin Martens**, University of Bremen, Germany; **Peter Mayer**, University of Bremen, Germany.

Titles include:

Joan DeBardeleben and Achim Hurrelmann *(editors)*
DEMOCRATIC DILEMMAS OF MULTILEVEL GOVERNANCE
Legitimacy, Representation and Accountability in the European Union

Klaus Dingwerth
THE NEW TRANSNATIONALISM
Transnational Governance and Democratic Legitimacy

Achim Hurrelmann, Steffen Schneider and Jens Steffek *(editors)*
LEGITIMACY IN AN AGE OF GLOBAL POLITICS

Achim Hurrelmann, Stephan Leibfried, Kerstin Martens and Peter Mayer *(editors)*
TRANSFORMING THE GOLDEN-AGE NATION STATE

Anja P. Jakobi
INTERNATIONAL ORGANIZATIONS AND LIFELONG LEARNING
From Global Agendas to Policy Diffusion

Kerstin Martens, Alessandra Rusconi and Kathrin Leuze *(editors)*
NEW ARENAS OF EDUCATION GOVERNANCE
The Impact of International Organizations and Markets on Educational Policy Making

Kerstin Martens, Alexander-Kenneth Nagel, Michael Windzio and Ansgar Weymann *(editors)*
TRANSFORMATION OF EDUCATION POLICY

Thomas Rixen
THE POLITICAL ECONOMY OF INTERNATIONAL TAX GOVERNANCE

Peter Starke
RADICAL WELFARE STATE RETRENCHMENT
A Comparative Analysis

Jens Steffek, Claudia Kissling, Patrizia Nanz *(editors)*
CIVIL SOCIETY PARTICIPATION IN EUROPEAN AND GLOBAL GOVERNANCE
A Cure for the Democratic Deficit?

Michael J. Warning
TRANSNATIONAL PUBLIC GOVERNANCE
Networks, Law and Legitimacy

Hartmut Wessler, Bernhard Peters, Michael Brüggemann, Katharina Kleinen-von Königslöw, Stefanie Sifft
TRANSNATIONALIZATION OF PUBLIC SPHERES

Hartmut Wessler *(editor)*
PUBLIC DELIBERATION AND PUBLIC CULTURE
The Writings of Bernhard Peters, 1993–2005

Jochen Zimmerman, Jörg R. Werner, Philipp B. Volmer
GLOBAL GOVERNANCE IN ACCOUNTING
Public Power and Private Commitment

Transformations of the State
Series Standing Order ISBN 978-1-4039-8544-6 (hardback) 978-1-4039-8545-3 (paperback)

You can receive future titles in this series as they are published by placing a standing order. Please contact your bookseller or, in case of difficulty, write to us at the address below with your name and address, the title of the series and one of the ISBNs quoted above.

Customer Services Department, Macmillan Distribution Ltd, Houndmills, Basingstoke, Hampshire RG21 6XS, England

This illustration is taken from the original etching in Thomas Hobbes' *Leviathan* of 1651. Palgrave Macmillan and the editors are grateful to Lucila Muñoz-Sanchez and Monika Sniegs for their help in redesigning the original to illustrate what "transformations of the state" might mean. The inscription at the top of the original frontispiece reads *"non est potestas Super Terram quae Comparetur ei"* (Job 41.33): "there is no power on earth which can be compared to him". In the Bible, this refers to the sea-monster, Leviathan. (Original Leviathan image reprinted courtesy of the British Library.)

Transformation of Education Policy

Edited By

Kerstin Martens
Associate Professor of International Relations, University of Bremen, Germany

Alexander-Kenneth Nagel
Assistant Professor of Sociology of Religion, Ruhr-University, Bochum, Germany

Michael Windzio
Professor of Sociology, Department of Social Sciences, University of Bremen, Germany

Ansgar Weymann
Professor of Sociology, Department of Social Sciences, University of Bremen, Germany

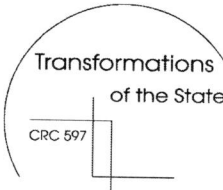

Editorial matter and selection © Kerstin Martens, Alexander-Kenneth Nagel, Michael Windzio, Ansgar Weymann 2010
All remaining chapters © respective authors 2010

All rights reserved. No reproduction, copy or transmission of this publication may be made without written permission.

No portion of this publication may be reproduced, copied or transmitted save with written permission or in accordance with the provisions of the Copyright, Designs and Patents Act 1988, or under the terms of any licence permitting limited copying issued by the Copyright Licensing Agency, Saffron House, 6-10 Kirby Street, London EC1N 8TS.

Any person who does any unauthorized act in relation to this publication may be liable to criminal prosecution and civil claims for damages.

The authors have asserted their rights to be identified as the authors of this work in accordance with the Copyright, Designs and Patents Act 1988.

First published 2010 by
PALGRAVE MACMILLAN

Palgrave Macmillan in the UK is an imprint of Macmillan Publishers Limited, registered in England, company number 785998, of Houndmills, Basingstoke, Hampshire RG21 6XS.

Palgrave Macmillan in the US is a division of St Martin's Press LLC,
175 Fifth Avenue, New York, NY 10010.

Palgrave Macmillan is the global academic imprint of the above companies and has companies and representatives throughout the world.

Palgrave® and Macmillan® are registered trademarks in the United States, the United Kingdom, Europe and other countries.

ISBN: 978–0–230–24634–8 hardback

This book is printed on paper suitable for recycling and made from fully managed and sustained forest sources. Logging, pulping and manufacturing processes are expected to conform to the environmental regulations of the country of origin.

A catalogue record for this book is available from the British Library.

A catalog record for this book is available from the Library of Congress.

10　9　8　7　6　5　4　3　2　1
19　18　17　16　15　14　13　12　11　10

Printed and bound in Great Britain by
CPI Antony Rowe, Chippenham and Eastbourne

Contents

List of Illustrations	vii
List of Abbreviations	ix
Acknowledgments by the Editors	xii
Series Editors' Preface	xiii
Notes on Contributors	xv

Part I Theory and Methods

1. Introduction—Education Policy in Transformation
   Alexander-Kenneth Nagel, Kerstin Martens, and Michael Windzio — 3

2. Measuring Transformation of Education Policy—a Mixed-Method Approach
   Alexander-Kenneth Nagel, Tonia Bieber, Anja P. Jakobi, Philipp Knodel, Dennis Niemann, and Janna Teltemann — 28

Part II Historical Settings

3. The Educating State—Historical Developments and Current Trends
   Ansgar Weymann — 53

Part III Country Case Studies

4. Turn of the Tide—New Horizons in German Education Policymaking through IO Influence
   Dennis Niemann — 77

5. Playing the Multilevel Game in Education—the PISA Study and the Bologna Process Triggering Swiss Harmonization
   Tonia Bieber — 105

6. What's England Got to Do with It? British Underestimation of International Initiatives in Education Policy
   Philipp Knodel and Heiko Walkenhorst — 132

7	Education Policy in New Zealand—Successfully Navigating the International Market for Education *Michael Dobbins*	153
8	A Contrasting Case—the U.S.A. and Its Weak Response to Internationalization Processes in Education Policy *Michael Dobbins and Kerstin Martens*	179

Part IV Comparative Analyses

9	Comparing Education Policy Networks *Alexander-Kenneth Nagel*	199
10	The Internationalization of Education Policy in a Cross-National Perspective *Anja P. Jakobi, Janna Teltemann, and Michael Windzio*	227

Conclusion

11	Education Policy, Globalization, and the Changing Nation State—Accelerating and Retarding Conditions *Michael Windzio, Kerstin Martens, and Alexander-Kenneth Nagel*	261

Index   277

Illustrations

Tables

1.1	Principled beliefs of education	16
3.1	University attendance in Europe, 1910–1995 (number of students compared to the number of 20–24-year-olds)	60
5.1	The instruments of the reform project "HarmoS"	114
9.1	Structural change, synopsis	206
9.2	Positional change	210
9.3	Sending ranks of international actors	214
9.4	Degrees of change	223
10.1	Welfare regimes in countries of this study	232
10.2	Change of selected indicators of secondary and tertiary education	236
10.3	Outcomes of secondary education policy—math achievement and inequality, OLS regressions	244
10.4	Output of secondary education policy—school autonomy indicators, OLS regressions	245
10.5	Determinants of delta-convergence—Finland's education policy as an ideal-type, OLS regressions	246
10.6	Institutional and political determinants of tertiary education policies—fixed and random effects models	248
10.7	Institutional and political determinants of tertiary education policies—random effects models, EU countries	249
10A.1	Output of secondary education policy—school autonomy indicators and level of teachers' input, OLS regressions	255

Figures

1.1	Theoretical model for explaining changing education policymaking	17
1.2	Research design and case selection	20
2.1	Methodological pluralism in a multidimensional setting	31
2.2	Mixed-methods network	46
3.1	Front-page coverage of education	68

3.2	International coverage of education (percentage of all front-page articles on education)	68
4.1	The education system of the Federal Republic of Germany	81
5.1	The Swiss education system	108
7.1	Relationships between key actors in the tertiary education system	166
9.1	National education politics: Modes of political interaction	203
9.2	Change of density	207
9.3	Change of centralization	208
9.4	International actors in the German policy network	216
9.5	International actors in the Swiss policy network	218
9.6	International actors in the English policy network	219
9.7	International actors in the New Zealand policy network	221
10.1	PISA reading achievement	237
10.2	Share of students in the working population	238

Abbreviations

AICGS	American Institute for Contemporary German Studies
ASPAC	Asia Pacific Network of Science and Technology Centres
B.A.	Bachelor's degree
BBT	Bundesamt für Berufsbildung und Technologie
	Federal Office for Professional Education and Technology
BFS	Bundesamt für Statistik
	Federal Statistical Office
BFUG	Bologna Follow-up Group
BMBF	Bundesministerium für Bildung und Forschung
	Federal Ministry of Education and Research
CEO	Chief Executive Officer
CRUS	Rektorenkonferenz der Schweizer Universitäten
	Rectors' Conference of the Swiss Universities
DAAD	Deutscher Akademischer Austausch Dienst
	German Academic Exchange Service
DCSF	Department for Children, Schools and Families
DIUS	Department for Innovation, Universities and Skills
ECTS	European Credit Transfer and Accumulation System
EDI	Eidgenössisches Departement des Innern
	Federal Department of Home Affairs
EDK	Konferenz der kantonalen Erziehungsdirektoren
	Swiss Conference of Cantonal Ministers of Education
ERASMUS	European Region Action Scheme for the Mobility of University Students
ERO	Education Review Office
ETH	Eidgenössische Technische Hochschule
	Swiss Federal Institute of Technology
EU	European Union
EUA	European University Association
EVD	Eidgenössisches Volkswirtschaftsdepartement
	Federal Department of Economic Affairs
FAZ	Frankfurter Allgemeine Zeitung
FE	Fixed Effects
FH	Fachhochschule
	University of Applied Sciences

GATS	General Agreement on Trade and Services
GCSE	General Certificate of Secondary Education
GDP	Gross Domestic Product
GEW	Gewerkschaft Erziehung und Wissenschaft *Union for Education and Science*
GNI	Gross National Income
HarmoS	Interkantonale Vereinbarung über die Harmonisierung der obligatorischen Schule *Intercantonal Agreement on the Harmonization of Obligatory Schooling*
HDI	Human Development Index
HEPI	Higher Education Policy Institute
HRG	Hochschulrahmengesetz *Framework Act for Higher Education*
IHEP	Institute for Higher Education Policy
IO	International Organization
IQB	Institut zur Qualitätsentwicklung im Bildungswesen *Institute for Educational Progress*
KFH	Rektorenkonferenz der Fachhochschulen der Schweiz *Rectors' Conference of the Swiss Universities of Applied Sciences*
KMK	Kultusministerkonferenz *The Standing Conference of the Ministers of Education and Cultural Affairs of the Länder in the Federal Republic of Germany*
M.A.	Master's degree
NCLB	No Child Left Behind Act
NRW	North Rhine-Westphalia
NZBRT	New Zealand Business Roundtable
NZQA	New Zealand Qualifications Authority
NZUSA	New Zealand Union of Students' Associations
NZVCC	New Zealand Vice-Chancellors' Committee
OAQ	Organ für Akkreditierung und Qualitätssicherung der schweizerischen Hochschulen *Center of Accreditation and Quality Assurance of the Swiss Universities*
OECD	Organisation for Economic Cooperation and Development
OFFA	Office of Fair Access
OLS	Ordinary Least Squares
OMC	Open Method of Coordination
PBRF	Performance Based Research Fund

PH	University of Teacher Education
Ph.D.	Doctor of Philosophy
PISA	Programme for International Student Assessment
PNA	Policy Network Analysis
PolCon V	Political Constraints Index
PT-Ratio	Pupil/Teacher Ratio
QA	Quality Assurance
quango	Quasi Nongovernmental Organization
RE	Random Effects
SATS	Key Stage National Curriculum Tests
SBF	Staatssekretariat für Bildung und Forschung *State Secretariat for Education and Research*
SE	Secondary Education
SGB	Schweizerischer Gewerkschaftsbund *Swiss Federation of Trade Unions*
SUK	Schweizerische Universitätskonferenz *Swiss University Conference*
TEC	Tertiary Education Commission
TES	Tertiary Education Strategy
TIMSS	Third International Mathematics and Science Study
UGC	University Grants Commission
UK	United Kingdom
UNESCO	United Nations Educational, Scientific and Cultural Organization
U.S.A./U.S.	United States of America
VERA	VERgleichsArbeiten in der Grundschule *Comparative Tests in Primary Education*
WHO	World Health Organization

Acknowledgments by the Editors

This volume is the result of a challenging endeavor: to study a recent and ongoing phenomenon such as the transformation of education policy from a dynamic and comparative perspective. This challenge could not have been met without close collaboration and the expertise and enthusiasm of many.

First of all, the editors are deeply indebted to Reinhold Sackmann, now Professor of Sociology in Halle, Germany, for his pioneering efforts and the programmatic and conceptual initiation of the research project. Work started in 2003 when the Collaborative Research Center "Transformations of the State" (*TranState Research Center*) was established.

Second, the volume draws closely from the work of former colleagues, namely Kathrin Leuze, now Assistant Professor at the Social Science Research Center, Berlin; Alessandra Rusconi, now Senior Researcher at the Social Science Research Center, Berlin; Carolin Balzer, now policy advisor for the internationalization of education for the Hanseatic City of Bremen; and Tilman Brand, now research fellow at the Criminological Research Institute of Lower Saxony, Hanover. Their conceptual contributions provided important steps for the considerations and results to be presented here.

Last, but not least, we owe a debt of gratitude to Dieter Wolf, Executive Manager of the TranState Research Center, and Stephan Leibfried, Director of the TranState Research Center for extensive advice and general support.

The TranState Research Center is funded by the German Research Foundation (Deutsche Forschungsgemeinschaft—DFG). We would like to thank Alexander Akbik, Paula van Aken, Anne Bock, Michael Dobbins, Frederik Elwert, Celia Enders, Julia Engelbrecht, Camille Farnoux, Andrew Gelbach, Steffen Hagemann, Jan Kellerhoff, Maren Liedmeier, Till Ludwig, Marie Popp, Patrick Rauch, Tobias Singer, Deike Striez, Svenja Stropahl, Gesa Schulze, Maren Sennhenn, and Philipp Weiskirch for their assistance during different conceptual and editorial stages.

Bremen and Bochum, December 2009
Kerstin Martens
Alexander-Kenneth Nagel
Michael Windzio
Ansgar Weymann

Series Editors' Preface

When we wonder about the future of the modern state, we encounter a puzzling variety of scholarly diagnoses and prophecies. Some authors predict nothing less than the end of the state as a prudent model of how to organize a society. They see a collapsing giant whose foothold has been eroded in a dynamic global economy and by a continuous flow of political decision-making powers up to supranational bodies. Others disagree profoundly. They point to the remarkable resilience of the state and its core institutions. Even in the age of global markets and politics, for them the state remains the ultimate guarantor of security, democracy, welfare, and the rule of law. These controversies raise vexing questions for the social sciences: What is happening to the modern liberal nation-state of the OECD-world? Is it an outdated model or still fit to serve or is it in need of modest or far-reaching reforms?

The state is a complex entity, providing so many different services and regulating so many areas of everyday life. There can be no quick and easy answer to these questions. In our series on the "Transformations of the State," we will try to disaggregate the tasks and functions of the state into four key, but manageable dimensions:

- the monopolization of the means of force,
- the rule of law as prescribed and safeguarded by the constitution,
- the guarantee of democratic self-governance, and
- the provision of welfare and the assurance of social cohesion.

At least in the OECD-world of the 1960s and 1970s it became the central characteristic of the modern state that these four institutional aspects had merged and that they supported each other and had turned into a 'synergetic constellation'. This series is devoted to empirical and theoretical studies exploring the transformations of this historical model and the promises it still holds for us today and in the future. The volumes will report on research on one or several of these dimensions, in all of which crucial change seems to be taking place. Although political science will often take the lead, many books will be interdisciplinary in nature and may also take the perspective of law, economics, history, and sociology. We hope that taken together these volumes will provide its readers with the "state of the art" on the "state of the state."

Achim Hurrelmann, Stephan Leibfried,
Kerstin Martens, and Peter Mayer

Notes on Contributors

Tonia Bieber is a Research Fellow at the TranState Research Center "Transformations of the State" at the University of Bremen, Germany.

Michael Dobbins is a Senior Researcher at the University of Konstanz and an associate of the TranState Research Center "Transformations of the State" at the University of Bremen, Germany.

Anja P. Jakobi is a Senior Researcher at the Peace Research Institute Frankfurt (PRIF/HSFK), Germany.

Philipp Knodel is a Research Fellow at the TranState Research Center "Transformations of the State" at the University of Bremen, Germany.

Kerstin Martens is Associate Professor of International Relations at the University of Bremen, Germany.

Alexander-Kenneth Nagel is Assistant Professor at the University of Bochum and an associate of the TranState Research Center "Transformations of the State" at the University of Bremen, Germany.

Dennis Niemann is a Research Fellow at the TranState Research Center "Transformations of the State" at the University of Bremen, Germany.

Janna Teltemann is a Research Fellow at the Institute for Empirical and Applied Sociology (EMPAS) and an associate of the TranState Research Center "Transformations of the State", both at the University of Bremen, Germany.

Heiko Walkenhorst is Head of Unit "Northern Europe" at the German Academic Exchange Service (DAAD) and an associate of the TranState Research Center "Transformations of the State" at the University of Bremen, Germany.

Ansgar Weymann is Professor of Sociology at the University of Bremen, Germany.

Michael Windzio is Professor of Sociology at the University of Bremen, Germany.

Part I
Theory and Methods

1
Introduction—Education Policy in Transformation

Alexander-Kenneth Nagel, Kerstin Martens, and Michael Windzio

2010 is an "education year": the results of the "Programme for International Student Assessment" (PISA)—the largest survey on students' performance—are being published again and will continue for another round of three evaluations; the Bologna Process—the largest project to provide Europe with a comparative higher education degree system—is supposed to be implemented within the region. Although the PISA Study and the Bologna Process have by now established themselves as prominent political issues with substantial impact on the political debate all over Europe and beyond, scholars of political science and political sociology have been rather reluctant to give this field the attention needed. This volume analyzes the significant changes in the field of education policy observable since the 1990s. It deals with the impact of the PISA Study and the Bologna Process as the most prominent examples with regard to the growing role of international organizations (IOs) and their impact on national education systems.

In this volume we therefore address the following question: how and to what extent are international initiatives, in particular the PISA Study and the Bologna Process, shaping national education systems? Whereas education policy was traditionally strongly connected to the nation state as part of domestic public politics, in recent years new developments in the international sphere have challenged the role of the state in this field. Therefore education policy no longer seems to be a domestic area in which government activity, supervision, and control are particularly strong and (almost) exclusive, rather these internationalization processes exert influence on national education systems. The PISA Study and the Bologna Process are currently the most outstanding examples of internationalization in education policy which may transform national policymaking in this field. They provide the framework for the cases studied in this volume:

- The PISA Study is the largest international comparative education study surveying the competencies and skills of 15-year-olds. According to the Organisation for Economic Cooperation and Development (OECD), it assesses "how far students near the end of compulsory education have acquired some of the knowledge and skills that are essential for full participation in society."[1] PISA covers reading, mathematical skills, and scientific literacy, with a particular emphasis on one of these subjects in each assessment cycle. Since the year 2000 it has been conducted every three years with the results being published the following year. More and more countries are joining the PISA Study: whereas in 2000 the survey was conducted in 43 countries, 66 are registered for participation in the fourth assessment in 2009/10.
- The Bologna Process for a European Higher Education Area is a political initiative within and beyond Europe to increase the compatibility of tertiary education in countries as diverse as Albania and the UK. Its "action lines" encompass implementing the three-cycle-system (B.A., M.A., Ph.D.), enhancing mobility and recognition, promoting quality assurance, and increasing employability, as well as strengthening the social dimension in higher education and enabling lifelong learning. The process was initialized in 1998 by four western European countries with the so-called Sorbonne Declaration and launched with the subsequent Bologna Declaration one year later. Since then it has expanded throughout Europe to a total of 46 member countries. The impact of the Bologna Process is backed and enhanced by the European Union (EU), which takes part as a full member and has implemented the process into its own agenda of education policy as a part of the Lisbon Strategy.

This introduction sets the stage for the book, which shows how education policy has increasingly become internationalized, in particular through the activities of IOs. It then provides the theoretical framework for the whole book, highlighting what we call "IO governance" as a driving force for change of national education policymaking and "national transformation capacities," which we conceptualize as veto players and points, as well as guiding principles of education policy, as the mediating factors which influence the direction and the degree of such change.[2] We thus combine well-established approaches from both

International Relations Theory and policy analysis research in order to explore the phenomena of internationalized education policy and its impact on national policymaking.

In the empirical part, our book comprises five in-depth country case studies on Germany, Switzerland, England, New Zealand, and—as a contrasting case—the United States (U.S.). These countries are members of different IOs and demonstrate different transformation capacities. We combine these case studies with comparative analyses in order to embed our results from the individual studies: network analysis allows for comparisons across the single country cases whereas quantitative regression analysis of the OECD world enables us to embed our results in a broader context of the industrialized world.

Internationalizing education policy

In the OECD world education policy is now considered to be a significant part of the "normative good" welfare which is provided by the state (Hurrelmann et al. 2007: 3). With the development of the modern state, education policy has increasingly been incorporated into national policymaking (for historical details see Weymann, Chapter 3 in this volume). The state integrates education policy into its realm of responsibilities as it prepares its citizens for participation in the polity and the labor market (Torres 2002). Nowadays, education policy is structured and paid for mainly by the nation state which is, in turn, responsible for outcomes in this sector.

However, with the growing demands of the labor markets, increasing costs for public education institutions, and demographic challenges, the education sector comes increasingly under pressure. As shown in previous publications of our group, one of the consequences of such developments is that education policy has developed into an internationalized field of policymaking since the 1990s when new arenas of governance emerged (Martens, Rusconi, and Leuze 2007). Our argument is that IOs initiated a process of internationalization of education policy outcomes. They did so by enhancing national viewpoints with an international comparative perspective. Additionally, IOs extended their responsibilities, competencies and their ability more or less specifically to recommend nation states to change their education policies.

The two examples of international initiatives in education policy to be examined in this book are particularly prominent cases in the wide reach of these education processes. The latest 2009 PISA Study includes not only the 30 members of the OECD, but also 36 nonmembers. For example Thailand, Qatar, and Uruguay are taking part in the examination; similarly, the Bologna Process also transcends the European region and includes countries on the Asian periphery such as Turkey and Azerbaijan. Moreover, universities outside the Bologna Process also are adapting to this framework. For example, the University of Melbourne was the first Australian university to tailor its degree system according to the Bologna scheme.

As a consequence of these processes, education policy has been in transformation in many countries over the last decade. Unlike previous international projects and programs, the PISA Study and the Bologna Process have been widely received at the national level. With its PISA Study, the OECD, for example, initiated heated debates about the effectiveness and efficiencies of the secondary school system in various countries (Bogdandy and Goldmann 2008/2009; Martens and Niemann 2009; Martens and Wolf 2006; Rinne, Kallo, and Hokka 2004). The Bologna Process and the closely related Lisbon Agenda of the EU even propose a completely new structure for the higher education systems for the participating countries (Balzer and Rusconi 2007; Corbett 2005; Walkenhorst 2008).

But how could IOs become prominent actors in education policy, despite the fact that education policy as a policy field is closely attached to nation states? As we argued in earlier work, the states themselves actually triggered such self-transformation processes (Hurrelmann et al. 2007; for education policy see Martens and Weymann 2007). With regard to PISA for example, national governments, in particular the U.S. and France, wanted to instrumentalize the OECD to promote national reforms and to overcome domestic opposition (Martens 2007; Martens and Wolf 2006). Similarly, the Bologna Process finds its roots in an agreement between France, Germany, Italy, and the UK which aimed to elevate higher education onto the European level in order to legitimize national reforms of their education systems (Balzer and Rusconi 2007; Toens 2008).

However, the IOs involved did not simply carry out the tasks as envisioned by the member states wanting them to do so, rather they developed "institutional dynamics," unforeseen by the states which originally initiated such international processes in education policy (for education see Martens and Wolf 2009; on the pathologies of IOs, see Barnett and Finnemore 2004). IOs developed their own agendas for the political tasks they were given by their member states.[3] As regards the PISA Study, countries did not anticipate that the OECD would develop its own tools for generating international education data and indicators to allow for easy comparison between countries with respect to system performance (Martens 2007). In the Bologna Process, initiating countries were not aware that action at the European level would weaken governmental influence in education policy as a whole.

But what effects does this internationalization of education policy have on national education systems? From the perspective of political science and sociology such questions have rarely been addressed; research on the impact of the PISA Study and the Bologna Process has just began (for PISA see for example Grek 2009, Rinne, Kallo, and Hokka 2004 and also http://www.knowandpol.eu for ongoing work on this issue; for Bologna see for example Dobbins 2010; Muche 2005; Reinalda and Kulesza 2005; Witte 2006). In a comparative way, however, internationalization processes such as the PISA Study or the Bologna Process have not been examined comprehensively (for an exception see Münch 2009). With regard to these ongoing internationalization processes in education policy, which affect national educational policymaking, it is in fact surprising that comprehensive research on these issues is still missing.

In this chapter we set up a parsimonious model to examine the interplay between the international and national levels in order to examine how and to what extent education policy is in transformation today as a result of the international initiatives of the PISA Study and the Bologna Process. We argue that IOs may exert influence on national education policymaking through a broad set of governance instruments. However, the impact of such IO governance is moderated by national capacities such as domestic veto players and guiding principles of education policy. These may hinder, block, or foster the initiatives promoted by IOs in the field of education policy. Our model thus combines constructivist approaches of soft governance with rationalist approaches in an eclectic mode in order to explain how and to what extent education policy is changing.

Transformations in national education policymaking

How can we grasp the change that is taking place in the field of education policy because of internationalization processes such as the PISA Study and the Bologna Process? In policy analysis, the three dimensions of *policy, politics*, and *polity* are generally distinguished in order to separate the political process taking place at the national level. Although these levels are obviously interlinked and interdependent, this differentiation allows us to split up the political process and to analyze distinctively the extent of change (see for example Schubert and Bandelow 2003). We argue that education policy can be transformed in all these dimensions by international initiatives such as the PISA Study and the Bologna Process.

First, national education *policy* may be affected through international initiatives as proposed by IOs. For example, through social learning IOs may introduce new political settings, instruments, and goals into the national context (Hall 1993: 288) by initiating debates and by promoting ideas. With its PISA Study, the OECD prominently highlights goals such as the better inclusion of children from low socioeconomic backgrounds or with a migrant background. In the context of the Bologna Process goals such as quality assurance and its surveillance have been emphasized with greater intensity than before.

Second, IOs may also have an impact on domestic education *politics*, and thus on the pattern of actors involved in the domestic decision-making process of a country. For example through the OECD's PISA Study the role of education experts in secondary education has been strengthened significantly. Similarly, the Bologna Process has led to the inclusion of new actors who influence the decisionmaking process in national education politics. For example, the participation of stakeholders, such as higher education institutions and accreditation agencies, has been expanded.

Third, the impact of IOs on national policymaking may indirectly affect the dimension of *polity*, which refers to the design of political institutions and entities, such as the constitution, the parliament, and the legal system. Changes in the dimension of polity may occur as a consequence of changes in policy and politics: for instance, the constitutional power relation between the federal state and the subunits might be reformed in order to implement the challenges triggered by the two international initiatives of the PISA Study and the Bologna Process. For example, in Switzerland, the Constitution was amended in 2006 so that the Confederation gained substantial competences in education policy at the expense of the cantons, while in Germany constitutional revision transferred responsibilities in higher education policy from the Federation to the *Länder* (Criblez 2008).

The proposed differentiation of national education policy is suitable to grasp the impact of different IOs on domestic policies, politics, and polities. Yet the formative power of IOs can only be fully understood from a *comparative perspective* across countries. Although IOs perhaps highlight the different problems of participating education systems they eventually propose one common model through their governance instruments. The OECD obviously promotes an economic view on how education systems are more effective and efficient (Brand 2006). Similarly the Bologna Process aims to introduce a commonly structured degree system allowing for easier access to a European job market (Martens and Wolf 2006).

Ultimately, if all countries successfully followed the models as proposed by international initiatives like the PISA Study or the Bologna Process, countries would obviously converge towards the common model (Heichel and Sommerer 2007; Holzinger and Knill 2005; Holzinger, Jörgens and Knill 2007). Thus, IOs and their governance instruments represent an important driving force which makes countries look more alike in their national education policymaking. Only when comparing the resulting change can we assess whether national policies for education have moved closer to the model as suggested by the IOs. However, *policy convergence* as stimulated by IOs can take different forms, most often differentiated as sigma-, delta-, and beta-convergence (see Heichel, Pape, and Sommerer 2005: 831).

First, *sigma-convergence* refers to the decrease in variation of domestic policies. For example, in the field of higher education, countries are becoming more alike because of the fact that many countries are introducing tuition fees in order to deal with tight state budgets and the rising number of students (Kohlrausch and Leuze 2007). However, increasing similarity between states does not necessarily mean that IOs are the source for convergence. Second, *delta-convergence*, instead, implies that countries are moving toward a common model, for example as suggested by IOs. As regards the PISA Study, such a common model is more implicit than explicit as the OECD does not set strict targets; however, it is possible to extract these targets in a hermeneutic way (see Popp 2010). With respect to the Bologna Process, the proposed model is spelled out rather clearly, for example by introducing a two-cycle degree system of a particular length, accompanied by accreditation and quality assurance. A further concept of policy convergence is beta-convergence. *Beta-convergence* denotes a process of "catching-up" of countries as regards education performance (see Jakobi and Teltemann 2009: 9). Countries that are already close to a certain standard or international goal might show slower change rates than countries that are still far away from this goal. This means that for example countries with a lower share of private expenditure in education tend to show higher increases in this respect than countries that are already relatively highly privatized (see also Sala-i-Martin 1996: 1327).

In brief, we conceptualize education policymaking in transformation by looking at the three dimensions of policy, politics, and polity in order to measure how international initiatives in this field such as the PISA Study and the Bologna Process may influence the national sphere. As such internationalization processes promote one common model, convergence would be the ultimate result. Thus, we would observe that countries restructure their education systems in order to diminish the distance to the internationally proposed models.

IO governance instruments as driving forces of transformations

How can the impact of IOs be grasped in theoretical and conceptual terms? From the perspective of International Relations Theory, the influence of IOs has been conceptualized mainly from a constructivist perspective. In particular, such scholars deal with the question of how IOs exert influence over their member states in the absence of legal means (Barnett and Finnemore 2004; Finnemore 1993, 1996).[4] Both the OECD's PISA Study and the Bologna Process are voluntary processes. In fact, as regards the continuation of the PISA Study, it needs to be renewed every couple of years. Countries may even opt out from the Bologna Process.

In order to measure the mechanisms of how IOs impact on national education policy, Jacobson (1979), for example, highlights five categories of informational activities. These are normative activities, rule-creating activities, rule-supervisory activities, and operational activities. For the case of education McNeely and Cha (1994) distinguish between exchange of information, charters and constitutions, standard setting instruments, and technical and financial resources. For the purposes of this volume, we build on our own earlier studies (Jakobi and Martens 2007; Martens and Balzer 2008) and develop a typology for analyzing the effects of the OECD's PISA Study and the Bologna Process in connection with the EU. For our purposes, we categorize IO instruments as norm setting, opinion formation, financial means, coordinative activities, and consulting services.[5]

First, *norm setting* refers to activities which aim to establish provisions for state policy. In this context, IOs set the standards against which national policies are evaluated and which create normative pressures for the national context of policymaking (Finnemore and Sikkink 1998: 891). As regards the PISA Study, the OECD formulates targets and goals for education systems (OECD 2009). Similarly, in the framework of the

Bologna Process participating countries have to adjust their higher education system along with several action lines, such as the Three-cycle System, Quality Assurance, Recognition, and Employability.

Second, *opinion formation* refers to the capacity of an IO to stimulate and inspire national policy debates by disseminating its own ideas, concepts, and models into national decisionmaking (Finnemore 1993; Finnemore and Sikkink 1998). In the case of the OECD, for example, the IO influences national secondary education through publications available in the context of the PISA Study, promoting more autonomous schools, and emphasizing the significance of integrating children with a migrant background. In the case of Bologna the so-called Trends Reports have been an important vehicle for opinion formation since 1999. Originally set up "in order to gauge the evolving positions and opinions of higher education institutions" (Crosier, Purser, and Smidt 2007: 46), the comparative reports have become a trigger for national discourses.

Third, *financial means* refer to the financial support given by IOs to states to allow them to put into practice programs suggested by the IO (Chayes and Chayes 1995: 25, Chayes, Chayes, and Mitchell 1998: 52–54; Martens and Balzer 2008: 89–90). Such resources may motivate countries to live up to the IO's standards and implement its ideas on the local, regional, and national levels. The OECD usually does not provide financial means; the EU instead has developed a broad set of education programs to foster mobility and the European dimension in education policy and therefore promotes the political agenda of the Bologna Process.

Fourth, *coordinative activities* refer to the capacity of an IO to organize and handle procedures which promote initiatives in a given policy field and therefore reflect "the special capacity of an international organisation to 'pull the strings together'" (Martens et al. 2004: 2). They indirectly influence policymaking by providing support with the implementation of programs and projects concerning, for example, the management and direction of the process (Martens and Balzer 2008: 89). Surveillance is a common tool for checking whether countries comply with the agreed policy targets (Conzelmann 2008; Schäfer 2006). The OECD and the EU, for example, create opportunities for international exchange by bringing together policymakers and scientific experts from different countries to discuss their ideas about how to best implement certain policies. By uniting all relevant actors the IO is able to promote and shape the organizational process.

Fifth, IOs can provide country-specific *consulting services*. Today, nation states might perceive a higher demand for consulting services, especially if the result of the benchmarking process unequivocally suggests a need for changing educational institutions. Even before the first wave of the PISA Study, for instance, the OECD composed a report on the "ecologisation of schools" in Austria (Posch 1998: 12), regarding the embeddedness of learning processes in social, economic, and technical environments. The OECD periodically conducts case studies on nation states and makes policy recommendations in its country reports. In fact, such peer-reviewing counts as a distinct "OECD technique" (Wallace 2000: 32). In the case of Bologna, so-called Bologna Promoters have been appointed to promote higher education reforms on an institutional level.

In brief, we argue that as regards the OECD's PISA Study and the Bologna Process as promoted in the context of the EU, these five governance instruments may be applied. However, it does not mean that they are all applied at the same time. Rather, only some of them may be applied in the context of the specific international initiative in education policy and they may also be applied in a temporary sequence.

National transformation capacities as mediating factors

What national factors account for national variations of change as promoted by IOs? If countries were all the same, international initiatives would have similar effects in all countries exposed to IO governance. Obviously, this is not the case. In order to explain the diversity of reactions to the same international initiatives, national transformation capacities have to be taken into account in order to reach valid results as to the impact of IOs on national education policymaking. Such domestic factors determine if, how, and to what extent IO governance affects the political dimensions in a country. To examine transformations in national education policymaking, we distinguish between two main theoretical approaches: from a rationalist perspective, analyses focus on actors and their institutional opportunities and constraints in the respective political system, while from a constructivist perspective, ideas, norms, and identities are the issues which mainly account for varying degree of change (Fearon and Wendt 2002).

National veto players and points in education as institutional modifiers

Veto players and veto points constitute a significant part of national transformation capacities. As part of the institutional setup, they reflect the overall ability to and willingness for change within a country. Veto players are those actors in a political system who have the power to block or hinder legislative initiatives. This approach usually refers to political actors directly involved in the political process (Tsebelis 1995; Wagschal 1999). Veto points are those institutional frameworks which hinder societal actors from influencing political decisions. This concept thus refers to the structures which enable such actors to participate within the political context (Crepaz and Moser 2004; Huber, Ragin and Stephens 1993; Immergut 1992; Schmidt 2000: 351–55). Rarely has this concept been applied to education policy (for an exception, see Klitgaard 2010). Such an approach helps us to analyze how and to what extent the formal characteristics of a political system influence changes in the field of education policy as promoted by IOs.

In line with Ganghof (2003: 2), we assume that "[t]he basic idea common to all veto player approaches is simple: if some individual or collective actor has veto power..., she will use it to further her interests. More specifically, she will veto policies that go against her interests." For our project in this volume, this means that the orientational frameworks as promoted by IOs are mediated by domestic veto players and their individual political interests or agendas. In the realm of education politics, federalism, which is strong in countries like Germany and Switzerland, creates a rich opportunity structure for veto players, like local ministries, and veto points, such as the Standing Conference of the Ministers of Education and Cultural Affairs ("Kultusministerkonferenz"—KMK) in Germany.

To operationalize veto players, we follow Tsebelis who defines veto players as those "individual or collective actors whose agreement is necessary for a change of the status quo" (1995: 301). In our volume we focus on institutional veto players who are those political actors who possess formal veto power according to a national constitution or alike, such as presidents, first chambers, second chambers, or senates (Tsebelis 1995: 302). For the concept of veto points, we use Immergut's definition:

> Political decisions require agreement at several points along the chain of decisions made in different arenas. The fate of legislative proposals [...] depends upon the number and location of opportunities for veto along this chain. The ability of interest groups to influence such legislative outcomes depends upon their access to the political representatives situated at the "weak links" or veto points in this chain. (Immergut 1992: 396)

The approach of veto players and points allows us "to examine how institutional constellations and individual and collective actors' interests mediate political change brought about by internationalization in the field of education" (Leuze et al. 2008: 13). Moreover, such domestic structures yield explanations as to how states react to IO governance as regards their transformation of education policy. With respect to the OECD's PISA Study and the Bologna Process in connection with the EU, the most important veto players are of course the national (or—in federalist countries—subnational) ministers who have to ratify all follow-up procedures by endorsing a new declaration.

In brief, we assume that the veto players and points of a country may significantly influence whether and to what extent international initiatives under the auspices of IOs, such as the PISA Study and the Bologna Process, are mediated in the national political context. Veto players and points may hinder the impact of IOs as they block such international influence from interfusing the national sphere. This argument is rather simple, but only on the face of it. If there is broad consensus on the acuteness of change in education policy needed to become part of the emerging globalized knowledge society, then actors probably establish new or enact existing institutions which can serve as functional equivalents to complex and interdependent modes of decisionmaking. By anticipating time-consuming policymaking, they could thereby circumvent veto players and points. If successful in doing so, they may be even more responsive to the orientational frameworks as promoted by IOs.

Guiding principles of education as ideational modifiers

Guiding principles are an essential part of a country's transformation capacities. As characterized in earlier work of our research group they are embedded "in the institutional structure and the collective interpretation scheme of a country and predetermine a country's further development to a certain extent by making some paths more likely than others" (Leuze et al. 2008: 14). Guiding principles—also labeled as *Leitideen* (Lepsius 1995; Lepsius 1997), interpretation frameworks (Gerhards and Rucht 2000), or cultural accounts (Meyer, Boli, and Thomas 1994)—present a country's ideational background. They "determin[e] the tracks along which action has been pushed by the dynamic of interest" (Weber 1968: 268).

Following Goldstein and Keohane (1993) ideational factors can be conceptualized on three different levels of concretion such as world views, principled beliefs, and causal beliefs. *World views* are fundamental concepts which "are embedded in the symbolism of a culture and deeply affect modes of thought and discourse" (ibid.: 8). An example for a world view in the realm of education may be that education is a public good in modern societies. *Principled beliefs* are "normative ideas that specify criteria for distinguishing right from wrong" (ibid.: 9). In terms of education policy a principled belief resembles basic understandings about the significance of education as a public good in modern societies, be it a competitive advantage over other countries or a matter of social cohesion. *Causal beliefs* "are beliefs about cause-effect relationships" (ibid.: 10), for example, if an actor believes in the principle of education being a matter of social cohesion he may consider free education a suitable means of expanding participation.

To operationalize national guiding principles we focus on principled beliefs as the more general view of education being a central value and public good that is likely to receive unanimous approval in all modern societies and thus is not apt to create variation across countries. We distinguish four ideal-typical principled beliefs of education. From an economic background education provides a helpful means of improving the competitiveness of a national economy. It serves as a tool to generate a nation's wealth by coordinating investments in human capital (Gellner 1983; Kiker 1966; Mann 1993). From a microperspective, education is a mechanism to increase the returns of private and public *human capital*; from a macroperspective, education is an enabling factor for the growth of productivity and *wealth of nations*. From a standpoint of social cohesion, education is crucial to create a national collective identity and thus to ensure social integration. In modern societies, education is perceived as a means for establishing or maintaining the political integration of a country by providing for a national curriculum, promoting a common language, and disseminating a common history through the education system (Archer 1979; Meyer, Ramirez, and Soysal 1992; Smith 1986). From a microperspective social cohesion thus implies an understanding of education as a means of *self-fulfillment* and personal refinement by taking part in a collective cultural enterprise. From a macroperspective education thus becomes a *social right* which is helpful to overcome the reproduction of social inequalities as it increases each individual's chances for participation in society (Marshall 1965 [1949]). In most developed countries education has also become a *social duty*, since it is considered as a prerequisite to becoming a member of the civilized community.

Table 1.1 distinguishes four types of principled beliefs of education between economy and social cohesion as well as a micro and a macro perspective.

We apply this classification of the guiding principles of education in an ideal-typical way in order to make cross-national variations of the means and concept of education policy visible. Such guiding principles cannot be identified as mere ideas, but are "'coagulated' in institutional settings and thus influence the incentive structure of the political actors and the transaction costs of a political choice" (Leuze et al. 2008: 16). This is so because

> Ideas have a lasting influence on politics through their incorporation into the terms of political debates; but the impact of some set of ideas may be mediated by the operation of institutions in which the ideas are embedded. Once the ideas have influenced organizational design, their influence will be reflected in the incentives of those in the organization and those whose interests are served by it. [...] In this sense ideas can have an impact even when no one genuinely believes in them as principled or causal statements. (Goldstein and Keohane 1993: 20)

In brief, guiding principles in education policy influence a country's capacity for change. As deeply rooted cognitive and normative patterns they shape the discursive environment for political intervention from the international level. Guiding principles resemble national schemes of reference to judge to the plausibility of policy proposals from IOs and thus reflect the ideational component of national transformation capacities.

In sum, we conceptualize a country's national capacities for transformation by integrating two approaches, namely a rationalist veto player/points approach and a constructivist approach on guiding principles.

Table 1.1 Principled beliefs of education

Focus	Economy	Social cohesion
Micro	Human Capital = education as a means to boost individual productivity	Self-fulfillment = education as a means of personal refinement
Macro	Wealth of Nations = education as a location factor of national economies	Social Right and Duty = education as a means of political and social participation

Both have to be taken into account when seeking to analyze how and to what extent international initiatives in education policy, such as the PISA Study and the Bologna Process are received at the national level.

Toward a model for assessing education policy in transformation

Our main argument in this book is that through their education initiatives, such as the OECD's PISA Study or the European Bologna Process with EU involvement, IOs use a wide set of governance instruments in order to influence national education policymaking. Such influence through IOs may lead to a transformation of national education policies, politics, or polities and ultimately to delta-convergence between participating countries, for example, to the best-performer according the benchmarking. However, a country's capacity and willingness to respond to international influences also depends on its national transformation capacities, which include veto players as well as existing guiding principles of education, both of which influence a country's capacity for transforming toward a common model in the different dimensions of policies, politics, and polities. Figure 1.1 illustrates our model of education policy in transformation.

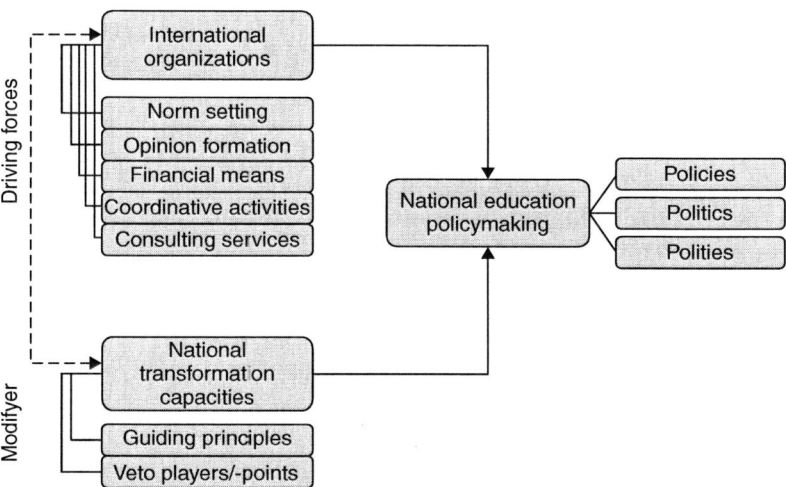

Figure 1.1 Theoretical model for explaining changing education policymaking
Source: Leuze et al. (2008: 19) with variations.

What are the causal relations between the variables we introduce here? We argue that IOs function as "entrepreneurs of (delta-) convergence" (Leuze et al. 2008: 18). Even with their soft governance mechanisms at hand they have the capacity to influence national education policymaking toward the common model they promote. As entrepreneurs, IOs establish an organizational field between participating states that allows for transnational communication, strengthens interaction, and increases the flow of information (DiMaggio and Powell, 1983; Holzinger and Knill 2005). The OECD has become a successful education policy entrepreneur with its PISA Study; as regards the EU in the context of the Bologna Process, the IO was able to jump on the bandwagon. Thus, the more a country is exposed to IO governance by its membership in that IO, the more we expect it to change its education policy.

However, we assume that transformations of national education policymaking occur only if there is a certain "misfit" between the models proposed by international organizations and the existing domestic guiding principles of education. According to Börzel and Risse misfit is a crucial precondition for change to take place in the interplay between the international and the national levels as it creates opportunities of political learning and a redistribution of power resources: "The lower the compatibility between [international and] European and domestic processes, policies and institutions, the higher the adaptational pressure" (Börzel and Risse 2000: 5). With regard to the internationalization of education politics we also assume that a certain misfit or dissonance between international models and domestic guiding principles of education is required to induce changes in national education policymaking at all. On the other hand we expect a curvilinear rather than a linear relation between compatibility and change: if the gap between international models and domestic principles and causal beliefs on education becomes too big, national states will behave like a wood louse and lock themselves up in idiosyncratic opposition.[6]

Drawing on the literature on veto players and points, we expect a lesser degree of transformation of national education policy to result from the OECD's PISA Study and the Bologna Process when there are multiple veto players and points in the decisionmaking process of a participating country (Tsebelis 1995: 293). To quote Börzel and Risse (2000: 7): "The more power is dispersed across the political system and the more actors have a say in political decisionmaking, the more difficult it is to foster the domestic consensus or 'winning coalition' necessary to introduce changes in response to [international and] Europeanization pressures." Institutional modifiers on the national level may significantly block or hinder the impulses of IOs and their governance instruments.

Summarizing our assumptions about national transformation capacities as extracted from the current literature, we expect national policies, politics, and polities to become more alike and converge towards the model proposed by IOs when a country is exposed to their governance. However, national transformation capacities modify how and to what extent IO governance influences changes in national education policy. The more veto players are involved in the political process, the more difficult change is as all reforms have to be approved by those with a say. Nonetheless, transformations are possible even in systems with many veto players if the misfit between the orientational framework as provided by IOs and the guiding principles of national education systems is great enough to create significant adaptive pressure.

Overall, the results of this volume show that a simplified view is not appropriate to the complex field of education policy. Countries like Germany and Switzerland had a backlog of reforms dating to the 1970s and 1980s and were influenced by guiding principles which do not best fit the market-based orientational framework of the OECD and the Bologna Process. However, there were far-reaching changes in their education policies, despite of their decentralized and interdependent polity structures. In these cases, actors actually have been able to cope with institutional constraints and could quickly implement new education policies in order to compensate their subjectively perceived misfits (see Conclusion of this volume).

Outline of the volume

In our research design we combine in-depth case studies with comparative cross-country analyses in order to embed the results from the individual studies. Network analysis allows for comparisons across our single country cases whereas quantitative regression analysis of the OECD world enables us to embed our results in the broader context of the industrialized world. By applying such a mixed-method approach of qualitative case studies and quantitative comparisons we seek to provide answers to the research question from different angles.

Figure 1.2 illustrates our research design and case selection.

This first chapter of the introductory part provides the theoretical framework for the whole book and sets the guidelines for each of the following four country cases (plus the chapter on the U.S.) and the two comparative chapters. In the second chapter of the introductory part Nagel and contributors to this book outline the methodological approach used to measure the transformation of education policy. It presents the mixed-methods design applied in this volume, which combines qualitative

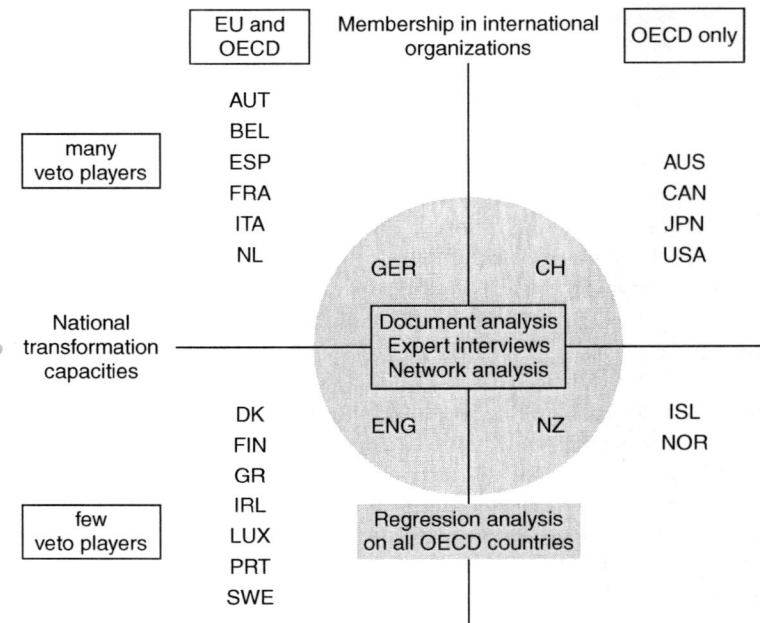

Figure 1.2 Research design and case selection
Source: Weymann and Martens (2006: 651).

methods (expert interviews and document analysis) with quantitative methods (network analysis and regression analysis). Chapter 3 introduces Part II, on the historical context. In his overview chapter Weymann looks at the interconnectiveness of education and the state, how it developed over time, and what challenges the state as the main education provider faces since education has become increasingly internationalized.

Part III contains individual case studies on Germany, Switzerland, England, and New Zealand (and as an excursus: the U.S.). The case selection reflects the logic of our causal model, with IO governance as independent and national transformation capacities as the intermediate variable to explain changes in national policymaking. With regard to IO governance, Germany and England are likely to be more exposed to the interference of the IOs addressed here as Germany and the UK are members of both the EU and the OECD. In contrast, Switzerland and New Zealand are members of the OECD only and therefore likely to be less exposed to pressures from the international level. With regard to veto players the federal systems of Germany and Switzerland exhibit a more rigid political pattern than the more centralized systems of England and New Zealand. According to our theoretical assumptions change in education policymaking should be the greatest in England—as the exposure to IOs is relatively strong since there are only a few national veto points or players—whereas it should be minimal in Switzerland, which is less exposed to IOs and is characterized by a highly federal system of decisionmaking. The fifth excursus country chapter on the U.S. reveals a contrasting nonresponse to the two international initiatives of the OECD's PISA Study and the Bologna Process dealt with in this volume.

Our studies show how countries reacted differently to the international initiatives in education policy of the Bologna Process and the PISA Study. In Chapter 4 Niemann argues for Germany that both processes significantly changed the education landscape of the country, resulting in structural changes of the education system: Bologna und PISA triggered reforms long overdue in Germany. Similarly, Chapter 5 on Switzerland by Bieber shows how IO governance has led to extreme change in the Swiss education system over the last decade. Most significantly, Swiss education actors used both international initiatives for legitimizing long overdue reforms. In Chapter 6 by Knodel and Walkenhorst on England the authors shows that England, by contrast, introduced reforms earlier than other countries, and IO governance does not have a major impact on the English system. However, policymakers in England also underestimated the pressure of these international processes and now have to deal with the question of conforming to them closely or not. Dobbins demonstrates in Chapter 7 how New Zealand—often overlooked because of its larger neighbor, Australia—has taken a different route and is today characterized by a great degree of flexibility and adaptiveness. Unlike the European cases in this book, New Zealand reformed its education system as early as the 1980s and now treats education as an export industry. As a contrasting case, Dobbins and Martens look at the U.S. in Chapter 8. Paradoxically, the U.S. has not shown much responsiveness to PISA, despite the fact that it continuously ranked as poorly as, for example, Germany, whereas the Bologna Process—although the U.S. is not party to it—is more prominently discussed, mainly for reasons of compatibility with the new European system.

Part IV deals with the internationalization of education policy and its impact on national education policy in a comparative way. Chapter 9 by Nagel analyzes the networks of education politics in the four main selected countries. It indicates that despite apparent changes in education policy the modes of political interaction, that is, actors and processes, have remained considerably stable in all countries. Obviously, the internationalization of education politics has not triggered the displacement of domestic actors, but has resulted in the attachment of international actors to the domestic sphere. Using time series plots as well as cross-sectional and longitudinal regression analyses, Chapter 10 by Jakobi, Teltemann, and Windzio investigates processes of internationalization and privatization of educational policies. Based on a comprehensive dataset of more than 20 countries over several years, it shows how both IOs and the characteristics of the nation states affect the process of change of national education policy.

In conclusion Chapter 11 by Windzio, Martens and Nagel summarizes the findings of the individual chapters and embeds the results of this volume in the broader context of the relationship between the state, society, and education. Based on the studies presented in this volume, the chapter provides a synopsis of the findings. Accelerating and decelerating conditions of change are identified and analyzed from both an agency-centered and structure-centered perspectives.

Notes

1. http://www.pisa.oecd.org/pages/0,3417,en_32252351_32235918_1_1_1_1_1,00.html (last access May 10, 2009).
2. For the conceptual framework see the initial research proposal of the group C4 "Internationalization of Education Policy" at the TranState Research Center (Weymann and Martens 2006: 644–49). This introduction also benefits considerably from an early elaboration on this framework as presented in a working paper of Leuze et al. (2008).
3. In another paper we used the metaphors of the Boomerang and Trojan Horse to circumscribe these effects (Martens and Wolf 2009).
4. With regard to the OECD's governance see in particular Marcussen (2004) and Martens and Jakobi (2010).
5. Others add technical assistants to this (Jakobi 2009; McNeely and Cha 1994), which is, however, not applicable to the OECD's PISA Study and the Bologna Process. So we adapted this point into "consulting services".
6. This assumption seems more appropriate to the idiosyncratic logic of national policymaking than the linear hypothesis "the more fit, the more change", which was put forward in earlier accounts of our research group (Leuze et al. 2008: 20).

References

Archer, Margaret S. (1979) *Social Origins of Educational Systems*, London and Beverly Hills, CA: Sage.

Balzer, Carolin and Alessandra Rusconi (2007) "From the European Commission to the Member States and Back—A Comparison of the Bologna and the

Copenhagen Process," in K. Martens, A. Rusconi, and K. Leuze, eds., *New Arenas of Education Governance—the Impact of International Organizations and Markets on Educational Policy Making*, Houndmills, Basingstoke: Palgrave Macmillan, 57–75.

Barnett, Michael N. and Martha Finnemore (2004) *Rules for the World: International Organizations in Global Politics*, Ithaca, NY: Cornell University Press.

Bogdandy, Armin von and Matthias Goldmann (2008/2009) "The Exercise of International Public Authority through National Policy Assessment. The OECD's PISA Policy as a Paradigm for a New International Standard Instrument," *International Organizations Law Review* 5 (2), 241–98.

Börzel, Tanja A. and Thomas Risse (2000) "When Europe Hits Home: Europeanization and Domestic Change," *European Integration Online Papers* 4 (11).

Brand, Tilman (2006) *Kontinuität und Wandel von bildungspolitischen Leitideen— Die EU und OECD im Vergleich*, Diploma Thesis, University of Bremen.

Chayes, Abram and Antonia Handler Chayes (1995) *The New Sovereignty. Compliance with International Regulatory Agreements*, Cambridge, MA: Harvard University Press.

Chayes, Abram, Antonia Handler Chayes, and Ronald B. Mitchell (1998) "Managing Compliance: A Comparative Perspective," in H.K. Jacobson and E. Brown Weiss, eds., *Engaging Countries. Strengthening Compliance with International Environmental Accords*, Cambridge, MA: MIT Press, 39–62.

Conzelmann, Thomas (2008) "Beyond the Carrot and the Stick: State Reporting Procedures in the World Trade Organization and the Organization for Economic Cooperation and Development," in J. Joachim, B. Reinalda, and B. Verbeek, eds., *International Organizations and Implementation—Enforcers, Managers, Authorities?*, London and New York: Routledge, 35–47.

Corbett, Anne (2005) *Universities and the Europe of Knowledge. Ideas, Institutions and Policy Entrepreneurship in European Union Higher Education Policy, 1955–2005*, Houndmills, Basingstoke: Palgrave Macmillan.

Crepaz, Markus M.L. and Ann W. Moser (2004) "The Impact of Collective and Competitive Veto Points on Public Expenditures in the Global Age," *Comparative Political Studies* 37 (3), 259–85.

Criblez, Lucien (2008) *Bildungsraum Schweiz. Historische Entwicklung und aktuelle Herausforderungen*, Bern, Stuttgart, Wien: Haupt.

Crosier, David, Lewis Purser, and Hanne Smidt (2007) *Trends V: Universities Shaping the European Higher Education Area*, Brussels: European University Association.

DiMaggio, Paul J. and Walter W. Powell (1983) "The Iron Cage Revisited: Institutional Isomorphism and Collective Rationality in Organizational Fields," *American Sociological Review* 48 (2), 147–60.

Dobbins, Michael (2010) "Towards Convergence of Higher Education Policy in Central and Eastern Europe," in A.P. Jakobi, K. Martens, and K.D. Wolf, eds., *Education Policy and Political Science—Discovering a Neglected Field*, London and New York: Routledge, 38–55.

Fearon, James and Alexander Wendt (2002) "Rationalism v. Constructivism: A Skeptical View," in W. Carlsnaes, T. Risse and B.A. Simmons, eds., *Handbook of International Relations*, London: Sage, 52–72.

Finnemore, Martha (1993) "International Organizations as Teachers of Norms: The United Nations Educational, Scientific, and Cultural Organization and Science Policy," *International Organization* 47 (4), 565–97.

Finnemore, Martha (1996) *National Interests in International Society*, Ithaca, NY and London: Cornell University Press.

Finnemore, Martha and Kathryn Sikkink (1998) "International Norm Dynamics and Political Change," *International Organization* 52 (4), 887–917.

Ganghof, Steffen (2003) "Promises and Pitfalls of Veto Player Analysis," *Swiss Political Science Review* 9 (2), 1–25.

Gellner, Ernest (1983) *Nations and Nationalism*, Oxford: Blackwell.

Gerhards, Jürgen and Dieter Rucht (2000) "Öffentlichkeit, Akteure und Deutungsmuster: Die Debatte über Abtreibung in Deutschland und den USA," in J. Gerhards, ed., *Die Vermessung kultureller Unterschiede*, Wiesbaden: Westdeutscher Verlag, 165–88.

Goldstein, Judith and Robert O. Keohane (1993) "Ideas and Foreign Policy: An Analytical Framework," in J. Goldstein and R.O. Keohane, eds., *Ideas and Foreign Policy. Beliefs, Institutions, and Political Change*, Ithaca, NY and London: Cornell University Press, 3–30.

Grek, Sotiria (2009) "Governing by Numbers: The PISA 'Effect' in Europe," *Journal of Education Policy* 24 (1), 23–37.

Hall, Peter (1993) "Policy Paradigm, Social Learning and the State," *Comparative Politics* 25 (3), 275–96.

Heichel, Stephan and Thomas Sommerer (2007) "Unterschiedliche Pfade, ein Ziel?— Spezifikationen im Forschungsdesign und Vergleichbarkeit der Ergebnisse bei der Suche nach der Konvergenz nationalstaatlicher Politiken," in K. Holzinger, H. Jörgens, and C. Knill, eds., *Transfer, Diffusion und Konvergenz von Politiken*, Wiesbaden: Verlag für Sozialwissenschaften, 107–30.

Heichel, Stephan, Jessica Pape, and Thomas Sommerer (2005) "Is There Convergence in Convergence Research? An Overview of Empirical Studies on Policy Convergence," *Journal of European Public Policy* 12 (5), 817–40.

Holzinger, Katharina and Christoph Knill (2005) "Causes and Conditions of Crossnational Policy Convergence," *Journal of European Public Policy* 12 (5), 775–96.

Holzinger, Katharina, Helge Jörgens, and Christoph Knill (2007) "Transfer, Diffusion und Konvergenz: Konzepte und Kausalmechanismen," in K. Holzinger, H. Jörgens, and C. Knill, eds., *Transfer, Diffusion und Konvergenz von Politiken*, Wiesbaden: Verlag für Sozialwissenschaften, 11–35.

Huber, Evelyne, Charles Ragin, and John D. Stephens (1993) "Social Democracy, Christian Democracy, Constitutional Structure, and the Welfare State," *The American Journal of Sociology* 99 (3), 711–49.

Hurrelmann, Achim, Stephan Leibfried, Kerstin Martens, and Peter Mayer (2007) "The Golden-Age Nation State and Its Transformation—a Framework for Analysis," in A. Hurrelmann, S. Leibfried, K. Martens, and P. Mayer, eds., *Transforming the Golden Age Nation State*, Houndmills, Basingstoke: Palgrave Macmillan, 1–23.

Immergut, Ellen M. (1992) "Institutions, Veto Points, and Policy Results: A Comparative Analysis of Health Care," *Journal of Public Policy* 10 (4), 391–416.

Jacobson, Harold K. (1979) *Networks of Interdependence*, New York: Knopf.

Jakobi, Anja P. (2009) *International Organizations and Lifelong Learning. From Global Agendas to Policy Diffusion*, Houndmills, Basingstoke: Palgrave.

Jakobi, Anja P. and Janna Teltemann (2009) *Convergence and Divergence in Welfare State Development: An Assessment of Education Policy in OECD Countries*, TranState Working Paper No. 93, Bremen: CRC 597.

Jakobi, Anja P. and Kerstin Martens (2007) "Diffusion durch Internationale Organisationen: Die Bildungspolitik der OECD," in K. Holzinger, H. Jörgens, and C. Knill, eds., *Politische Vierteljahresschrift—Special Issue: Transfer, Diffusion und Konvergenz von Politiken*, 247–70.

Kiker, Billy F. (1966) "The Historical Roots of the Concept of Human Capital," *The Journal of Political Economy* 74 (5), 481–99.

Klitgaard, Michael Baggesen (2010, forthcoming) "Veto-Points and the Politics of Introducing School Vouchers in the US and Sweden," in A.P. Jakobi, K. Martens, and K.D. Wolf, eds., *Education Policy and Political Science—Discovering a Neglected Field*, London and New York: Routledge, 23–37.

Kohlrausch, Bettina and Kathrin Leuze (2007) "Implications of Marketization for the Perception of Education as Public or Private Good," in K. Martens, A. Rusconi, and K. Leuze, eds., *New Arenas of Education Governance—the Impact of International Organizations and Markets on Educational Policymaking*, Houndmills, Basingstoke and New York: Palgrave Macmillan, 195–214.

Lepsius, Rainer M. (1995) "Institutionenanalyse und Institutionenpolitik," in B. Nedelmann, ed., *Politische Institutionen im Wandel*, Opladen: Westdeutscher Verlag, 392–403.

Lepsius, Rainer M. (1997) "Institutionalisierung und Deinstitutionalisierung von Rationalitätskriterien," in G. Göhler, ed., *Institutionenwandel*, Opladen: Westdeutscher Verlag, 57–69.

Leuze, Kathrin, Tilman Brand, Anja P. Jakobi, Kerstin Martens, Alexander Nagel, Alessandra Rusconi, and Ansgar Weymann (2008) *Analysing the Two-Level Game—International and National Determinants of Change in Education Policy Making*, TranState Working Paper No. 72, Bremen: CRC 597.

Mann, Michael (1993) *The Sources of Social Power. Volume II. The Rise of Classes and Nation-States, 1760–1914*, Cambridge: Cambridge University Press.

Marcussen, Martin (2004) "OECD Governance through Soft Law," in U. Mörth, ed., *Soft Law in Governance and Regulation*, Cheltenham, Northhampton: Edward Elgar, 103–28.

Marshall, T.H. (1965) [1949] "Citizenship and Social Class," in T.H. Marshall, ed., *Class, Citizenship, and Social Development. Essays by T. H. Marshall*, Garden City, New York: Anchor Books, 30–39.

Martens, Kerstin (2007) "How to Become an Influential Actor—the 'Comparative Turn' in OECD Education Policy," in K. Martens, A. Rusconi, and K. Leuze, eds., *New Arenas of Education Governance—the Impact of International Organizations and Markets on Educational Policy Making*, Houndmills, Basingstoke: Palgrave Macmillan, 40–56.

Martens, Kerstin and Carolin Balzer (2008) "All Bark and No Bite? The Implementation Styles of the European Union and the Organization for Economic Cooperation and Development in Education Policy," in J. Joachim, B. Reinalda, and B. Verbeek, eds., *International Organizations and Implementation—Enforcers, Managers, Authorities?*, London and New York: Routledge, 88–101.

Martens, Kerstin and Anja P. Jakobi (2010) "International Organisations as Institutional Entrepreneurs: The OECD and Education Policy," in I. Dingeldey and H. Rothgang, eds., *Governance of Welfare State Reform—a Cross National and Cross Sectoral Comparison of Policy and Politics*, Cheltenham: Edward Elgar, 90–108.

Martens, Kerstin and Dennis Niemann (2009) "Governance by Comparison—How Ratings & Ranking Can Impact National Policy Making in Education," paper presented at the "International Studies Association," meeting, New York City, New York, February 15–18.

Martens, Kerstin and Ansgar Weymann (2007) "The Internationalization of Educational Policy—towards Convergence of National Paths?" in A. Hurrelmann, S. Leibfried, K. Martens, and P. Mayer, eds., *Transforming the Golden Age Nation-State*, Houndmills, Basingstoke: Palgrave Macmillan, 152–72.

Martens, Kerstin and Klaus Dieter Wolf (2006) "Paradoxien der Neuen Staatsräson—Die Internationalisierung der Bildungspolitik in der EU und der OECD," *Zeitschrift für Internationale Beziehungen* 13(2), 145–76.

Martens, Kerstin and Klaus Dieter Wolf (2009) "PISA als Trojanisches Pferd—die Internationalisierung der Bildungspolitik in der OECD," in S. Botzem, J. Hofmann, S. Quack, G. F. Schuppert, and H. Strassheim, eds., *Governance als Prozeß*, Berlin: Nomos, 357–76.

Martens, Kerstin, Carolin Balzer, Reinhold Sackmann, and Ansgar Weymann (2004) *Comparing Governance of International Organisations—the EU, the OECD and Educational Policy*, TranState Working Papers, No. 7, Bremen: CRC 597.

Martens, Kerstin, Alessandra Rusconi, and Kathrin Leuze, eds. (2007) *New Arenas of Education Governance—the Impact of International Organizations and Markets on Educational Policy Making*, Houndmills, Basingstoke: Palgrave Macmillan.

McNeely, Connie L. and Yun-Kyung Cha (1994) "Worldwide Educational Convergence through International Organisations: Avenues for Research," *Education Policy Analysis Archives* 2.

Meyer, John W., J. Boli, and George M. Thomas (1994) "Ontology and Rationalization in the Western Cultural Account," in W.R. Scott and J.W. Meyer, eds., *Institutional Environments and Organizations: Structural Complexity and Individualism*, Thousand Oaks, CA, London, New Delhi and Singapore: Sage, 9–26.

Meyer, John W., Francisco O. Ramirez, and Yasemin N. Soysal (1992) "World Expansion of Mass Education, 1870–1980," *Sociology of Education* 65 (2), 128–49.

Muche, Franziska, ed. (2005) *Opening Up to the Wider World: The External Dimension of the Bologna-Process*, Bonn: Lemmens.

Muche, Franziska, Maria Kelo, and Bernd Wächter (2004) *The Admission of International Students into Higher Education. Policies and Instruments*, Bonn: Lemmens.

Münch, Richard (2009) *Globale Eliten, lokale Autoritäten: Bildung und Wissenschaft unter dem Regime von PISA, McKinsey and Co.*, Frankfurt am Main: Suhrkamp.

OECD (2009) *Education Today. The OECD Perspective* (Online: http://browse.oecdbookshop.org/oecd/pdfs/browseit/9609021E.PDF, last access: May 2, 2009).

Popp, Marie (2010, forthcoming) *Viel Lärm um PISA: Eine qualitative Medienanalyse zu den Reaktionen auf die PISA-Studie in Deutschland, Österreich, Spanien und Mexiko*, TranState Working Paper. Bremen: CRC 597.

Posch, Peter (1998) "The Ecologisation of Schools in Austria," *PEB Exchange. The Journal of the OECD Programme on Educational Building* 34 (June), 12–15.

Reinalda, Bob and Ewa Kulesza (2005) *The Bologna Process—Harmonizing Europe's Higher Education*, Opladen: Budrich.

Rinne, Risto, Johanna Kallo, and Sanna Hokka (2004) "Too Eager to Comply? OECD Education Policies and the Finnish Response," *European Educational Research Journal* 3 (2), 454–85.

Sala-i-Martin, Xavier (1996) "Regional Cohesion: Evidence and Theories of Regional Growth and Convergence," *European Economic Review* 40 (6), 1325–52.

Schäfer, Armin (2006) "A New Form of Governance? Comparing the Open Method of Coordination to Multilateral Surveillance by the IMF and the OECD," *Journal of European Public Policy* 13 (1), 70–88.

Schmidt, Manfred G. (2000) *Demokratietheorien*, Opladen: Leske + Budrich.

Schubert, Klaus and Nils C. Bandelow, eds. (2003) *Lehrbuch der Politikfeldanalyse*, Munich, Vienna: R. Oldenburg Verlag.

Smith, Anthony D. (1986) *The Ethnic Origins of Nations*, Oxford/Malden, MA: Blackwell.

Toens, Katrin (2008) "Die Sorbonne-Deklaration. Hintergründe und Bedeutung für den Bologna-Prozess," *die hochschule. Journal für Bildung und Wissenschaft* 2007 (2), 37–53.

Torres, Carlos Alberto (2002) "Globalization, Education, and Citizenship: Solidarity versus Markets?" *American Educational Research Journal* 39 (2), 363–78.

Tsebelis, George (1995) "Decision Making in Political Systems: Veto Players in Presidentialism, Parliamentarism, Multicameralism and Multipartyism," *British Journal of Political Science* 25 (3), 289–325.

Wagschal, Uwe (1999) "Blockieren Vetospieler Steuerreformen?" *Politische Vierteljahresschrift* 42 (4), 628–40.

Walkenhorst, Heiko (2008) "Explaining Change in EU Education Policy," *Journal of European Public Policy* 15 (4), 567–87.

Wallace, Helen (2000) "The Institutional Setting: Five Variations on a Theme," in H. Wallace and W. Wallace, eds., *Policy Making in the European Union*, Oxford: Oxford University Press, 3–37.

Weber, Max (1968) "The Social Psychology of the World Religions," in H.H. Gerth and C. Wright Mills, eds., *From Max Weber*, New York: Oxford University Press, 267–301.

Weymann, Ansgar and Kerstin Martens (2006) *Internationalisierung von Bildungspolitik*, Research Proposal of the TranState Research Center "Transformations of the State," University of Bremen (Online: http://www.staat.uni-bremen.de/pages/fcrProjektBeschreibung.php?SPRACHE=de&ID=14, last access: May 10, 2009).

Witte, Johanna (2006) *Change of Degrees and Degrees of Change—Comparing Adaptations of European Higher Education Systems in the Context of the Bologna Process*, Enschede: CHEPS (Center for Higher Education Policy Studies).

2
Measuring Transformation of Education Policy—a Mixed-Method Approach

Alexander-Kenneth Nagel, Tonia Bieber, Anja P. Jakobi, Philipp Knodel, Dennis Niemann, and Janna Teltemann

> *But there comes a moment when the atmosphere changes. The significance of the unreflectively utilized viewpoints becomes uncertain and the road is lost in the twilight. The light of the great cultural problems moves on. Then science too prepares to change its standpoint and its thinking apparatus and to view the streams of events from the heights of thought.*
>
> Weber 1949 [1904]: 55

In his famous essay, "The Methodology of the Social Sciences" Max Weber indicated that new social and cultural phenomena bring along new academic problems. These new academic problems, however, call for an adjustment of the paradigmatic and methodological apparatus. In this chapter, we point to the methodological challenges arising from new and complex social phenomena in the realm of internationalizing education policy and how they can be addressed by a systematic combination and pooling of different methods with their particular strengths and limitations. Basically, new analytical problems can be dealt with in three different ways. The first and least desirable way is to downsize the phenomenon in question to make it accessible within a given methodological framework. The second is to refine a given methodological framework to make it cover more aspects of the phenomenon in question, thus to increase the validity of the respective type of data. The third is to deepen the overall validity of analysis by a systematic rearrangement of the methodological framework. Such an arrangement should combine both qualitative and quantitative methodological strategies with descriptive and explanative logics of research. A carefully arranged mixed-method approach can not only account more deeply for more facets of the phenomenon in question, but can also connect the methods involved in an appropriate way in order to counterbalance their limits and to pool their strengths.

Since King, Keohane, and Verba's publication on methodology (1994), social science has witnessed a vivid debate on methodology. Given the aim of generalizable conclusions in most research in political science, the quantitative focus and its way of testing and proving is, at first sight, in a favored position. While King, Keohane, and Verba intended to transfer the quantitative logic to qualitative research, others have raised arguments for the specific logic of qualitative research and pointed towards weaknesses of large-N quantitative studies (Brady and Collier 2004; in particular Brady, Collier, and Seawright 2004; George and Bennett 2005). Although the debate revealed cleavages between different methodological traditions, it is however, not unusual or unorthodox to combine both strands of methods; in fact they can fruitfully interact with each other (Read and Marsh 2002).

Yet, a mixed-method approach is not an end in itself and the mere combination of methodological strategies does not necessarily improve the validity or scope of empirical analysis. The term "mixed-method designs" has been defined "as including at least one quantitative method (designed to collect numbers) and one qualitative method (designed to collect words)" (Caracelli and Greene 1993: 195). In their earlier work, Greene et al. distinguished five ideal-types of mixed-method designs, namely *triangulation, complementarity, development, initiation,* and *expansion* (Greene, Caracelli, and Graham 1989: 258). While triangulation "seeks convergence [...] of results from the different methods," expansion "seeks to extend the breadth and range of inquiry by using different methods for different inquiry components" (ibid.: 258). Mixed-method designs are thus distinguished as to their degree of functional differentiation as well as to their temporal logic. Functional differentiation refers to the extent to which methods focus exclusively on certain facets of the phenomenon in question; the temporal logic can either be *concurrent* or *sequential* (ibid.: 264). A sequential mixed-method setting implies a chronological order for the methodological strategies involved, for example, a qualitative prestudy to elucidate key variables and explanatory factors for a subsequent larger quantitative project (Barton and Lazarsfeld 1955). In contrast, a simultaneous mixed-method setting is characterized by the concurrent implementation of different methods. Greene and McClintock assert that a simultaneous application of methodological strategies is crucial for purposes of triangulation (Greene and McClintock 1985).[1]

In this chapter, we present the mixed-method design of our project and provide detailed insights to operationalization, procedures, and data as well as the interplay of the respective methodological strategies applied. Besides the scope of our research project in this volume we aim to make a contribution to the debate on mixed-method designs in general by bringing into focus the temporal logics of such designs. We assume that the concurrent application of different methodological strategies yields particular advantages compared with the sequential application as long as the intermethodological links and communication are properly arranged.

As pointed out in the introductory chapter of this volume our central research question is whether, how, and to what extent transformations of national education policymaking occur as a result of the influence of international initiatives in education policy, in particular the Programme for International Student Assessment (PISA) of the Organisation for Economic Cooperation and Development (OECD) and the Bologna Process in the context of the European Union (EU). We hypothesize that international organizations (IOs) have an impact on national policymaking through different governance instruments and thereby trigger transformations within and possibly convergence across countries. This process, however, can be enhanced or restricted by national institutions such as veto players and points as well as guiding principles of education. Such transformation of the state can be seen as an important dimension of social and cultural transformation in societies and how they are organized. We explore our research question with comparative case studies of four countries (Germany, Switzerland, England, and New Zealand)[2] based on document analysis and expert interviews as well as policy network analysis and time series cross-section (TSCS) regression models of all OECD countries.

Figure 2.1 illustrates how the general research question is decomposed into different variables and phenomena (for more detail see the introductory chapter of this volume), that is, units, which can be observed empirically. As for these phenomena, we distinguish between *five instruments* which IOs have on hand to influence national politics: norm setting, opinion formation, financial means, coordinative activities, and consulting services. The concept of *transformation capacities* is linked to the expected degree of change, and these capacities are distinguished in institutional factors as veto players and points as well as more ideal factors as guiding principles of education.

It is obvious that the methodological strategies applied—expert interviews, network analysis, and regression analysis—can account for different, yet overlapping, phenomena. The mixed-method design of this project can be characterized using the design-characteristics proposed

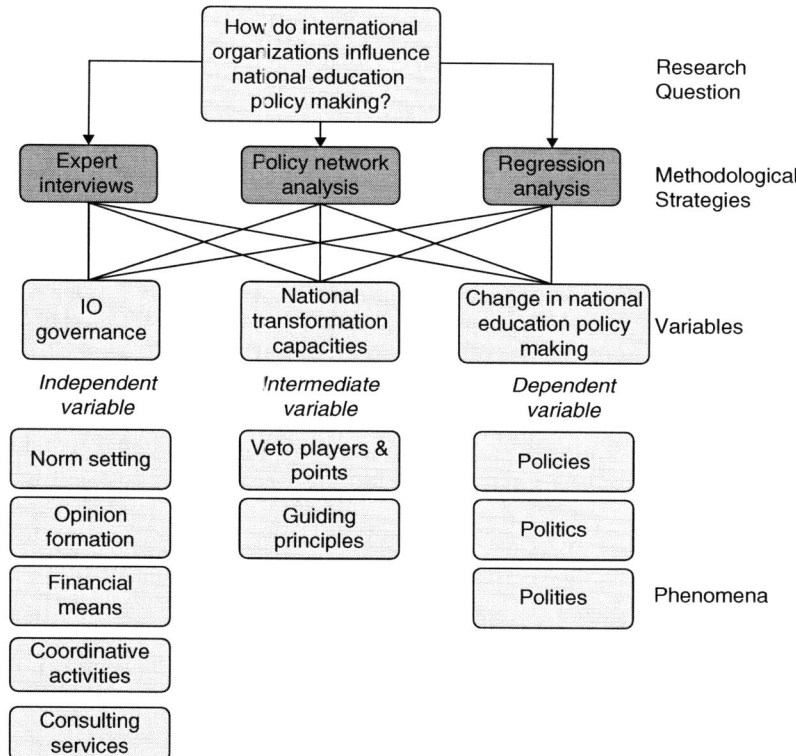

Figure 2.1 Methodological pluralism in a multidimensional setting

by Greene, Caracelli, and Graham (1989). They distinguish mixed-method designs with regard to methods, phenomena, paradigms, status, implementation interdependence, implementation timing, and status (ibid.: 262).

The dimension of *methods* refers to the "degree to which the qualitative and quantitative methods selected for a given study are similar to or different from one another in form, assumptions, strengths, and limitations or biases" (ibid.: 262). The methodological strategies applied in our project are different, both with regard to their qualitative or quantitative nature and, subsequently, their form, strengths, and limitations. Furthermore, there is a difference with regard to the underlying assumptions and research logics: regression analysis aims at formal causal explanations, network analysis can provide a systematic quantitative description, and expert interviews can elucidate causal mechanisms and help to develop a more general understanding of the phenomena in question.

The dimension of *phenomena* "refers to the degree to which the qualitative and quantitative methods are intended to assess totally different phenomena or exactly the same phenomenon" (ibid.: 262–63). In our project we decompose the general research questions into several empirically accessible phenomena, such as instruments of IO governance, veto players and points, and guiding principles of education, as well as national education policies, politics, and polity. These phenomena include both our independent variable (IO governance), our intermediate variable (national transformation capacities, i.e. veto players and points as well as guiding principles), and our dependent variable (transformation of national education policy, politics, and polity). In our mixed-method design all methodological strategies cover as many of these phenomena as possible and it might thus be called a holistic approach. At the same time, each method can account for different facets of a given phenomenon.

The dimension of *status* "represents the degree to which a study's qualitative and quantitative methods have equally important or central roles vis-à-vis the study's overall objectives" (ibid.: 264). As a result of their inherent differences as to form, assumptions, strengths, and limitations, there is no hierarchical order of the methodological strategies applied in our project. In the sense of triangulation as mentioned above, each method fully and directly accounts for the phenomena instead of being a mere pretest or prestudy.

For the temporal logics of mixed-method designs, the distinction between implementation interdependence and implementation timing are of particular importance. While interdependence refers to "the degree to which the qualitative and quantitative methods are conceptualized, designed, and implemented interactively or independently" (ibid.: 264), timing means that "a given pair of methods is typically implemented concurrently or sequentially, not in between" (ibid.: 264). In our project, expert interviews, network analysis and regression analysis have been conceptualized and designed interactively in a collective endeavor of specification of concepts and operationalization. The implementation itself was then independent because of the different nature of data and operations involved. Thus, all methodological strategies were implemented concurrently and in mutual awareness of each other.

In the following section we will discuss the particular strengths and limitations of each methodological strategy employed in our project, thus to illustrate their particular division of labor in our mixed-method design. In the concluding section, we will focus on linkages and interfaces within our set of methods and consider both special (i.e. project-specific) and general opportunities of cross-fertilization in a simultaneous, high-variation mixed-method design.

Methodological strategies applied

In this section we will address the different methodological strategies and logics employed in our project, that is, expert interviews and document analysis, policy network analysis, and time series cross-section regression models. Instead of a self-referential and isolated description of the respective empirical approach we aim at a comparative and relational perspective. For this purpose, all methods that are part of our mixed-method design will be outlined according to the same scheme: first, the characteristic perspectives and strengths will be presented. Further on we address questions of operationalization, to show how different methodological strategies account for different facets of the phenomena in question. Finally, the collection and handling of data as well as procedures and models of data analysis will be discussed as different methods entail different logics of research (e.g. explorative, explanative, or descriptive). In a concluding remark we deal with particular limitations of each methodological strategy and reflect on how they can be counterbalanced in the context of our mixed-method design.

Expert interviews and document analysis

A qualitative approach allows us to examine a particular issue of interest in depth and to trace causal processes. In our project, we concentrate on document analysis and expert interviews as qualitative methods. Document analysis serves to capture the basic fundaments for change in a policy field (Schnell, Hill, and Esser 1999: 375). Expert interviews[3] are known to be a particularly suitable method in the social sciences for gaining qualitative information (Froschauer and Lueger 2003; Martens and Brüggemann 2006; Mayer 2004). They enable us to discover new or important aspects of the issue at stake according to structures or actors in the policy field. Both methods offer an analytical tool to assess the influence of IOs on national education policymaking in the four examined countries (Germany, Switzerland, England, and New Zealand). In the following, we will explain our operationalization of the independent, intervening, and dependent variables, and describe the database and approach.

Operationalization

To assess qualitatively the variables of our project, *document analysis* provides a good starting point and we consulted diverse types of publications. While official IO publications or activities reflect governance instruments *per se*, veto players and points as well as national guiding principles were identified by exploring the national reactions to IO activities. However, document analysis alone is obviously not suitable for exploring all dimensions of internationalization of education policy because it is rather limited in capturing concepts like guiding principles on education. Furthermore, it is impossible to measure all relevant variables by analyzing documents because not all relevant variables emerge in the context of official publications. The analysis of documents is an approach for scrutinizing governance instruments and their impact on national policymaking, but it needs further input from other data collection instruments, such as expert interviews, to assess the whole range of IO influence.

For the *expert interviews*, we formulated questions on each variable of our theoretical concepts to obtain otherwise inaccessible, comprehensive expert knowledge about the influence of IOs on national education policymaking. In the following, we illustrate this approach.

1. *IO Governance instruments*: In order to assess the independent variable "IO governance instruments," the interviewees are asked, e.g. which activities of the EU have had an impact on education reform process in the respective country. However, expert interviews are necessary but not sufficient by themselves in detecting the whole spectrum of IO governance instruments. As regards the instrument of financial means, specific figures are better identified by studying documents which reflect, for example, the accurate amount of transferred money. Expert interviews are more suitable for identifying the impact of financial support.

2. *National transformation capacities*: In our conceptualization, such national political-institutional factors as veto players and points, as well as guiding principles, are decisive intervening variables of how the internationalization of policies is framed and implemented on the national level. Explicit questions concerning specific educational traditions and legacies in each of the four countries examined served to identify national guiding principles. For example, with the question, "How well do the ideas of EU/OECD fit to the national philosophy of your country?", we assess if national principles on education block or support reform efforts by IOs.

3. *Transformation of national education policymaking*: Changes with regard to the dependent variable "transformation of national education policymaking" resulting from IO influence are supposed to take place in the dimension of policy, politics, and polity. By asking multiple questions, we seek to gather qualitative data to cover both dimensions. For example, to capture the policy dimension we ask about the main changes in the field of education reforms. Changes with regard to politics are covered by questions about the process of education policymaking itself. By doing this, it is possible to arrive at a differentiated assessment of how national policymaking in education has changed and which dimensions this change encompasses.

Data

The selection of documents requires the researcher to have a comprehensive preconception of the research object at stake. In our project, documents are selected regarding their importance for the political process and policymaking. We thus choose documents authored or edited by those institutions that are influential in, and responsible for, the issue of education policymaking.

The selection process of interview partners is aimed at covering all national and subnational stakeholders relevant to decisionmaking who can shape national education policies in the context of internationalization. Following Bogner and Menz (2002: 66), the expert is to be understood as "a person who, due to special competence, has a certain status or operates in a certain capacity that allows him/her to determine the orientation of actions or definition of situations." The status of an expert is therefore not necessarily status *per se*, but is conferred upon the person through the relevant research. In our study, experts are political and administrative actors and scientists in the policy field of education. The selection reflects a three-step process. First, not all institutions that principally deal with education policy are suitable to be interviewed because their actual influence on national policymaking is often negligible, for example pure interest groups without any formal means of exerting influence. Thus, it was inevitable that the scope of national expert organizations would be reduced. Second, after narrowing the scope of the research objects, representatives in charge of internationalization issues within the relevant national institution were identified. Third, the experts chosen were contacted via a standard email. By request, they were sent the questionnaire in advance to provide more detailed information.[4] Limitations of the method consist in a self-selection bias of interview partners that may have country-specific reasons, for example different nonresponsiveness rates of professionals of different countries. The selection bias is avoided by counterbalancing missing information by the use of document analysis regarding the specific institution or actor. This serves to reduce the problem of lacking validity in cross-country analysis.

Procedure

Both document analysis and expert interviews are suitable for gaining descriptive information and for causal analysis. A striking feature of expert interviews is that they often reveal causal mechanisms in domestic policymaking and provide more and deeper insights into the processes responsible for influencing national politics and policies (Schnell, Hill, and Esser 1999: 380). In light of domestic factors (transformation capacities) and IO initiatives (IO governance instruments), expert interviews allow us to trace policymaking processes in an area where causal interrelations are not well explored. Moreover, in a personal interview it is likely that interviewees reveal implicit knowledge and provide an insider's perspective. In line with this argument, in our project we use document analysis primarily for the description of changes in the role of the state with regard to education and expert interviews for explaining decisions in policymaking and causes of change. Thus, our qualitative analysis proceeds in two steps. First, a stocktaking of change is carried out (*description* of change) and secondly, the relationship between IO governance, national transformation capacities and transformation of national education policymaking is explored (*explanation* of change).

Documents like statutes and position papers are explored with respect to the above-mentioned dependent, independent, and intervening variables and thus shed light on transformation of national education policymaking. Documents reflect the positions of actors and in a temporal dimension and can indicate if changes regarding these positions have occurred. Regulative documents as laws or decrees refer especially to altered polities. Hence, drawing on this type of document is useful for the phase of orientation and selection of experts, as well as controlling and supplementing information from the experts. Analyzing documents also encompasses the danger of certain interpretation errors. For example, the same word may have different meanings in different national contexts or in different countries.

Personal interviews of approximately 50 minutes' length were conducted with national experts of the four countries examined, using a half-standardized questionnaire that leaves room for multifaceted answers. The recorded interviews were transcribed in their entirety. A qualitative data-analysis program (MaxQDA) was used for coding and analyzing the interview transcripts with a predefined coding scheme.

In a nutshell, *qualitative methods* are particularly appropriate for analyzing recent educational reforms in OECD and EU countries and identifying causal factors for internationalization processes. They help to confirm or to question research results from different approaches and to include different perspectives on the research object. In general, *document analysis* is an instrument that provides diverse insights that enable further data collection and specific questions in the expert interviews. *Expert interviews* enable the formulation of more sophisticated causal hypotheses insofar as causes of change of national education policymaking are identified in the interviews with the expert.

These methods are not suitable for testing the whole array of alternative explanations because social interaction bears limited options. In general, conducting interviews is a time- and cost-intensive method and therefore the possibility of adding further variables and gathering information retrospectively is rather restricted. This increases the importance of an accurate design for the research project. Our research design enables the control of third variables, for example, by choosing two EU and two OECD countries to trace a process back to one IO.

For our project, *document analysis* provides background information, while *expert interviews* are important because some data on our variables are either not yet available as latest appraisals of developments by experts, or hardly quantifiable, for example guiding principles. Without these methods we could not detect hidden effects. Privileged access to information via experts gives us deeper insights into the influence of international actors, such as the EU and OECD, and national political-administrative institutions, such as veto powers, normative expectations, and cultural-cognitive interpretation schemes for country-specific principles of education, on national policymaking. It is especially beneficial to combine the advantages of qualitative methods with advantages of quantitative methods in order to assess the field of education policy from a triangulative perspective.

Policy network analysis

Policy network analysis can account for the complexity and informality of change in national education politics induced by internationalization and privatization and thus provides a specific view on the various phenomena and facets of our research question. The main characteristic is the type of data which is used. Unlike other methodological strategies, such as expert interviews or regression analysis, policy network analysis is based on relational data, that is, the relations or interactions between (corporative) actors rather than particular attributes, such as age, size, or mission statement (Jansen 2003: 53–59). Formally, a policy network consists of actors (nodes) and their relations (edges). The added value of policy network analysis as a structural analysis in our mixed-method design is the systematic description of political actors and their patterns of cooperation and exchange. Thus it can be used to combine micro- and macroperspectives by analyzing intermediate structures (ibid.: 15–21). In the following section the opportunities and constraints of policy network analysis as well as its function in our research design are shown by describing operationalization, data collection, and process.

Operationalization

To cover the complexity and diversity of the political process, the operationalization of the phenomena in question (IO governance, national transformation capacities, and transformation of national education policymaking) rests on a classification of relevant actors and relations. Based on former studies and own explorative work (Knoke et al. 1996; Nagel 2006; Nagel 2008) on policy networks, categories of actors and relations have been created.[5] The operationalization of independent, intervening, and dependent variables rests on our category systems as well as the research logic of policy network analysis.

1. *IO governance instruments*: We investigate several IO governance instruments as an independent variable of our research design; these instruments are then conceptualized and measured as relations between IOs and national corporate actors from a network-analytical perspective. Governance by opinion formation, for instance, can be operationalized as relations based on lobbying and symbolic interaction. Lobbying relations encompass the purposeful and instrumental interventions of corporate actors on other actors within the policy network. The scope of intervention may vary between mere suggestions, demand, and pressure. Relations of symbolic interaction are expressed in affirmative speech acts of actors, such as granting membership or declaring programmatic congruence. In analogy, a network analytical operationalization of governance by financial means involves relations of transaction, which encompass both direct monetary transfers and the organization and realization of seminars and conferences by IOs to the extent that they require personal and financial expenses.

2. *National transformation capacities*: National configurations of actors and guiding principles of education moderate the effect of IO governance on national decisionmaking. While guiding principles cannot be operationalized in an actor-by-actor network model, the study of veto players is perfectly in line with the logic of policy network analysis.[6] Our typology of actors includes a broad scope of organizations participating in the education policy network. Following Tsebelis' veto player approach (1995) only actors endowed with constitutional veto power are considered. In policy network analysis, these veto players in the strict sense of the word are covered by the following categories of actors: national state actors, federal state actors and parties, and legislative actors.[7]

3. *Transformation of national education policymaking*: Policy change at the national level occurs in the dimension of policies and politics. In policy network analysis we put particular emphasis on education politics, that is, structural changes in the set of actors as well as processes of decisionmaking. From a network-analytical perspective the phenomenon of politics can be operationalized by looking at the composition of national policy networks with regard to the actors involved regardless of whether they are private, national, or international and the types of relations these actors maintain with each other. Variation in the composition of either actors or relations in a given network is an indicator for change in national decisionmaking in the dimension of politics. Even if the composition of these policy networks remains relatively stable, we may account for changes on a more structural level regarding the intensity of interaction and its overall hierarchization.

Data

A systematic structural description of political change requires dynamic network data. Both the generation and handling of longitudinal network data have been crucial topics in the methodological debate on network analysis (Suitor, Wellman, and Morgan 1997). A major complaint in this debate is that elaborate panel designs are very demanding in terms of time and money: "Although the limitations of such a single snapshot approach have been recognized, financial and organizational constraints have limited efforts to study the inevitable changes that occur in networks over time" (Morgan, Neal, and Carder 1997: 1). To minimize costs and effort we therefore employ another strategy of data collection which has so far mainly been used in historical network analysis: a content-analytical approach to gather dynamic network data (Seibel and Raab 2003). Here, we systematically scan a body of policy documents for relational data making use of a semiotic method of structural connotation (Nagel 2008). As a result, we obtain weighed and directed network data for several relational contents (see above). In contrast to surveys or interviews, there are no biases of reactivity and retrospectivity as political change can be extrapolated from the publication dates. Thus, in our project data collection in policy network analysis resembles a (sequential) mixed-method approach within a bigger (concurrent) mixed-method design.

Procedure

In the previous section we emphasized the network-analytical measurement and operationalization of variables. The specific strength of policy network analysis, however, is its capacity to analyze relational data by means of matrix-algebraic procedures.[8] First of all, networks can be visualized, which provides some prima-facie evidence that may guide further analysis. Moreover, several coefficients can be calculated with regard to general patterns of interaction as well as subgroups and influential actors. For example the *density* of a network describes "the general level of linkage among the points in the graph" (Scott 2003: 69). It shows the distribution of lines and at the same time the openness or closeness of a network. Measures of *centrality and prestige* help to locate network actors in central and marginal positions. We assume that a central position in the network allows access to particular resources—depending on the relational content—and thereby a higher degree of control or power. For example a high centrality index of IOs within the transaction network indicates the prevalence of financial means as a governance instrument.[9] Aside from single actors, substructures can be analyzed as groups or positions. Here, *clique analysis* aims to identify cohesive subgroups in the network (Jansen 2003: 193). Thus, patterns of collaboration—and exclusion—as well as their development can be identified and compared. By using clique analysis, for example, in the cooperation network, we can assess the relations between international and national actors concerning joint action in educational politics. Second, *blockmodel analysis* will be used to elucidate positions of structural equivalence. Here, similar actors are clustered according to common positions with regard to similar external relations.

In brief, analyzing the phenomena of the internationalization of education politics, in particular with regard to IO governance instruments and the role of transformation capacities, requires different logics of explanation. With the specific view of policy network analysis on intermediate structures of social action, patterns of cooperation, or exchange between corporate actors, for example, OECD, EU, and national actors, can be analyzed. The underlying methodological challenge of explaining new and complex social phenomena can thus be fruitfully complemented with policy network analysis.

However, policy network analysis brings along specific limitations. The usage of relational data and the focus on interaction between actors makes ideational factors, such as national guiding principles and the substantial dimension of education policies, a blind spot in an actor-by-actor network model. Moreover, the research logic of policy network analysis aims at structural description rather than explanation. To give it an explanative twist, network analytical results therefore have to be put in a comparative perspective and are thus dependent on the parameters of theoretical sampling as well as case selection. Given both its weaknesses and its particular strength, policy network analysis appears to be an ideal candidate for mixed-method designs where its results can be complemented with causal hypotheses extracted by expert interviews or regression analysis. In doing so, we cover multiple levels of analysis by combining different methodological approaches and provide a dynamic, complementary view on the phenomena of internationalized education politics at the same time.

Time series cross-section regression models (TSCS)

In our quantitative empirical analysis we aim to estimate effects of explanatory variables on dependent variables of policy output and outcomes. Provided that the database allows for a longitudinal perspective, we are interested not only in stable characteristics of nation states, which we compare in a cross-sectional perspective. In contrast, when we address inherently dynamic research questions, our focus is on the effects of changing determinants on changing outcomes of the dependent variable within countries. This is especially important with respect to the analysis of convergence processes, but also with regard to the effect of becoming a member of an international or intergovernmental organization like the EU or the OECD. As argued in the following, TSCS, as well as panel regression models, provide powerful tools for the investigation of processes of change.

Operationalization

Quantitative methodology uses numeric data and generates information from calculations and estimations. The interpretation of regression models leads to statements like "the more of the independent variable x, the more of the dependent variable y." Regression analyses are not restricted to a specific sort of data but can be based on metric as well as categorical data.

1. *IO governance instruments*: From the viewpoint of quantitative analysis a standard approach for measuring our independent variable "IO governance" is membership and its duration, assuming closer congruency with the organization's aims if a country is a member for a longer time. Our approach considers this possibility, but also strives to differentiate between the various governance instruments an organization has at hand. For example, for the instrument of financial means we consider the flow of money from the EU to a country as being an important indicator of its governance capacity. The calculation of such values is based on EU budgets over several years.[10] Activities consist of participation in events such as the Bologna Process, the Open Method of Coordination, and PISA or OECD education policy reviews. To generate this indicator, we code the participant list of these activities.

2. *National transformation capacities*: The intervening variables of the theoretical model, national transformation capacities, are split into institutional factors as veto players and ideational factors as specific guiding principles of education. We operationalize the institutional factors by an indicator as to whether a political system is open or less open to policy change.[11] The variable "veto player" mainly refers to the number of veto players, conceiving political change as more or less difficult, depending on the number of possible veto options.

3. *Transformation of national education policymaking*: The dependent variables represent political change provoked by IOs and can show two different patterns. A first possibility is that countries do more in the respective area. In our case this could mean that, for example, more resources are devoted to education. Second, as a result of common policy change across countries, states can converge with regard to central policy aims. This means that they become more similar with respect to education systems. We include as dependent variables indicators that relate to an expected increase and those that relate to convergence. Examples of variables linked to an increase would be the share of the gross domestic product (GDP) in secondary or higher education or the percentage of pupils in private schools. Examples of indicators linked to an assumption of convergence are the hours of teaching or the age of leaving secondary education.

As we carry out a quantitative large-N analysis, we can also test *alternative explanations*, thus variables that explain political change better than IOs, veto players, and points, as well as guiding principles, the factors assumed as driving forces in our theoretical model. Such variables could, for example, be the size and type of the economy or the qualification and age of the labor force. Such tests are necessary since it is plausible to assume that, since education serves the purpose of forming a labor force, related factors may well influence education policy in a very functionalist sense (Rubinson and Browne 1994, also naming other factors). Additionally, the size of a country might determine whether IO influence can easily impact on national processes, or whether it is more difficult: large countries may be much more inwardly oriented than small ones (Katzenstein 1985). Finally, the political orientation of the government can also be assumed to be an influential factor in education policymaking (e.g. Busemeyer 2007). Therefore we also control for this factor. We operationalize these variables by indicators such as the gross national income per capita, the share of the service sector as part of the GDP, the number of inhabitants, or the political majority in parliament.

Data

The data used are presented in detail in this chapter. In general, we draw on different sources to compile our dataset, since there is no existing database that contains information for all the indicators we are interested in. One of the main sources is obviously the comprehensive database that is provided by the OECD itself. The OECD statistics division publishes data on several topics, which it collects from member states. We used the OECD database to generate indicators for our dependent variables—as such they mostly measure outcomes of education policy. With regard to our intervening variables, one source in this context is published by the Quality of Government Institute, which conducts and promotes research on the causes, consequences, and nature of governance. In a comparable manner, we used data from the World Bank and other international sources. We additionally acquired some data by coding several policy documents. For example, the Eurydice Information Network provides a wide array of information on the educational systems and policies of European countries and the European University Association publishes Trends reports on particular issues. The UNESCO International Bureau of Education provides data on education, as well as country dossiers and other policy related documents that we use to assess if a country had implemented certain means, or to describe the structure of the educational system, for example the two-cycle structure in higher education.

Procedure

The specific approach of regression analysis depends heavily on the models constructed and calculated, which are, in turn, also dependent on the databases. As argued above, the dataset contains countries as well as measurements within countries as units of observation. A longitudinal approach allows not only the analysis of change over time, but also more elaborated testing of causal relationships. As a general pitfall in causal analysis, an investigation of the impact of veto players on the outcome of interest is hampered by the problem of not being able to control for any other relevant characteristics which possibly are associated with the outcome of interest. However, the longitudinal framework of the project offers the opportunity to estimate the impact of changes in *the independent variables* on changes of *the dependent variables* using a so-called fixed effect approach (see Nagel et al. 2009 for details on the method; for specific calculations see Jakobi, Teltemann and Windzio, Chapter 10 in this volume).

Such a regression analysis operates with clear assumptions of causal relationships and proves their effects. It can do so for a large number of countries and can also include alternative explanations. Limitations of the method can be distinguished as general limits, or those related specifically to operationalization, data, or modeling. Generally, quantitative assessments have a clear-cut idea of what the assumed causes and effects are before the process starts and remodel the complex social world in simple figures. This has the advantage of proving relationships between variables, but the disadvantage that the figures themselves provide only limited insights into the complexity of the "real world," a critique that qualitative researchers have often raised.

More specific weaknesses in operationalization concern independent, intervening, and dependent variables: opinion formation, for example, can in fact be shown only by linking IO activity to an outcome at the national level (e.g. that states also mention autonomy as important issue). In our specific case, there is no process of opinion formation that can be expressed in numbers. Finally, some aspects of the dependent variable, namely new processes existent at the national level, can be assessed only indirectly, by observing new actors, and deducting from their existence changed processes.

Possible problems with the dataset are its "fit" and the different sources. Analyses that are not based on primary data often bear several problems with respect to the "fit" of the data with the research phenomena. In our case it is even more problematic as we draw on many different sources to compile the dataset. That means that we have to rely on data that were gathered by different means. However we made sure to use the same source for one indicator, which was not possible with regard to the data that we gathered by document analysis. Moreover, the database of the OECD delivers a broad set of different kinds of information, but it also carries problems, because the OECD is only partly able to set binding standards for obtaining the data. This could lead to limits to the validity of certain indicators.

In addition, our analyses are limited to OECD countries. Due to the nonavailability of the respective data for many non-OECD countries we are not able to include a control group of countries that are not members of the EU or OECD. Moreover, most of the data that we rely on are not available for the time before the mid- or late 1990s. This means that we can only assess changes that occurred in a relatively short period. While longer periods of time are generally preferred, this short period nonetheless represents the temporal corridor in which we can assume that most changes should have occurred. The time frame investigated is thus a direct consequence of a research question that deals with a relatively recent phenomenon.

In sum, even given the specific difficulties of the method, an advantage of quantitative assessments is the better control for alternative reasons for a specific development. Unlike the other two methodological strategies applied in our research project—expert interviews and policy network analysis—the method can also test how IO influence and transformation capacities relate to other factors. Moreover, taking regression analysis out of the methodological portfolio would have the consequence that the findings of the country studies could not be related to any larger sample size.

Mixed-method design: A synthesis

In the previous sections we have outlined several methodological strategies to study the internationalization of education policy and its impact on national policymaking. Their obvious variation with regard to operationalization, procedure, and data points to the potentials of cross-fertilization between three approaches as different as expert interviews and document analysis, policy network analysis, and TSCS regression models. In the concluding section we will now take the step from the particular methods to a more general perspective on mixed-method designs. Initially, we proposed that *implementation timing* was a crucial characteristic of mixed-method designs and pointed to the concurrent or sequential implementation of the methodological strategies involved.

A sequential design implies a chronological step-by-step procedure, for example, an explorative qualitative study guiding a quantitative large-N survey, or a quantitative description followed by a qualitative in-depth case study. In contrast, a concurrent design is characterized by ongoing and reciprocal communication between the respective methods. Instead of a fixed unidirectional setting, different methodological strategies and logics are loosely coupled here as a dynamic mixed-method network.

Figure 2.2 illustrates that different methodological strategies and logics can be interlinked as a "network of methods." Interfaces between the respective approaches can now be institutionalized as follows. *Expert interviews* may inform network analysis to add some new actors who have not been accounted for by the more standardized selection procedures of policy network analysis, but who are nevertheless considered important by some interview partners. With respect to regression analysis, expert interviews may point to causal mechanisms guiding the expectations and action of political actors which may then be incorporated into existing statistical models or be used to reshape the strategy of modeling as a whole to improve their goodness of fit.

Policy network analysis as an approach of structural description may guide the selection of experts to be interviewed and contextualize the perception of interviewees of important (or meaningless) actors in the policy field. With respect to regression analysis, policy network analysis may account for the centrality (or marginality) of ideal-typical actors (such as IOs or veto players) in a certain country and over a given period of time. These measures can be used as an additional, more refined variable for the prominence of the respective actors or to inform the construction of models.

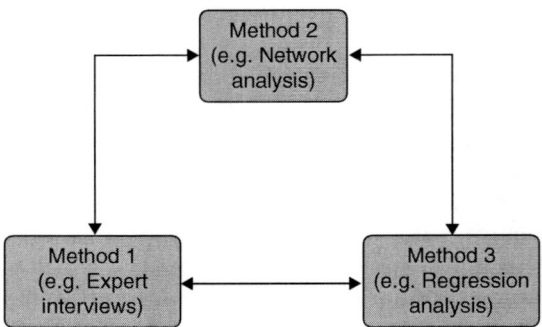

Figure 2.2 Mixed-methods network

Finally, *regression analysis* may respond to the question whether and to what extent anecdotic evidence from expert interviews and policy network analysis can be generalized beyond the case study where it was encountered. This refers to causal mechanisms as well as to influential actors. Moreover with respect to expert interviews, regression analysis may point to alternative explanations (e.g. of political change) which can then be included in the questionnaire to be considered in following interviews. As far as policy network analysis is concerned, regression analysis may point to certain causal factors (such as economic growth) that may have significance in the set of actors (e.g. a high prevalence of trade associations).

Obviously, the metaphor of a "mixed-method network" does not only allude to the chances of fruitful collaboration, but also to certain challenges inherent in mixed-method approaches in general and in a concurrent implementation timing in detail. Such a design requires a high level of expertise in at least two of the methodological strategies applied and makes great demands on communicative skills. Thus, the potential gains of validity and reliability of results are not for free, but bring along considerable transaction costs. Moreover, an interdependent setting of methods may not only be apt to pool their respective strengths, but also their weaknesses and pitfalls. Errors in data collection or analysis in one method may thus "infect" the empirical enterprise as a whole. Yet, these challenges do not call into question the endeavor of mixed-method designs in general. Rather, the acceleration of social change, on the one hand, and the disciplinary specialization of social sciences, on the other call, for cooperation, not isolation.

Finally, methodological strategies such as expert interviews, network analysis, and regression analysis differ not only as to their operationalization of theoretical concepts, gathering and handling of data, and procedures of analysis. Beyond these technical features, each method resembles a distinct *logic* of research, and this should be taken into account when a mixed-method approach is designed. In our example, explorative (expert interviews), descriptive (network analysis), and explanative research logics (regression analysis) have been combined to address the phenomenon of political change. This understanding as a "mixed-logics approach" finally allows for adjustment and adaptation in other fields of research. Expert interviews thus become a mere placeholder for methods with a qualitative, idiographic, and explorative shape, such as participant observation or discourse analysis whereas network analysis might easily be replaced by other relational and descriptive approaches, such as analyses of process known from historical institutionalism. The flexible and easily adaptable arrangement of methodological strategies and logics, however, cannot be realized in a tight sequential setting. On the other hand, the mere parallelism of various methods in a simultaneous design is somewhat arbitrary and self-referential. In contrast, a "network of methods" comprising some preconceptions as to the interactions of strategies and logics involved without exerting them in a hierarchic way, may be a fruitful model for multimethod arrangements in an era of rapid social and academic change.

Notes

1. In accordance with this, Kelle and Erzberger note the parallel application of qualitative and quantitative strategies as a characteristic for a triangulative setting (Kelle and Erzberger 2000: 300).
2. The U.S.—as a contrasting case—is only examined with qualitative methods.
3. Also often referred to as "elite interviews" or "special interviews" (Dexter 1970: 5).
4. On the one hand, it is beneficial if experts know the questions in advance to prepare their statements in a detailed and more sophisticated way. On the other hand, the disadvantage consists in a loss of spontaneous answers by the expert, who might then answer according to social desirability (Schnell, Hill, and Esser 1999).
5. We distinguish 16 types of actors and six types of relations. The *actors* are international organizations, supranational organizations, third-state actors, national state actors, federal state actors, parties and legislative actors, quality assurance agencies, research agencies, higher education institutions, training agencies, public interest groups, student representatives, professional associations, schools´ and teachers´ representatives, labor unions, and economy representatives. These actors may be connected to each other by *relations* of information and knowledge transfer, monetary transaction, symbolic affirmation, cooperation, and collective action, as well lobbyism and control.
6. There are options to include ideas and preferences in a network-analytical research design, e.g. by using a two-mode-network (Wasserman and Faust 1994: 39). As our method of data collection was actor-centered rather than topic- or issue-orientated, we decided to work with an actor-by-actor network only.
7. Certainly the number of veto players varies in the different countries, e.g. there are no federal actors in New Zealand.
8. For visualization and calculation of the network data we used the software UCINET.
9. The number of outgoing relations of an actor in the network is called its *outdegree*. This measure determines the centrality of an actor in the network, whereas the *indegree*, that is, the number of incoming relations of an actor, may resemble its reputation.

10. We consider the money explicitly dedicated to education, as well as the overall sum given to the country over time (taking out subsidies to the agrarian sector, since this constitutes a large part of the overall budget, but is traditionally not linked to any educational means).
11. The indicator PolCon III of the Political Constraint Index Dataset by Henisz (2002).

References

Barton, Allen H. and Paul F. Lazarsfeld (1955) "Some Functions of Qualitative Analysis in Social Research," *Frankfurter Beiträge zur Soziologie*, 1, 321–61.

Bogner, Alexander and Wolfgang Menz (2002) "Das theoriegenerierende Experteninterview. Erkenntnisinteresse, Wissensformen, Interaktion," in A. Bogner, B. Littig, and W. Menz, eds., *Das Experteninterview. Theorie, Methoden, Anwendungen*, Opladen: Leske+Budrich, 33–70.

Brady, Henry E. and David Collier, eds. (2004) *Rethinking Social Inquiry. Diverse Tools, Shared Standards*, Lanham and others: Rowman and Littlefield Publishers.

Brady, Henry E., David Collier, and Jason Seawright (2004) "Refocusing the Discussion of Methodology," in H.E. Brady and D. Collier, eds., *Rethinking Social Inquiry. Diverse Tools, Shared Standards*, Lanham and others: Rowman and Littlefield Publishers, 3–20.

Busemeyer, Marius (2007) "Determinants of Public Education Spending in 21 OECD democracies, 1980–2001," *Journal of European Public Policy* 14 (4), 582–610.

Caracelli, Valerie J. and Jennifer C. Greene (1993) "Data Analysis Strategies for Mixed-Method Evaluation Designs," *Educational Evaluation and Policy Analysis* 15 (2), 195–207.

Dexter, Lewis Anthony (1970) *Elite and Specialized Interviewing*, Evanston, IL: Northwestern University Press.

Froschauer, Ulrike and Manfred Lueger (2003) *Das qualitative Interview. Zur Praxis interpretativer Analyse sozialer Systeme*, Vienna: WUV.

George, Alexander L. and Andrew Bennett (2005) *Case Study Research and Theory Development in the Social Sciences*, Cambridge: MIT Press.

Greene, Jennifer C. and Charles McClintock (1985) "Triangulation in Evaluation: Design and Analysis Issues," *Evaluation Review* 9 (5), 523–45.

Greene, Jennifer C., Valerie J. Caracelli, and Wendy F. Graham (1989) "Toward a Conceptual Framework for Mixed-Method Evaluation Designs," *Educational Evaluation and Policy Analysis* 11 (3), 255–74.

Henisz, Withold J. (2002) "The Institutional Environment for Infrastructure Investment," *Industrial and Corporate Change* 11 (2), 355–89.

Jansen, Dorothea (2003) *Einführung in die Netzwerkanalyse*, Opladen: Leske+Budrich.

Katzenstein, Peter J. (1985) *Small States in World Markets: Industrial Policy in Europe*, Ithaca, NY: Cornell University Press.

Kelle, Udo and Christian Erzberger (2000) "Qualitative und Quantitative Methoden: kein Gegensatz," in U. Flick, E. v. Kardoff, and I. Steinke, eds., *Qualitative Forschung. Ein Handbuch*, Hamburg: Rowohlt, 299–309.

King, Gary, Robert O. Keohane, and Sidney Verba (1994) "Designing Social Inquiry. Scientific Inference," *Qualitative Research*, Princeton, NJ: Princeton University Press.

Knoke, David, Franz Urban Pappi, Jeffrey Broadbent, and Yutaka Tsujinaka (1996) *Comparing Policy Networks. Labor Politics in the U.S., Germany, and Japan*, Cambridge: Cambridge University Press.

Martens, Kerstin and Michael Brüggemann (2006) *Kein Experte ist wie der andere— Vom Umgang mit Missionaren und Geschichtenerzählern*, TranState Working Paper No. 39, Bremen: CRC 597.

Mayer, Horst (2004) *Interview und schriftliche Befragung—Entwicklung, Durchführung und Auswertung*, Munich: Oldenbourg.

Morgan, David L., Margaret B. Neal, and Paula Carder (1997) "The Stability of Core and Peripheral Networks Over Time," *Social Networks* 19 (1), 9–25.

Nagel, Alexander-Kenneth (2006) *Der Bologna-Prozess als Politiknetzwerk. Akteure, Beziehungen, Perspektiven*, Wiesbaden: DUV.

Nagel, Alexander-Kenneth (2008) *Analysing Change in International Politics. A Semiotic Method of Structural Connotation*, TranState Working Paper No. 70, Bremen: CRC 597.

Nagel, Alexander-Kenneth, Tonia Bieber, Anja P. Jakobi, Philipp Knodel, Dennis Niemann, and Janna Teltemann (2009) *Measuring Transformation: A Mixed-Method Approach to the Internationalization of Education Politics*, TranState Working Paper No. 83, Bremen: CRC 597.

Read, Melvyn, and David Marsh (2002) "Combining Quantitative and Qualitative Methods," in D. Marsh and G. Stoker, eds., *Theory and Methods in Political Science*, Houndmills, Basingstoke: Palgrave, 231–48.

Rubinson, Richard, and Irene Browne (1994) "Education and the Economy," in N.J. Smelser and R. Swedberg, eds., *Handbook of Economic Sociology*, Princeton, NJ: Princeton University Press, 581–99.

Schnell, Rainer, Paul Hill, and Elke Esser (1999) *Methoden der empirischen Sozialforschung*, Munich: Oldenbourg.

Scott, John (2003) *Social Network Analysis: A Handbook*, London: Sage Publications.

Seibel, Wolfgang and Joerg Raab (2003) "Verfolgungsnetzwerke. Zur Messung von Arbeitsteilung und Machtdifferenzen in den Verfolgungsapparaten des Holocaust," *Kölner Zeitschrift für Soziologie und Sozialpsychologie* 55 (3), 197–230.

Suitor, Jill, Barry Wellman, and David L. Morgan (1997) "It's About Time: How, Why, and When Networks Change," *Social Networks* 19 (1), 1–7.

Tsebelis, George (1995) "Decision Making in Political Systems: Veto Players in Presidentialism, Parliamentarism, Multicameralism and Multipartyism," *British Journal of Political Science* 25 (3), 289–326.

Wasserman, Stanley and Katherine Faust (1995) *Social Network Analysis. Methods and Applications*, Cambridge: Cambridge University Press.

Weber, Max (1949 [1904]) *The Methodology of the Social Sciences*, Glencoe: Free Press.

Part II
Historical Settings

3
The Educating State—Historical Developments and Current Trends[1]

Ansgar Weymann

Education policy is considered a classic prerogative of the modern nation state. In the twenty-first century, we have seemingly entered a period of transformation of the state toward internationalization in the field of education policy. How do the forces of national legacies and the forces of global universalism interact in times when international organizations (IOs) are designing and implementing concepts for international education policies and trying to shape national education policy outputs? This chapter contends that nation states respond in idiosyncratic ways to the new international influences as a result of pecularities in path-dependencies which determine—what we call—national transformation capacities. Two principle dynamics of development are possible.

Archer's (1979: 1) thesis holds that national power groups compete permanently to set political goals for education policy and to control the implementation of educational systems. New goals can be pursued successfully only by those power groups who have won the national power struggles. They are the ones who can modify previous practices effectively. Thus, the shape of present education policies is the product of power struggles throughout history. Depending on national history, educational systems vary significantly. And because future political action has to take place within the restrictions and opportunities of the structure of historically shaped types of educational systems, national differences have a natural tendency to persist. Education policy is shaped by the nation and is therefore nationally path-dependent. This "... does in no way necessitate the belief that educational institutions are converging, either during or after the emergence of state systems" (ibid.: 44).

Collins (1979) also argues that modern education policy is a universal element of state building, but state building itself is driven by universal forces. Educational credentials represent what Weber once coined as closure, "Schließung." The access to status distribution is closed by means of credentials. The success of individuals in the education system regulates supply on the labor market. When the number of successful social climbers is growing rapidly, credentials will be devaluated. Education policy and market actors respond to this inflation with offers of more specialized credentials and with offers of ever higher ranking credentials. Each opening up of the educational system to new social groups is followed by newly erected wings and annexes of educational institutions and curricula (ibid.: 66; Bourdieu 1988). New types of credentials are proposed as soon as the customer loses confidence in the old types.

We must assume that in the course of globalization and with the accompanying transformation of education policy, previously national paths become denationalized and blurred. As a result, a shift takes place towards technically useful knowledge, career-specific qualifications, a general performance orientation, and transnational communicative competence (Baker and LeTendre 2005; Koselleck 2006; Schriewer 2000; Schriewer 2005). Weber's ideal-type of western rationality seemingly establishes itself among actors in industry, trade, finance, transport, communication, law, bureaucracy, science, and technology (Elias 2000). This development towards one world culture is strengthened by professional actors in the field of education policy who design education systems with isomorphic curricula and institutions of teaching (McEneaney and Meyer 2000; Meyer 2007; Meyer and Rowan 1977). Finally, international organizations like the Organisation for Economic Cooperation and Development (OECD) and the European Union (EU), as well as professional associations which are supported by transnational elites, are also impacting education policy (Martens and Weymann 2007; Weymann et al. 2007).

This chapter will examine early world views of education policy which argued for and against stimulating economic prosperity and social cohesion by means of—what I call—the educating state. The chapter then will outline the institutional formation of the educating state in the history of nation-building since the eighteenth century. The thesis contends that the political economy of the educating state does indeed explain the value of the utilization of education for improving power, wealth, and integration of competing nations as universally driving forces in history. Finally, a study of front-page coverage of education policy in leading American, UK and German newspapers shows how interacting forces of national path-dependencies and universal forces are represented in the public discourse in the second half of the twentieth century.

World views on education policy

In terms of world views (see the introductory chapter to this volume), the European understanding of education is not at the beginning bound to the notion of an educating state. John Locke's (2000 [1693]) thoughts on education follow from the humanistic ideals of the gentleman, but not from the state's purpose. Hume (2005 [1739/40]) writing on human nature, Rousseau's *Emile* (2003 [1762]), and Herder (2004 [1774]) on the history of the education of mankind do not describe a theory of state responsibility within the realms of upbringing and education, although they do deal with the circumstances and interrelations of the state, society, and citizens. In each of these publications, education is neither a self-evident prerogative of the state nor a key element of the theory of the state.

In contrast to these eighteenth-century philosophers' and political scientists' points of view, the economist Adam Smith (1974 [1776]) advocates the rise of the educating state in his *Wealth of Nations*. His Anglo-Saxon utilitarian argument focuses on the externalized costs of the accelerating, capital-driven economy that creates the new wealth of nations—but not for all. The competitive division of labor of individuals, institutions, and nations within ever larger and more capital-intensive markets triggers not only unprecedented economic growth but also creates losers from competition whose personal decline may damage the nation in many forms: military unsuitability, laziness, stupidity, delinquency, herd-mentality, religious fanaticism, and ideological gullibility. It is here that the educating state steps in. While the gentleman regards his costs of higher education as his own, the state must take the deracinated agrarian population which was transformed into a new industrial underclass populace under its strict care and implement free elementary schooling, work training, and public access to basic culture through state-financed and state-regulated measures. Smith's educating state, however, did not preside over a monopoly of education policy, but rather was obligated to set its leading ideas, legal, and financial frameworks.

Long-term differences exist between the English class-structured ideas and institutions of education, and the German corporatist ones (Clark 2006). The German idealist Humboldt (2008 [1792/93]) does not advocate the educating state, which was already looming large in his days. In his book about the limits of the state, Humboldt emphasizes the preservation of liberty in the realms of education against state usurpation. He writes that public education violates the legal bounds of the state. Education shall not be used by the state to promote the prosperity of the economy or the accumulation of individual human capital. Education should not be applied to integrate the population through homogenization. Instead, a maximum of personal pluralism and creativity of the learned should be the guiding principle of education. And definitely, education should not be misused as an institution of a caring welfare state, which protects sections of the population or protects itself from them.

Again, Smith's utilitarian and Humboldt's idealistic concepts of education are different from the strictly nation state focused arguments in France. August Comte, (1968 [1842]) who gave sociology its name, pursues this point with enthusiasm. The sociological supervision of positivistic scientific education serves as a panacea against the multifaceted social ills of modern society. Only the state, through its role in upbringing and education, can correct the permanent danger of the disintegration of society. Durkheim (1972 [1922]; 1977) also had a keen eye on the role of education aimed at the creation of a maximally homogenious population. Furthermore, in context of the rivalry between France and Germany, schools and universities played a special role in the competition for national success, in a period in which Germany's education system, especially the universities, were seen as superior compared to other nations. The French absolutist and Jacobian policy of producing national elites in extremely centralized and highly specialized institutions continues to exist till today (Bourdieu 1988).[2]

The universal, overarching European résumé is given by Weber, who understood the relationship between the state and education to be shaped by the universal concept of western rationality. Higher education establishments, especially, he argues, are strongly influenced by the need for specialist schooling, which disseminates technocratic knowledge for the expanding bureaucracy (Weber 1978). For Weber, it is no longer problematic if and how state bureaucracies and market capitalism can produce the requisite social character within their populations, but rather, how rational subjects can preserve their personal liberty against the forces of bureaucratic and capitalist domination and successfully thwart the consolidation of the "iron cage" (Weber 2009).

The institutional development of the educating state in history

In terms of institution building in the history of international comparative education, the first steps towards the educating state were taken with the formation of the secular and centralized state. The highly selective education of the religious and aristocratic elites and the highly selective education of citizens in urban Latin Schools were gradually supplemented by the more inclusive and expanding education of the entire population in leading European regions (Day 2001; Fraser and Brinckmann 1968; Grendler 2001; Stearns 2001).

In Germany, in the fifteenth century, municipalities of 1000 inhabitants and more had established Latin schools for children of higher social standing. In the sixteenth to seventeenth centuries, education was used by the emerging modern state, which was confronted with religious conflicts and clashes, to integrate the multicentered and multicultural population by means of literacy, religious lectures, basic arithmetic, and a common language and narrative. In the German empire, the territorial states were in charge of providing education. Before the Reformation, 18 universities were founded and given privileges. Step by step, education turned into a normative good of statehood, transcending the boundaries of Christendom, feudal territories, and local authorities. The state's maintenance, governance, or supervision of education has had increasingly strong effects on the structure and development of opportunities over the lifespan and on the rationale of individual decisionmaking during the lives of a growing share of the populace (Hammerstein and Herrmann 2005).

A second step in the formation of the educating state was made with the formation of the nation state. Starting in the UK in the second half of the eighteenth century and in France at the turn of the century, the nation state became the most important "container" of modern society (Jeismann and Lundgreen 1987). The nation state was taken as a stronghold of civilization, progress, and protection and was seen as a key instrument of rational economic policy and decisionmaking. The state became a prime tool of the rising bourgeois political power elites, and the most important social construction of community. The nation state subordinated religion, gender, class, ethnicity, and the family as institutions of community to its rules of governance. Education—already used as an instrument of distinction and status admission in the clergy, guilds, and professions—was now also used as a mercantilist instrument of the state to improve the industrialism and human capital of the sovereign's people. These goals could only be achieved through compulsory and comprehensive education of the lower classes (Smith 1974) that was added to the time-honored selective municipal Latin school of citizens and the private education of the nobles. In Germany, compulsory elementary schooling was introduced in the early eighteenth century[3], but it took more than 100 years to enforce the policy of compulsory schooling for all citizens. For a long time, nonattendance was widespread among the poor, peasant families, and the growing industrial proletariat (Albrecht 2005).

In the nineteenth century, the educating state also played a key role in democratization and in social policy (Swaan 1988: 52–117). Nation building was a liberating force, which broke the power of feudalism, regionalism, and religion and benefited large national economies and central administrations. More and more, society was based on universal rights of citizenship, a national economy, inclusive communication, and a national curriculum of education. The nation state also nurtured nationalism, ethnosymbolism, and political Messianism as secular religions and ideologies (Smith 1998). The inclusion of the lower classes in primary and lower secondary education became a prime tool of the developing democratic state and an instrument of its welfare regime and social policy. Increasingly, education was perceived as a social right (see the introductory chapter of this volume). At the end of the nineteenth century, education served as a social right of the constitutional state, as a fundament of democratic self-determination, and as a means of providing wealth and security.

The twentieth century finally may be called the human capital century (Golding and Katz 2008; Heckman and Krueger 2003). At this point in history the United States (U.S.) became the leading nation in the race between competing states. The U.S. opened higher secondary school education earlier and more consistently to all citizens than European nations did and they turned the time-honored European university education into a much less selective and generalized system of higher education.

Today, education policy is considered a classic prerogative of the modern nation state. As a means of integrating society, as a key tool to improve economic growth, and as a social right it constitutes a core element of the nation state's sovereignty and autonomy. Mass education is employed to foster national unity, capitalizing on the resources of a national language, literacy, and homogenous arithmetic skills. Mass education is based on public- or state-financed and supervised institutions and on standardized curricula. Education enforces discipline in the personal conduct of all citizens according to the municipal middle-class archetype. Education supports the construction of cultural homogeneity and the identification with the national community. Education improves the smooth exchange of goods, persons, and services on expanding markets. Education is seen as the key resource of nations in successfully competing for wealth and power. Education is perceived as the fundament for national achievements in science and technology.

Education is applied to integrate migrants and minorities into society. Education serves as an instrument to fight lawlessness by resocialization, correction, and rehabilitation. Moreover, improvements in education are also supposed to promote democratic participation. And last, but not least, education legitimizes the unequal distribution of status among citizens by means of the acquisition of standardized and publicly acknowledged credentials that govern opportunities which are allocated in the labor and marriage markets.

Looking back at the development of higher education in Europe in the twentieth century, the expansion of education and the progressive inclusion of ever higher shares of the population into secondary education are striking. In 1950, western and central European populations were completely literate. By contrast, the illiteracy rates of Mediterranean countries still were high: Portugal 44 percent, Spain 18, Italy 14, Yugoslavia 27, Greece 26, Bulgaria 24, and Romania 23. By 1980, the rate of illiteracy had fallen to under 5 percent—with the exception of Turkey (21 percent).[4] Within one generation, mandatory schooling became the standard of personal development all over Europe, exerting a strong impact on life opportunities and influencing the rationale of decisionmaking of the entire population. In addition, the years spent in education expanded rapidly and permanently. Kindergartens and preschools were widely introduced and at the same time secondary education expanded more and more. Whereas in 1950 secondary schooling was a privilege of small elites, in the 1970s junior secondary schooling had already become the standard of education and senior secondary education the standard grade of a majority. And while in 1950 academic higher education encompassed only 4 percent of European cohorts and 17 of U.S. ones, in 1995 the figure was around 42 percent in Europe and 75 in the U.S. The share of women in higher education surpassed 50 percent, but the inclusion of the working class and migrants was much less successful. Table 3.1 displays university attendance rates in Europe from 1910 to 1995.

The political economy of the educating state: Power, wealth and integration

Education, which has enabled full literacy, full participation in secondary education, and a growing participation in higher education, substantially promoted the human development of individuals and nations. The indicators of the Human Development Index (HDI), measuring the Gross National Product per capita, unemployment rate, mortality, life

Table 3.1 University attendance in Europe, 1910–1995 (number of students compared to the number of 20–24-year-olds)

Country	1910	1950	1960	1970	1980	1990	1995
Albania			5	8	8	10	10
Belgium	1	3	9	18	26	40	54
Bulgaria	1	5	11	15	16	31	39
Germany (FRG)	1	4	6	14	26	34	44
Denmark	(1)	6	9	18	28	37	45
GDR		2	10	14	23	22	–
Finland	1	4	7	13	32	49	70
France	1	4	7	16	25	40	51
Greece	0	3	4	13	17	25	43
Great Britain	1	3	9	14	19	30	50
Ireland		4	9	14	18	29	39
Italy	1	4	7	17	27	31	41
Yugoslavia		4	9	16	28	16	18
Netherlands	1	8	13	20	29	40	49
Norway	1	3	7	16	26	42	59
Austria	4	5	8	12	22	35	47
Poland		6	9	11	18	22	25
Portugal	0	2	3	8	11	23	37
Romania	1	3	5	10	12	10	23
Sweden	1	4	9	21	31	32	46
Switzerland	2	4	6	8	18	26	33
Spain	1	2	4	9	23	37	49
Czechoslovakia		4	10	10	18	16	22
Hungary	2	3	7	10	14	14	24
Europe	1	4	8	14	22	30	42
Variation Coefficient Europe	65	34	31	26	27	33	30
Western Europe	1	4	7	15	22	34	48
Variation Coefficient Western Europe	66	36	33	27	26	21	20
USSR/Russia			11	25	52	52	43
Turkey			3	6	5	13	18
U.S.A.	3	17	21	31	56	75	81
Japan			9	17	31	30	–

Source: Kaelble 2007: 392.

expectancy, literacy rate, and tertiary and higher education participation, show the increasing contribution of human capital to the total level of human development (Wagner 2008).

The assumed potential of education to improve human development makes education policy highly important within the spectrum of national policy fields. The legitimacy of spending on education is mainly based on the trust of the public in the returns of educational investments. The application of economic criteria to education has gained weight at the expense of humanist considerations about education as personal development (Pechar 2006). The rationale is that a knowledge-based economy requires a high level of public and private investment in lifelong education; the continuous mobilization of scarce human resources; and the control of quality, efficiency, and effectivity of educational investments. Today, it is seen as normal to monitor and evaluate the utilization of education in order to ascertain whether goals have been achieved in the fields of political power, economic prosperity, and social integration.

Legitimate political power and credential meritocracy

Education policy is a valuable ideological source of power. Like other ideological sources of power, education policy is well suited to shape broad areas of society homogeneously. Ideological powers like education can be transformed into economic, military, and political powers of the state (Hall and Schroeder 2006; Mann 1986).

Modern societies have an integration and loyalty problem that lies with the issue of permanently reallocating the right people to the right places. Societies must arrange for lifelong socialization, so that the orientations and motives necessary for integration must be continuously learned anew by old and new members alike through the institutions of family, kindergarten, schools, universities, resocialization, rehabilitation, and correction. As a consequence, this development comprises an enduring field of life-long education, on the one hand, and unequal results through permanent individual educational competition on the other.

Over the course of centuries, education became a means for the meritocratic distribution of opportunities for individuals and groups and an uncontested condition for entry into the clergy, the state administration, professions, vocations, and skilled jobs. The growing educated middle-classes successfully conquered all ranks and spheres of private and state employment with educational degrees as the meritocratic basis for claims. That, in turn, made educational degrees attractive for the newly ascending social strata. Progressive general education breached the principles of inheritance of legal and material status, position, and class barriers and increasingly based the status of social groups on the principle of meritocracy.

Social climbers have to scale long ladders of educational achievements before they are admitted for competition on the segmented labor market. More than the market, meritocracy through credentials is widely accepted as a legitimate basis for the distribution of worldly goods and commodities throughout the population. The fight for educational credentials mirrors the fight for social positions in society and reflects the balance of the main power groups in society. As a consequence, the struggle with credential inflation is a permanent political problem for the state. State policies of consolidation stretch from credential capitalism to credential Keynesianism to credential socialism (Collins 1979: 195).

Education is a trusted instrument for achieving loyalty within mass societies. With full literacy (and a growing purchasing power of the population) the circulation of mass media increases. Complete literacy allows mass mobilization at the national level. Education supports or even constitutes the ideology of the nation and of the nation state through its claim to provide the definitive interpretation of world views, values, and the meaning of existence. The necessity for mass education persistently increases as a result of urbanization, industrialization, and migration. Additionally, by expanding higher education, the state becomes a venue, an instrument, and a partisan of conflicting interests between powerful groups.

This process reveals a paradox: besides loyalty, education can also foment or spur conflict. Education can enable ascending classes to partake in the nation state or make them known enemies of it. Both outcomes are possible as evidenced in history and in the present. An example is the Austrian monarchy's policy of promoting literacy through education, creating a greater awareness of the national and ethnic identity of minorities within the empire (Mann 1993). Furthermore, education fosters not only the intended identification of the individual with the state and society, but also the identification with special interest groups. Mass education and the welfare state call to the fore the notion of better services and extended rights in return. Gradually, citizens become experts in an acute and professionally organized struggle for the distribution of the public goods collected by means of taxes, fees, and dues. Political parties become specialized interest groups during this distributional struggle and must be certain that they carefully serve their active members and respective clientele in order to maintain their dominant roles within the state apparatus. Therefore, ever better organized special interest groups, clientelism, and a high impact of public choice on the distribution of collective goods are both the signs of a highly developed educating state and one of the causes of national path-dependency (Olson 1982).

The alliance between capitalism and human capital

In the nineteenth century, the hierarchy of the ruling classes was ultimately transformed from the dominance of the aristocracy and military to new bourgeois classes, institutions, and resources. A prosperous capitalist economy became a crucial factor of power in civil societies. With the takeover of power by civil society, investments in capital and in human capital became central elements of state policy. The acquisition of a disciplined work ethic and everyday standards of behavior through general education became important policy goals. General education was introduced in order to transform lower-class habits into working and middle-class habits. Vocational knowledge and skills increasingly comprised an important part of educational curricula. Vocational and academic credentials set incentives for career achievements. In the twentieth century, national human capital policy and the individual economizing on human capital became a rationale perceived as natural (Heckman 2008; Schultz 1981).

The transformation of education is driven by the options and sanctions of the capitalist economy and by the distributive consequences of the credentialism of education certificates. This goes along well with the institutionalist argument that institutions which manage the inexpensive preconditions for cooperative solutions to complex exchanges stimulate economic growth (North 1990).

The nation, globalization, and integration

The rise of the educating state played and still plays a crucial role in nation building. Agrarian societies cannot be considered "nations" as a result of their many competing elites within the nobility, churches, military, and bureaucracy, and because of the large proportion of illiterate rural populations without rights. As a result of urbanization and mass migration, the rural populations, often still organized in clans, tribes, or extended families, are transformed into an alienated and community-less urban proletariat. Conflicts between the old residents and the newcomers, between the rich and the poor, and between classes and ethnicities threaten the integration of state and society. Against the background of these developments, education policy is one of the best means for the construction and binding character of a unified national public, for which primary schools are above all useful institutions (Gellner 1983). For example, the common national language is practiced as the core element of national culture. The maintenance of the national language and the national culture is promoted among the settled population as well as the migrants. Education plays a role in the construction of cultural homogeneity and the acceptance of the national community. In this context, education, together with the mass media and intellectuals, serves as a producer of national myths.

Modernization has often stimulated countermovements in history and contemporary globalization processes have also provoked re-ethnization and religious reawakenings, reterritorialization, and strong reversion to nationalism (Conrad 2006; Conrad 2007; Guibernau and Hutchinson 2001; James 2001; Smith 1998: 215). The educating state plays a substantial role in this ambivalent dynamic of globalization and countermovements. For example, the use of dialects or foreign languages became punishable in many nineteenth-century European states with the purpose or latent function of leveling cultural differences between dialects, traditions, religions, regions, and lifestyles.[5] A historical narration of national origin and a national myth are also part of the standard curriculum. National feelings are awoken through singing the national anthem and honoring the national flag (Hechter 2000: 24–5, 64–6).

The education of unity within the nation state is more difficult to realize among the lower classes than within the middle classes, as the latter mostly see themselves as the carriers and beneficiaries of national advancement and the nation state. In contrast, among the underclasses, a break with familistic traditions, localism, religion, and the use of children and youth within family businesses must be achieved. School truancy is traditionally a problem with which the educating state must cope. For example, in the nineteenth century, corporal punishments of children and fines for parents were used to fight truancy of lower-class children especially from farming and proletarian families. Only slowly and gradually, did the pride in education expand from the upper classes to the lower ones. The more the lower classes are dependent on the state and welfare policy, the more easily this process is completed (Hechter 2000: 60).

Front-page coverage of education policy in American, UK, and German newspapers 1950–2004

It took centuries before education policy became an unquestioned prerogative of the modern state. As a means of integrating the nation state and as a key tool in improving political power and economic growth, it constitutes a core element of its sovereignty and autonomy. The currently increasing inclination of western states to engage in international (OECD) or supranational (EU) cooperation and benchmarking reflects a major change in the national policy arenas because this change will lead to a loss of power over educational control at the national level for the leading groups. The state's power, which it acquired through winning domestic power struggles in history, is at stake. This profound challenge to the balance of power of national groups should be reflected in the public discourse in newspapers. The international orientation of education coverage on the front pages of newspapers should be expected to increase at the expense of nationally oriented coverage.

We will check this assumption by investigating the front pages of leading German, UK and American newspapers since 1950, the *Frankfurter Allgemeine Zeitung* (Germany), *The Times* (UK), and the *New York Times* (U.S.A.). Can we observe a growing number of rhetorical references to globality in the national discourses and inputs of international ideas, curricula, and institutions (Janssen, Kuipers, and Verboord 2008; Roose 2008; Schriewer 2000; Schriewer 2005)? Do articles refer to shifts of power, wealth, and integration at the national level in the wake of globalization? Is national path-dependency reflected? The analysis of front-page coverage of education policy is based on a quarterly sample of Saturday editions. It includes front pages of the first week of January, April, July, and October. This makes a total of 604 front pages, 224 editions of *The New York Times* and the *Frankfurter Allgemeine Zeitung* each, and 165 editions of *The Times* printed over a period of 54 years.[6]

A total of 64 articles written exclusively about education policy or giving reference to education policy can be found on the front pages of the *Frankfurter Allgemeine Zeitung*. This is a relatively high share of 28 percent of all front pages published. Out of these 64 articles only 15 refer to issues of *international* education policy. The coverage of education policy is predominantly national. The traditional conflicts of rivaling classes and groups over power, wealth, and integration of the nation are the key issues of education coverage: selectivity and inequality of the tracking system vs. comprehensive schools, the defeat of humanist traditions and religious education, migration and education, the quality of teaching and the competences achieved by graduates, over- and undersupply of graduates, budgets and financial shortages, and finally federalist peculiarities and rivalries of the Länder and the Federation as well as competing political parties and movements. These issues reflect the vested interests in education and the precarious balance of power between interest groups and classes, the outcome of educational investments in terms of individual and national competitiveness and returns, and problems of social integration of classes and interest groups. Articles on education with international references report on successes and failures of education in foreign countries, but they do not refer to international actors on education policy.

Within the period of observation 56 front-page articles in *The Times* deal with education policy, of which only five refer to international education policy. Compared to the *Frankfurter Allgemeine Zeitung* there is less coverage of international education policy. This does not change over time. International education articles deal with foreign exchange, colonial students' accommodation, the American-British battle for greater productivity and the German idea of a two-year probatory period attached to school entries of teachers. The coverage of national issues is broadly similar to the *Frankfurter Allgemeine Zeitung*, but there is a much stronger concentration on class conflict. Many articles deal with either cuts or budget shortages, with the miserable state of buildings, and lack of facilities. They deal with the poor salaries and living standards of teachers and often mention strikes. Public policymakers are blamed for ignoring intolerable conditions of hard labor among the members of the depressed class of teachers. The balance of power is reflected in battles over primary versus comprehensive schools and over university access regulations. Furthermore, it is argued that individual human development and the prosperity of the nation are endangered by a lack of quality and skills among graduates and by the undersupply of technical skills that industries demand. Finally, a number of articles were found on specific issues like school or university TV and celebrations, which is not the case in the *Frankfurter Allegemeine Zeitung*.

In the *New York Times*, 76 articles cover education policy. Again, little reference is made to international issues. Eight articles deal with international education policy. The broad majority of articles deal with school segregation of black students. This is the central theme guiding all five decades of education policy coverage. Articles report about educator associations like the National Education Association which back the ban on segregation. They refer to court rules and judge orders on state and federal levels and to problems of implementation. Other articles comment on political programs, social movements, racial clashes, and the opening and closing of black-run (charter) schools and colleges. In this context, poverty is a big and persistent issue. A second broadly discussed issue covers finance and governance of public schools and colleges. In this field of education policy financial restrictions and the strained relation between cities, the states, and federal government are of major importance. "The task force offers programs for all education levels over the next $4^1/_2$ years. Opposition is expected" (*New York Times*, January 7, 1961). A third category of articles presents arguments on the alleged affiliation or sympathy of teachers and professors with the communist party or with communist groups inside and outside the U.S. This McCarthy issue ranks third in the coverage of education policy on front pages. It was frequent in the 1950s and 1960s. In contrast, in the 1980s and 1990s a growing number of articles about monitoring and the evaluation of outcomes of education can be observed. In 2001 (April 7) the alarming front page news is that from 1992 to 2000 the gap between the best and the worst students widened in the nationwide fourth-grade reading test of the National Assessment of Educational Progress. "Two-thirds of students tested fell below the level the federal government considers proficient, and 37 per cent fell below even basic knowledge of reading, meaning they could read little beyond simple words and sentences and could not draw conclusions from what they read."

From a comparative perspective the front page coverage of education policy between 1950 and 2004 can be summarized as follows. Of a total of 604 editions of the *New York Times*, *The Times*, and the *Frankfurter Allgemeine Zeitung* 196 front-page articles cover education policy (33 percent). International coverage is limited to 28 articles. This is 5 percent of the total of all front pages or 14 percent of all education coverage. The international coverage of education policy spans from 23 percent for the *Frankfurter Allgemeine Zeitung* to 10 for the *New York Times*, and 9 for *The Times*.

Two general trends may be concluded from Figures 3.1 and 3.2. First, the front-page coverage of education generally reached a climax in the late 1960s and early 1970s. Over later years, the interest in education has decreased or has remained stable at best. Second, the coverage of international education policy is small and characterized by booms and busts. There are years without any reference to international education policy. No growth of international coverage of education policy can be observed within the window of observation. Figures 3.1 and 3.2 show the numbers and percentage of articles on education in selected print media from 1955 to 1999.

The trinity of national education policy

About a century ago, the coevolution of power, capital, and integration by utilizing education policy had reached the state of affairs we still are used to today. In February 1927, John Maynard Keynes in a BBC discussion became involved in a debate with Ernest Walls, an industrial leader, and with Ernest Benn, publisher and journalist, on "University Men in Business."

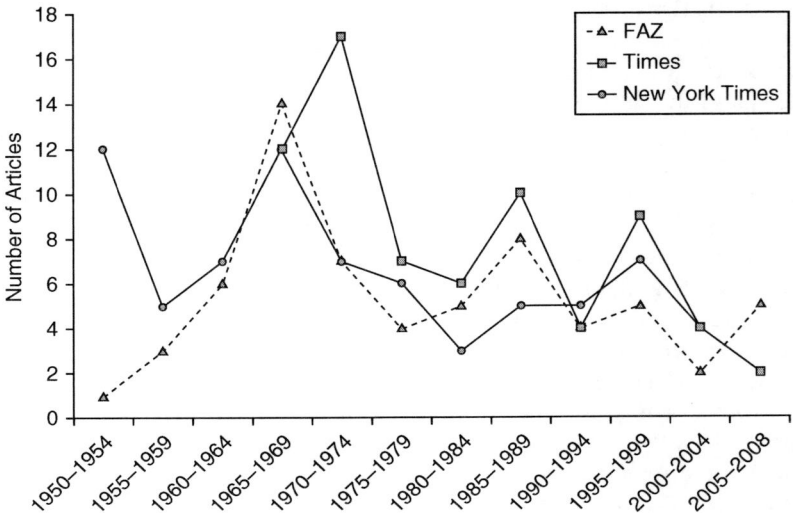

Figure 3.1 Front-page coverage of education

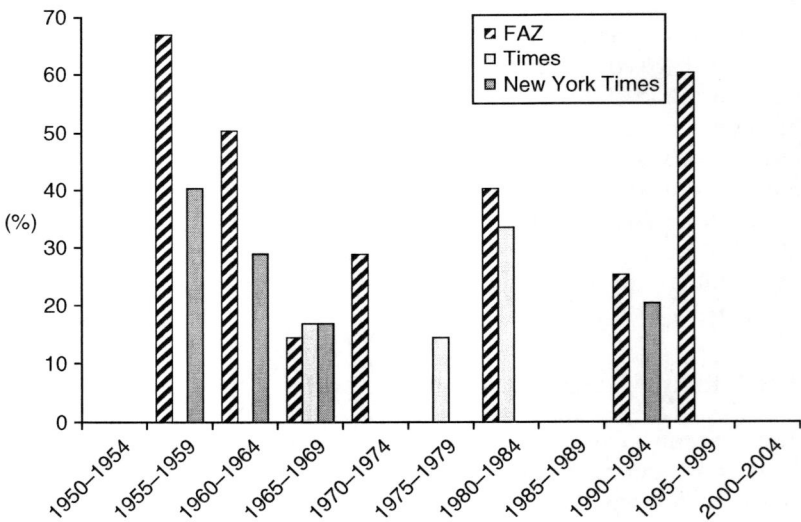

Figure 3.2 International coverage of education (percentage of all front-page articles on education)

There is unanimous consent among them that an ongoing trend towards a closer relationship between capital returns, expanding education, and successful social integration can be observed. This process is driven by both sides because it combines the interests of capital and human capital. Industry and business have a growing demand for well educated graduates from higher education to stimulate further creativity, innovation, flexibility, professionalism, multilingualism, and context sensitivity in a prosperous global economic world. Internationally active companies look for more university-educated personnel to hire worldwide.

The second argument is that these graduates of higher education increasingly have a middle-class background. They are social climbers from the upper and lower middle classes. They increasingly replace the former system of filling industrial leadership positions by hereditary succession. University education turns skilled business and industrial jobs into professions of a meritocratic credential society.

Alongside these two arguments, a third general conclusion holds which says: "Surely no one will deny that industrial peace would be easier of achievement if both branches of the industrial army possessed a higher degree of education?" (Keynes 1981: 649).

Even though articles about education are not omnipresent on the front pages of newspapers, they reflect basic issues and changes of education policy well over time. The national paths of dealing with education policy profoundly influence the perception of problems, forces, and issues of education at stake. In terms of political power, front pages might rather vigorously defend or attack the national paths of the educational system of a country, for example, tracking and corporatism, class structure and conflicts, or minority segregation and legitimacy. In terms of capital, front pages reflect more universal issues of education policy like fiscal input-outcome balances, demand and supply of labor, and economic and human capital investments and returns—sometimes from the perspective of international comparison. With respect to international coverage the front pages reflect some awareness of national competitiveness, universal developments, and problems. But they look at international issues through path-dependent national experiences and interests.

From the analysis of international coverage of education policy, it looks like there is no simple or rapid transformation from national to international education policy in sight. The transformation of the educating state is primarily seen in the light of the premises of how national transformation capacities are geared, successfully or unsuccessfully, to confront the forces of international competitiveness of economies and the rivalry of states. Internationalization is a historical process that has an impact over extended historical periods of time and requires long-term observations in order to be fully understood. It is all the more essential to pursue in-depth country case studies as well as comparative analysis in the light of an encompassing perspective of *longue duree* to reach a broad understanding of recent transformations of education policy.

Notes

1. This chapter was written at the Social Science Research Centre Berlin (WZB) in summer 2009. The author is very grateful to the WZB's President Jutta Allmendinger for the invitation, and owes the librarian Birgit Wobig and to his student Gabriel Bartl much gratitude.
2. Germany, France, and England have served as models in the history of European education policy, while the U.S. still continues to be an influential model. Nevertheless, in view of the case selection in this volume, France will be excluded from further considerations in this chapter.
3. In Germany, the origins of public schooling date back long before the sixteenth century. An overview is given in Hammerstein and Herrmann (2005).
4. Figures are taken from Kaelble (2007: 386–87).
5. In Turkey and in other countries, this is still the case.
6. *The Times* does not have a front page before July 1966.

References

Albrecht, Peter (2005) "Fürsorge und Wohlfahrtswesen," in N. Hammerstein and U. Herrmann, eds., *Handbuch der deutschen Bildungsgeschichte, Band II.: 18. Jahrhundert. Vom späten 17. Jahrhundert bis zur Neuordnung Deutschlands um 1800*, Munich: C.H. Beck, 421–41.
Archer, Margaret Scotford (1979) *Social Origins of Educational Systems*, London and Beverly Hills, CA: Sage.
Baker, David P. and Gerald K. LeTendre (2005) *National Differences, Global Similarities: World Culture and the Future of Schooling*, Stanford, CA: Stanford University Press.
Bourdieu, Pierre (1988) *Homo Academicus*, Stanford, CA: Stanford University Press.
Clark, William (2006) *Academic Charisma and the Origins of the Research University*, Chicago, IL and London: University of Chicago Press.
Collins, Randall (1979) *The Credential Society. A Historical Sociology of Education and Stratification*, Orlando and London: Academic Press.
Comte, Auguste (1968) *System of Positive Philosophy*, New York: B. Franklin.
Conrad, Sebastian (2006) *Globalisierung und Nation im Deutschen Kaiserreich*, Munich: C.H. Beck.
Conrad, Sebastian (2007) *Competing Visions of World Order: Global Moments and Movements, 1880s–1930s*, Houndmills, Basingstoke and New York: Palgrave Macmillan.

Day, Charles R. (2001) "Higher Education", in *Encyclopaedia of European Social History from 1350 to 2000*, Volume 5, New York: Charles Scribner's Sons, 353–64.

Durkheim, Émile (1972) *Erziehung und Soziologie*, Düsseldorf: Schwann.

Durkheim, Émile (1977) *Die Entwicklung der Pädagogik. Zur Geschichte und Soziologie des gelehrten Unterrichts in Frankreich*, Weinheim and Basle: Beltz.

Elias, Norbert (2000) *The Civilizing Process: Sociogenetic and Psychogenetic Investigations*, Oxford: Wiley-Blackwell.

Fraser, Stewart and William W. Brinckmann (1968) *A History of International and Comparative Education*, Pennsylvania: Scoot & Co.

Gellner, Ernest (1983) *Nations and Nationalism*, Ithaca, NY: Cornell University Press.

Golding, Claudia and Lawrence F. Katz (2008) *The Race between Education and Technology*, Cambridge and London: The Belknap Press of Harvard University Press.

Grendler, Paul F. (2001) "Schools and Schooling," in *Encyclopaedia of European Social History from 1350 to 2000*, Volume 5, New York: Charles Scribner's Sons, 329–51.

Guibernau, Montserrat and John Hutchinson (2001) *Understanding Nationalism*, Cambridge: Polity Press.

Hall, John A. and Ralph Schroeder (2006) *An Anatomy of Power*, Cambridge: Cambridge University Press.

Hammerstein, Notker and Ulrich Herrmann, eds. (2005) *Handbuch der deutschen Bildungsgeschichte. Band II. 18. Jahrhundert. Vom späten 17. Jahrhundert bis zur Neuordnung Deutschlands um 1800*, Munich: C.H.Beck.

Hechter, Michael (2000) *Containing Nationalism*, Oxford and New York: Oxford University Press.

Heckman, James (2008) *Schools, Skills, and Synapses*, Cambridge, MA: National Bureau of Economic Research.

Heckmann, James J. and Alan B. Krueger (2003) *Inequality in America. What Role for Human Capital Policies?*, Cambridge, MA and London: MIT Press.

Herder, Johann Gottfried (2004) *Another Philosophy of History and Selected Political Writing*, Indianapolis, IN: Hackett.

Humboldt, Wilhelm von (2008) *The Limits of State Action*, Cambridge: Cambridge University Press.

Hume, David (2005) *A Treatise of Human Nature*, New York: Barnes & Noble.

James, Harold (2001) *The End of Globalization. Lessons from the Great Depression*, Cambridge, MA and London: Harvard University Press.

Janssen, Susanne, Giselinde Kuipers, and Marc Verboord (2008) "Cultural Globalization and Arts Journalism: The International Orientation of Arts and Culture Coverage in U.S., Dutch, French, and German Newspapers, 1955 to 2000," *American Sociological Review* 73 (5), 719–40.

Jeismann, Karl-Ernst and Peter Lundgreen (1987) *Handbuch der deutschen Bildungsgeschichte. Volume III. 1800–1870. Von der Neuordnung Deutschlands bis zur Gründung des Deutschen Reiches*, Munich: C.H.Beck.

Kaelble, Hartmut (2007) *Sozialgeschichte Europas. 1945 bis zur Gegenwart*, Munich: C.H. Beck.

Keynes, John Maynard (1981) "University Men in Business," BBC, February 16, 1927, in: *Collected Writings*, 19, 649–61.

Koselleck, Reinhart (2006) *Begriffsgeschichten. Studien zur Semantik und Pragmatik der politischen und sozialen Sprache*, Frankfurt: Suhrkamp.

Locke, John (2000) *Concerning Education*, Oxford: Oxford University Press.
Mann, Michael (1986) *The Sources of Social Power. Volume I. A History of Power from the Beginning to 1760*, Cambridge: Cambridge University Press.
Mann, Michael (1993) *The Sources of Social Power, Volume II: The Rise of Classes and Nation States, 1760–1914*, Cambridge: Cambridge University Press.
Martens, Kerstin and Ansgar Weymann (2007) "The Internationalization of Educational Policy—Towards Convergence of National Paths?" in A. Hurrelmann, S. Leibfried, K. Martens, and P. Mayer, eds., *Transforming the Golden-Age Nation-State*, Houndmills, Basingstoke, New York: Palgrave Macmillan, 152–72.
McEneaney, Elizabeth and John W. Meyer (2000) "The Content of the Curriculum. An Institutionalist Perspective," in M.T. Hallinan, ed., *Handbook of the Sociology of Education*, New York: Kluwer/Plenum (Springer), 189–211.
Meyer, John W. and Brian Rowan (1977) "Institutionalized Organizations: Formal Structure as Myth and Ceremony," *American Journal of Sociology* 83 (2), 340–63.
Meyer, John W. (2007) Reflections. Institutional Theory and World Society, Stanford University: Unpublished paper.
North, Douglass C. (1990) *Institutions, Institutional Change and Economic Performance*, Cambridge: Cambridge University Press.
Olson, Mancur (1982) *The Rise and Decline of Nations. Economic Growth, Stagflation, and Social Rigidities*, New Haven, CT: Yale University Press.
Pechar, Hans (2006) *Bildungsökonomie und Bildungspolitik*, Münster, New York, and Munich: Waxmann.
Roose, Jochen (2008) "In nächster Nähe so fern? Grenzübergreifende Regionalberichterstattung als Aspekt von europäischer Integration," *Zeitschrift für Soziologie* 37 (4), 321–41.
Rousseau, Jean-Jacques (2003) *Emile: Or Treatise on Education*, Amherst: Prometheus Books.
Schriewer, Jürgen (2000) *Discourse Formation in Comparative Education*, Frankfurt: Peter Lang.
Schriewer, Jürgen (2005) "Wie global ist institutionalisierte Weltbildungsprogrammatik?" *Zeitschrift für Soziologie—Special Issue: Weltgesellschaft*, Stuttgart: Lucius & Lucius, 415–41.
Schultz, Theodore W. (1981) *Investing in People*, Berkeley, Los Angeles, New York, and London: University of California Press.
Smith, Adam (1974) *The Wealth of Nations*, Harmondsworth: Penguin Books.
Smith, Anthony D. (1998) *Nationalism and Modernism. A Critical Survey of Recent Theories of Nations and Nationalism*, London and New York: Routledge.
Stearns, Peter N. (2001) "Culture. Leisure. Religion. Education. Everyday Life," *Encyclopedia of European Social History from 1350 to 2000*, Volume 5, New York: Charles Scribner's Sons.
Swaan, Abram de (1988) *In Care of the State. Health Care, Education and Welfare in Europe and the USA in the Modern Era*, New York: Oxford University Press.
Wagner, Andrea (2008) *Die Entwicklung des Lebensstandards in Deutschland zwischen 1920 und 1960*, Berlin: Akademie Verlag.
Weber, Max (1978) *Economy and Society. An Outline of Interpretive Sociology*, Berkeley, Los Angeles, and London: University of California Press.

Weber, Max (2009) *The Protestant Ethic and the Spirit of Capitalism*, New York: Oxford University Press.
Weymann, Ansgar, Kerstin Martens, Alessandra Rusconi, and Kathrin Leuze (2007) "International Organizations, Markets and the Nation State in Education Governance," in K. Martens, A. Rusconi, and K. Leuze, eds., *New Arenas of Education Governance*, Houndmills, Basingstoke: Palgrave Macmillan, 229–41.

Part III
Country Case Studies

4
Turn of the Tide—New Horizons in German Education Policymaking through IO Influence

Dennis Niemann

The recent years of German education policymaking have been characterized by immense changes and continuing reform dynamics. Particularly in comparison to previous decades, which were a period of stagnation and marginal adjustments, far-reaching reforms in both secondary and higher education have taken place since the late 1990s. However, national factors did not provide the main impulse for this rediscovery of education policy. First and foremost, initiatives on the international level promoted by international organizations (IOs) were responsible for putting issues of education back on the agenda. In secondary education, the Programme for International Student Assessment (PISA), as carried out by the Organisation for Economic Cooperation and Development (OECD), influenced themes and debates in matters of education policy (Jakobi and Martens 2007; Martens 2007). PISA revealed the mediocrity of Germany's education system compared to other industrialized countries in late 2001 and triggered an intensive discourse about improving secondary education. It became obvious that reforms to modernize the German school system were inevitable. For higher education, efforts at the European level to create a common university sector undertaken under the label "Bologna Process" gradually became linked to the European Union (EU)[1] and stimulated an ongoing process of reorganization of the German system (Hahn 2004). In this context, the Bologna Process and the EU significantly influenced the shape of higher education policymaking (Balzer and Rusconi 2007) although education remained a topic of subsidiarity (Reinalda 2008). Considering this trend, the German higher education system underwent extensive changes with regard to both academic and administrative matters. As this chapter shows, without the influence of international initiatives and institutions the boost of interest and the reform processes undertaken would certainly not have been able to occur to the extent experienced. The OECD and its PISA Study, as well as the Bologna Process in the EU context, were successful in influencing the directions of reform processes.

The impact of IOs on national education policymaking is theoretically explained by different types of IO governance instruments as outlined in the introductory chapter of this volume. These governance instruments basically comprise five modes, each of which resembles a different channel to influence national policymaking: norm setting, opinion formation, financial means, coordinative activities, and consulting services. While governance capacities refer to the instruments IOs have at hand to influence behavior of domestic actors, national transformation capacities are factors that might block or enhance IO influence. As explored in the introduction to this volume, as an intermediating factor, national preconditions thus determine to what extent IO governance is able to influence national policymaking. National transformation capacities encompass veto players and points as well as guiding principles about education. Being member of the OECD and the Bologna Process, Germany is—unlike New Zealand or Switzerland—exposed to the influence of both international processes. However, in the case of Germany, many veto players and points—first of all, the federal structure of Germany's education system with the institutionalized veto power of each federal state (Land, pl. Länder) in collective decisionmaking—makes changes in education policymaking less likely. Furthermore the traditional German noneconomic guiding principle of education stands in contrast to the orientational framework of the OECD. In spite of this, the case of Germany shows low probability of change through IO governance. Hence delta-convergence—that is, when German policymaking in secondary education or higher education moves closer to the orientational framework of IOs—is not expected to take place.[2]

Against this background I demonstrate that the influence of IOs on German secondary and higher education was exceptionally strong and fostered comprehensive reforms. Despite the existence of national veto points and players as well as competing guiding principles, IO governance instruments managed to overcome these obstacles and exerted significant impact on the German education system. In fact, IOs succeeded in even converting national principles according to their own orientational framework. Because the competence for education is situated within the German Länder, this level is taken into account by focusing on Bavaria and North Rhine-Westphalia (NRW). Both are suitable for analysis because they are comparatively similar in terms of population. In contrast, the political preconditions are significantly different in each. While NRW's political structure is shaped by a more social-democratic tradition, Bavaria is influenced by conservative political forces. To conduct the analysis I drew on the methods of document analysis and expert interviews (see Nagel et al., Chapter 2 in this volume). Primary documents were taken from official publications of IOs and the German institutions of education policymaking. Additionally, 13 semi-standardized expert interviews were conducted with German education experts, comprising representatives of Federal and Länder ministries of education, officials from coordinating administrative institutions, education-related unions, and education researchers.

In the next section of this chapter the systems of secondary and higher education in Germany are described by focusing on the political dimension of education policymaking. Against the background of historical developments in both areas the basic features of Germany's education system—and thus its national transformation capacities—are summarized. The third section focuses on implemented secondary and higher education reforms in Germany since the 1980s and highlights the most important changes on the level of policy, politics, and polity. Here, a clear distinction between a pre-PISA/Bologna period and a post-PISA/Bologna period can be drawn. The emergence of both international processes triggered comprehensive reform dynamics in Germany. The fourth section of this chapter directly links the reform processes to both IO governance instruments and national transformation capacities. I analyze how the impact of international initiatives is mediated through national factors and how IOs succeeded in influencing secondary education as well as higher education. The conclusion contrasts the empirical findings with the introduced theoretical framework and gives an outlook for further research.

German education policymaking—developments and embeddedness in the international context

According to the very fundamental principle that Germany is organized as a Federal State (Article 20 (1) Basic Law), the 16 Länder possess "cultural sovereignty" and thus have the ability to exercise governmental powers and to fulfill governmental responsibilities as far as the

Basic Law does not provide or allow for any other arrangement or does confer legislative power on the Federal Government (Article 70 Basic Law). Considering this primacy of the Länder regarding education policymaking, the highest political level constitutes the State's Ministry for Education and Cultural Affairs, which is responsible for issues of secondary education, as is the Ministry for Science and Research in the field of higher education.[3] At the federal level, the Federal Ministry of Education and Research (BMBF) nowadays mainly has competences in funding research programs and in coordinating educational planning in cooperation with the Länder. The required consistency between the 16 Länder is first and foremost provided by nonconstitutional institutional arrangements. As one of the main arenas for cooperation and conciliation, the Standing Conference of the Ministers of Education and Cultural Affairs (KMK) was established in 1948 to create a common education area in Germany (KMK 2008). It unites the ministers of the Länder responsible for education policy and can be interpreted as an instrument of self-coordination of the Länder (Massing 2003: 34, 37). The Conference of Prime Ministers also has relevance for education policymaking: because it is a self-regulatory committee among the Länder its decisions can be transferred into legislation to be ratified in the Länder parliaments (Rürup 2007: 23–24). However, it has to be taken into account that decisionmaking at the federal level requires a consensus among the Länder. Overarching decisionmaking is therefore formally highly vulnerable to the veto power of each Land in the Bundesrat (federal council) and in other coordinating committees. In the Länder, decisionmaking in education policy is principally influenced by the formal veto points of (constitutional) courts. Thus, political decisions have to be in accordance with the underlying laws and can be legally appealed.

Secondary and higher education in Germany—a brief overview

The secondary education system consists structurally of four basic school types. Three types are ranked according to the students' ability and the fourth type is an all-encompassing comprehensive school. The crucial feature of this system is a selection depending on the ability of all children for one of the three types of school (Ertl and Phillips 2000: 393). Most schools are state-run institutions, which are principally free of charge, but the establishment of private schools is also constitutionally guaranteed (Article 7 (4) Basic Law) as long as they are approved by the state authorities (KMK 2008: 99). As one of the major ongoing problems, the tripartite school system makes Germany the "champion" of social selection (Interview GER07) and thus the performance disparity between students of different school types is very significant. But it has to be mentioned that the possibility of mobility between the school types is provided.

Following Teichler (2005: 26–27) higher education in Germany can be characterized by four basic features: the historically evolved focus on science including the unity of research and teaching, the *de jure* same qualitative standard of all German institutions of higher education,[4] the aim to train for a specific profession, and the traditionally high political influence of the state on universities. Higher education in Germany encompasses basically three types of institutions: universities, "Fachhochschulen" (established in 1970), and Colleges of Art and Music. Regarding financing, most of them are maintained by the Länder but private institutions are also allowed and—like private schools—approved and supervised by the state. Figure 4.1 illustrates the education system of the Federal Republic of Germany.

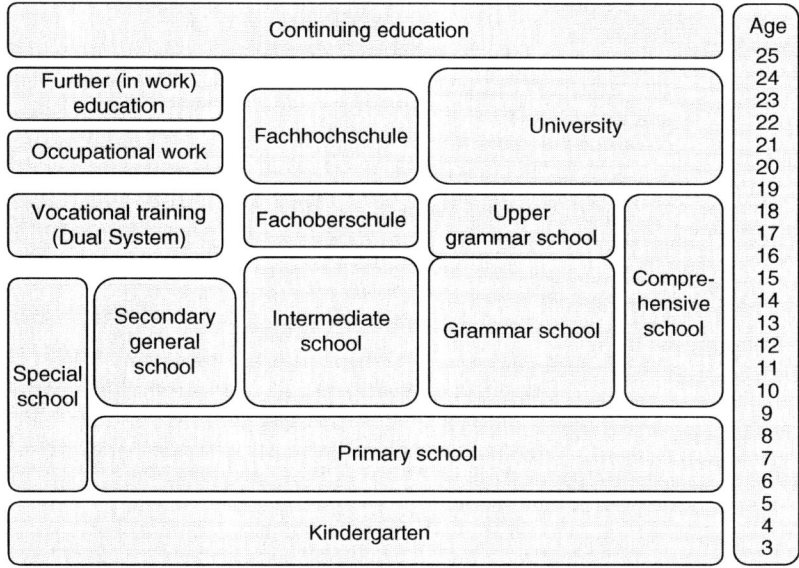

Figure 4.1 The education system of the Federal Republic of Germany

Source: Own account based on: BMBF (Online: http://www.bmbf.de/pub/bildung_in_deutschland.pdf, last access: November 13, 2008).

Historical evolution of the German education system

The current repercussions of reforms in German education policy need to be seen in the light of historical developments in order to understand the evolution of national transformation capacities that impact on the implementation of present reforms. Overall, the role of public authorities in matters of education was always very strong in Germany and it "can be regarded as a state-centred system" (Pritchard 2006: 92). In this way, education fulfilled manifold functions: national integration, social inclusion, and democratization (see Weymann, Chapter 3 in this volume). Additionally, today's federal structure of education policy is a legacy of prior state configurations from periods of different power distribution between the central government and the Länder (Führ 1997). With few exceptions education in Germany was always organized at the regional Länder level.

No comprehensive reformation of the German education system took place after the Second World War.[5] In the light of unilateral and uncoordinated reform approaches in which each Land started to develop its own education structures, the first cautious attempts to coordinate education policy were ventured and finally led to the establishment of the KMK. As education policy was solely under Länder's competence, the Federal Government gained its first diffident competences regarding higher education policy in the early 1950s.[6] One major step toward coordinating secondary education was taken by the KMK with the "Düsseldorf Agreement" in 1955, amended in 1964 and 1971 by the "Hamburg Agreements" that provided the opportunity to implement a different organizational structure for schools and defect from the tripartite principle (Baumert et al. 2003: 55). In the mid-1960s the publication of Georg Picht's "The German Education Catastrophe" (1964) induced the first education "shock" in Germany—and sparked a decade of reforms (Gehrmann et al. 2003: 108). In the aftermath several measures were undertaken to extend secondary and higher education for the newly emerged middle class and to provide equal academic opportunities among students of all social classes in order to secure economic competitiveness (Massing 2003: 19; Mayer 2005: 586–87).

On the administrative side, the expansion of higher education called for a stronger coordinative role for the Federal Government; in particular financial assistance was needed. As a result of this changed environment, the Basic Law was amended in 1969: higher education institutions became joint tasks of the Länder and the Federal Government. In line with this development, the Framework Act for Higher Education (HRG) was established in 1976 and provided a point of reference for a common higher education policy, which "the Länder subsequently fleshed out with their own legislation" (KMK 2008: 145). In short, the HRG defined the basic tasks of higher education institutions, their legal status, the requirements for accessing higher education, and other overall provisions (Künzel 1982; Mushaben 1984). With the creation of the Federal Ministry of Education and Science, the Federal Government finally established a ministry "in a policy area where it originally did not have constitutional jurisdiction" (Erk 2003: 308). At this point education policy had become an issue of joint activity of the Länder and the Federal Government.

In a nutshell, some basic historically evolved principles can be derived that are keystones for understanding developments in recent educational reform processes. First of all, the federal structure of Germany and the supremacy of the Länder in education policy make coordinative, consensus-based cooperation among them inevitable. Under the dictum that Germany is a decentralized state with a centralized society (Katzenstein 1987: 15) the provision of uniform education standards is indispensable but at the same time difficult to achieve. On the one hand the federal structure empowers the Länder to act autonomously and function as veto players concerning common agreements on standards. On the other hand Germany's homogenous society emphasizes the basic need for an equally homogenous education system. In higher education the establishment of modern and still valid structures could be traced back to the early eighteenth century and to the efforts in Prussia of Wilhelm von Humboldt, who laid the structural framework for the German higher education system, which persists to this day (Schramm 1980: 605–606). His principles include the internal autonomy of universities despite their being funded by the state and the freedom and unity of teaching and research (KMK 2008: 144). Moreover, the principled belief of the German higher education system generally corresponds with the category of self-fulfillment. It is important to note that this guiding principle lasted nearly two centuries and is still today a leading paradigm in Germany's higher education.

Trends of internationalization—German participation in the PISA Study and the Bologna Process

Overall, German participation in comparative studies in the mid-1990s was a new phenomenon in its education policymaking because it had not taken part in any international education assessments before. Thus, the conducting of the Third International Mathematics and Science Study (TIMSS) in 1995 reflected a turning point for Germany regarding participation in international education comparisons (Wößmann 2002: 97). Furthermore, with the "Konstanz Agreement" in 1997, German stakeholders agreed on regular participation in international comparative education studies and to use the results to improve the education system. The aim was to assess the strengths and weaknesses of German students in core areas of competence. Participation in PISA was one facet of this new strategy. Thus, a process of evaluating education from an outside perspective was initiated.

The intensity and extent of the debate initiated in Germany after PISA was astonishing. Unlike TIMSS, which had already alerted at least the elite in education policymaking about the mediocrity of German students in math and sciences, the broad public was not aware of the situation. As a result, the publication of PISA "led to a public outcry in Germany" (Ammermüller 2004: 2). The often cited "shock" was caused by PISA's pinpointing of Germany's status as a laggard—and not as expected as a leader—in the quality of education and framed shortcomings in education as highly crucial for general state performance (Martens and Niemann 2009). In essence, PISA managed to put the issue of education back on the public and political agenda.

The first PISA report, which was published in 2001, revealed that in the areas of academic competence tested (reading, mathematics, and science) the performance of German students at the age of 15 was significantly below the OECD average (Baumert, Stanat, and Demmrich 2001).[7] Besides the poor general results, it became also obvious that Germany was among the OECD countries with the highest level of performance variation between students. In no other industrialized country is academic success determined as much by socioeconomic background or migrant status as in Germany (Ertl 2006: 620; Kiper and Kattmann 2003: 32) and the education system seems unable to reduce existing social inequality (Loeber and Scholz 2003: 246). Thus, the aspired goal of education, that is, to provide every child—independent of its socio-economic background—with basically the same opportunities for academic success and advancement, was nullified. Although Germany improved slightly in the PISA studies of 2003 and 2006, it was still far away from ranking among the top countries in education quality and the variation still remained high (Carey 2008; Prenzel 2007; Prenzel et al. 2005).

In contrast to PISA, in Germany the Bologna Process was originally given relatively little attention, and this was mainly restricted to the part of the public who were affected by the changes in higher education. From 2002 the Bologna Process began to be discussed increasingly in German newspapers. Bologna could be characterized as a reform process initiated by a political discourse that did not emerge spontaneously, as the issue of secondary education did, but evolved gradually over time. After positive feedback from other European countries regarding the Sorbonne Declaration, in June 1999 Germany became one of the initiating countries of the Bologna Process, aiming to create a common European area of higher education by 2010. The implementation of the Bologna objectives into the German sector of higher education will be partially complete in 2010. Most prominently, by early 2009 around 75 percent of study programs were converted into B.A./M.A. structures and comprehensive measures for implementing quality assurance were introduced (BMBF 2008).

Changes in German education policymaking since 1980

After the fundamental reform processes of the late 1960s and early 1970s, Germany's education policy was characterized by a "deadlock of legal transactions since the mid-1970s onward" (Interview GER01).[8] Only small adjustments took place while the underlying structure remained stable and basically followed the same organizational patterns. Even the process of German reunification in the early 1990s brought about a major reform undertaking only for the eastern Länder while the west's pattern of education remained uncontested. The opportunity to reform the whole educational system was not seized. Instead the west German education system was simply imposed on the eastern part. Thus, it is fair to speak of an expansion of the Federal Republic of Germany's education system and a missed chance for comprehensive reforms (Wilde 2002).

However, from the end of the 1990s the field of education was characterized by multiple changes regarding both policies and politics: the years of nonreform and disregard of education policy in Germany finally came to an end. Far-reaching reform processes took place and substantially reshaped secondary and higher education. The public began to focus more intensively on the topic of education: "the awareness became prevailing that it is generally better to start investing early instead of repairing afterwards" (Interview GER09). The reforms in Germany generally reflect a paradigmatic change, which entailed an increased orientation toward an output perspective on education and a turn away from the previously predominant input dimension.

The empirical turn—reforms in secondary education

"Reform enthusiasm" concerning secondary education started in the late 1990s when three topics came to attention: quality assurance, modernization of administration according to criteria of efficiency and effectiveness, and transparency alongside accountability in the educational system (Baumert et al. 2003: 137). The slowly spreading reform awareness was finally boosted by the developments initiated by the international comparison results of the OECD's PISA Survey. In the light of the negative results, in December 2001—the same month PISA was officially published and almost three decades after the last comprehensive secondary education reform—the responsible Länder representatives agreed within the KMK upon an action plan that provided a framework for substantial reforms. The main emphasis was placed on early education in order to create a better basis for academic performance and to counterbalance the socioeconomic background of children (Carey 2008: 17–21). Furthermore, the catalog of action included the advancement of unprivileged students (especially those with an immigrant background). It also stipulated the expansion of quality assurance, improvements in the methodological and diagnostic skills of teachers, and increased opportunities for education and advancement by the extension of all-day service offers (KMK and BMBF 2008).

In order to improve the quality of education– the most important issue in reforming secondary education—the KMK agreed in 2002 on the introduction of educational standards and the establishment of a central agency for monitoring compliance with these standards (Nieke 2003: 201).[9] The Federal Government and the Länder decided to assess the performance of the German education system systematically and to act politically in respect of the empirical recommendations. From 2009 the Länder will continuously review the achievement of the educational standards in a national comparison (KMK and BMBF 2008). In general, the emphasis in secondary education policymaking shifted to empirical evaluations. In order to evaluate and interpret comparative results researchers' expertise was demanded and educational research now plays an important role in shaping and justifying education policymaking. Education policymaking does not simply concentrate on the fulfillment of certain principles. Instead, it integrates "evidence based policymaking" where political stakeholders are supported by scientific advisors. For instance, the KMK has created the "scientific advisory body," which provides advice regarding the implications of comparative studies. It is not just international comparisons that have become focal points of interest—assessments of the Länder's performances also were increasingly subject to evaluation. Moreover, the "Institute for Educational Progress" (IQB) was founded in 2004 to support all 16 Länder in their endeavors to ensure that the quality of education is monitored and continually improved upon (IQB 2009).

Overall, the state pulled back from detailed steering in favor of providing a framework for secondary education. In this regard the close relations to the new developments of output orientation become obvious again: while prior to the reforms the state authority regulated curricula and dictated what had to be taught, now it prescribes what competences a student should have at the end of a school year or at the end of his or her individual educational program.

(R-)Evolutions—recent reforms in higher education

The reform process in German higher education was multifaceted. An ostensible intention was to make German universities more competitive on the global level. Therefore, the "fiction of equality" (Interview GER06) that all German institutions of higher education are basically on the same (high) level was replaced by an intensified process of qualitative diversification. This changed understanding was first and foremost reflected by attempts to stimulate and mimic market mechanisms in the higher education sector and by the conception that education is a product that can be sold (Interview GER08). The stimulation of competitiveness induced a situation where single universities have to offer their goods (education) and the price varies regarding the performance of each institution. The German "excellence initiative," which provides a large amount of financial state support for a small number of institutions, was one additional aspect of this new development.[10] Beyond these developments, two basic streams of reforms that led to a fundamental reorganization of higher education can be identified: a far-reaching structural change resulting from the agreements of the Bologna Process and a shift in responsibilities accompanied by an increase in autonomy for higher education institutions themselves, mainly stimulated by the Federalism Reform.

Participation in the Bologna Process implied for Germany a far-reaching readjustment of national higher education structures. Since the Bologna Process aimed to introduce a consecutive study model with two main cycles (undergraduate/graduate)[11] and Germany's traditional study programs were one track, comprehensive efforts have had to be undertaken to realize the objectives of Bachelor's and Master's (B.A./M.A.) study programs. The first major step had already been taken in 1998 by an amendment of the HRG which ruled out a tentative introduction of B.A./M.A. study programs and thus provided the groundwork for a more encompassing reform of higher education (Maassen 2004: 14–15). In March 1999, the KMK, as the central political actor in coordinating education policy, published the "Structural Guidelines" (KMK 2001) which provided basic principles for accrediting B.A./M.A. programs. In line with the Bologna provisions the European Credit Transfer and Accumulation System (ECTS) was introduced to ensure the transferability of study achievements across European universities. Even though the restructuring of study courses according to the two-cycle structure and the introduction of the European credit system resembled a profound transformation of the German traditions, the implementation of both reform aspects was introduced relatively quickly and effortlessly (Interview GER11).

As in secondary education, quality assurance was generally underdeveloped in German higher education. In 1998 this aspect of evaluation was incorporated into the HRG in order to be transferred into the Länder's legislation. A corresponding process of quality orientation was initiated: accreditation. The accreditation system was supposed to ensure that both academic curricula and academic degrees of diverse study programs meet standard requirements, which had previously been defined by state authorities. Another intention was to improve and assure the quality of teaching by discovering the strengths and weaknesses of single institutions and their study programs. In 1998 the Federal Government and the Länder, in cooperation with the German Rectors' Conference, launched a program for matters of quality assurance. A KMK agreement enacted in 2002 the replacement of the old system of coordination and regulation with a decentralized system of accreditation. To be accredited, a study program must accomplish minimum standards in terms of structure, subject, and content, as well as in terms of professional relevance.

In September 2006 the most comprehensive reform of the German Basic Law since its establishment in 1949 came into force: the Federalism Reform that decartelized competences between the Federal Government and the Länder. With the amendment of 25 articles of the Basic Law the allocation of rights and duties concerning jurisdiction between the Federal Government and the Länder was reorganized. Educational policy was also affected by this fundamental reformation of the federal structure. In simple terms, the Federal Government lost most of its already limited competences to influence education policy. In detail, the amendment of Article 91b of the Basic Law defines how the Federal Government and the Länder cooperate in matters of education. The

Federal Government was no longer entitled to provide direct financial assistance or finance programs in education policy on its own, although it still continues to have the option to fund research projects beyond regional importance in cooperation with the Länder.[12] Because of the reallocation of competences in the education sector, existing cooperative institutions were abrogated, for example the task of "Joint Education Planning." Furthermore, the coordinating board between the Federal Government and the Länder was dissolved and instead in January 2008 the Joint Science Conference was created, and this mainly focuses on special matters of research. Furthermore, the HRG, which served as an instrument for securing a uniform sector of higher education across all Länder, was abolished in October 2008. In consequence, there are currently no panels where the Federal Government and the Länder can coordinate issues of education on a coequal basis. Thus, the Federalism Reform led to a decrease in the capacity of the Federal Government and the Länder to cooperate regarding education policymaking.

Through the Federalism Reform the federal character of education policy was fostered, the autonomy of the Länder in respect of higher education was strengthened, and the de facto withdrawal of the Federal Government was underscored. Unlike in Switzerland (see Bieber, Chapter 5 in this volume), it is fair to speak of the federalization of the entire education policy in Germany. The newly constituted relationship between the Federal Government and the Länder in higher education policymaking promoted new channels of governance. Formerly governance was predominantly carried out through laws. Since the Federalism Reform this pattern has widely changed: the Federal Government is no longer able to govern primarily through legal norm setting. Nevertheless it can be observed that the Federal Government has reentered the governance process in higher education on a different level. Today federal governance is conducted by means of positive incentives (providing financing). In other words, "the Federal Government still has a say because it has the money" (Interview GER03). This new mode of governance through financial incentive generally reflects an indirect tendency of the Federal Government to promote its interests in higher education.

The Federalism Reform was intended to release universities from detailed state control and grant them more autonomy by abolishing the Federal Government's competence to pass framework legislation. Beyond the direct impact of the Federalism Reform, the increase of autonomy for the Länder to govern issues of higher education also increased the autonomy of the institutions of higher education themselves. Thus, institutions of higher education can act as enterprises vis-à-vis the state and society. They elaborate aims and strategies on their own, manage their own budgets, and also develop study programs on their own (Müller-Böling 2006: 197). They can also adopt their own statutes, which need to be approved by the Land's Ministry of Education or the Ministry of Science and Research. Institutions of higher education are no longer perceived as state-owned agencies.

In NRW the enactment of the Higher Education (Liberty) Law of 2007 ("Hochschulfreiheitsgesetz") was the most far-reaching provision. This act enabled universities to operate autonomously without being affected by the Land's administration. Up to now NRW is the only Land which has made its institutions of higher education completely autonomous. De jure, universities were converted from pure state-run institutions into public corporations under sponsorship of the Land. The growth of competences empowered them with independent financial, personal, and organizational planning. But in order to receive state funding, they have to arrange target and performance agreements with the ministerial administration (MIWFT 2007). In contrast to previous procedures, this arrangement reflects a process of negotiation rather than an enactment of directives in a hierarchical relationship. The new modus operandi can be classed in terms of governance by funding and negotiating on a coequal level.

Bavaria also expanded the autonomy of its higher education institutions—but not to the same extent as NRW. The universities are still much more closely linked to the state. The topic of autonomy entered the political agenda in Bavaria comparatively late but has experienced a boost of interest in recent years (Interview GER05). For instance, the amendment of the "Bavarian Act on Higher Education" in 2006 limits the influence of the state administration basically to aspects of fundamental interests and to financial elements. With regard to operational affairs, the institutions of higher education became autonomous (STMWFK 2006). Within the framework legislation Bavaria assured to provide the higher education institutions with financial means while the universities agreed to modernize themselves. This process aims at developing a university profile with an elaborated concept of study programs. In addition, the individual higher education institutions signed a target agreement (Pritchard 2006: 100–101) with the Ministry of Research in June 2006 that laid down the development objectives which a university should achieve in the coming years (STMWFK 2005).

In sum, the German state now governs rather strategically and provides a framework for higher education, while the universities have gained enhanced autonomy. The administrations increasingly relied on setting a broad framework in which individual higher education institutions can act autonomously but need to develop sustainable concepts in order to receive funding. In this context the expression of an "unleashed university" (Müller-Böling 2000) emerged as a concept to describe the new role of higher education institutions. The Länder still govern by financial means. But in contrast to the prior situation, universities are today no longer part of the Land's budget plan; they have their own budgets (Interview GER11).[13]

Summarizing German education reforms—changes in policy, politics, and polity

The German system of secondary and higher education changed significantly in the past decade in the dimensions of policy and politics. The polity dimension was also affected in higher education by recent reform processes, but to a minor degree. Although both witnessed substantial changes the reform processes did not follow the same paths. While the reorganization of higher education is subsumed under at least two main comprehensive reforms—the Bologna Process and the Federalism Reform—the changes in secondary education reflect single adjustments without the overarching umbrella of a specific reform.

Regarding secondary education, the introduction of quality assurance, educational standards, and evaluation mechanisms, subsumed under the term "empirical turn," reflects major changes on the policy dimension. The sphere of politics was also affected by these new policies. Political stakeholders increasingly bring the expertise of consulting institutions and scientific advisors in the decisionmaking process. This new mode of steering can be labeled as "evidence based policymaking." The interplay of actors in secondary education policymaking shifted in line with the new output orientation.

Furthermore, in higher education a far-reaching change on the dimension of policy can be observed. This process involved the alteration of the study structures as well as the establishment of quality assurance, accreditation, and other output-oriented measures. As in secondary education, the higher education sector witnessed a shift toward evaluating outputs instead of merely controlling the inputs. These changes modified the whole decisionmaking process in higher education to a substantial degree. The Federal Government lost its formal competences and now increasingly relies on governance by informal mechanisms, like offering funding. At first glance, the Länder gained competences in higher education. But the increased autonomy of higher education institutions allows only for framework legislation by the Länder via target agreements and accreditation procedures. Thus, for the German state authorities it has become difficult to govern higher education institutions on a formal basis. The minor adjustments on the polity level resulted from the provisions of the Federalism Reform. The amendment of the Basic Law generally redistributed the competences between the Federal Government and the Länder and formally effectuated the clear distinction of competences in favor of the Länder in higher education.

Moreover, a watershed in German education policymaking can be clearly identified by the emergence of international processes. In the pre-PISA/Bologna era no education reforms took place. But since international developments entered the scene of education policymaking, comprehensive reforms have been implemented in Germany.

Assessing the influence of IOs and national transformation capacities on German education policymaking

The PISA Study regarding secondary education and the Bologna Process in higher education can be interpreted as the starting points for far-reaching education reforms in Germany. These reform processes cover structural aspects of policymaking as well as a paradigm change. Considering the comprehensive potential of veto players to influence policymaking and the deeply rooted guiding principles in German education policymaking, it is remarkable that both IOs were successful in exerting influence.

The PISA Study and German secondary education

Almost the entire German reform dynamic regarding secondary education was sparked when the poor PISA results of German students were published in late 2001. By showing that other industrialized countries were doing much better in certain respects related to education, the OECD provided examples of best practices, made indirect recommendations, and simultaneously raised the issues of how to improve the domestic education system. The OECD essentially affected changes with regard to the structure and principles of German secondary education.

The changes on the structural level encompass, on the one hand, an "empirical turn" that emphasized the role of evaluation including output orientation and, on the other hand, concrete changes in school settings in order to resolve the highlighted weaknesses. In detail, the OECD promoted the concept of monitoring and had substantial influence on the output orientation in German education policymaking that assesses achievement of specified goals instead of controlling just the input (Interview GER04). Generally, by coordinating the evaluation of the national system and comparing it to other countries (peer reviewing), the OECD created immense informal pressure on German policymakers to improve secondary education. But this pressure did not directly impact on the political level; it mobilized the public, who in turn called for far-reaching reforms. Although experts had already foreseen that the German comparative results would be below the average, it was a shock for Germany as a whole. The poor performance in education was directly translated into anticipated risks for future economic prosperity (Interview GER04). Thus, with the PISA Study the OECD successfully linked the topic of education to economic issues and created public demand for political reforms in order to sustain Germany's overall performance (Martens and Niemann 2009). By mobilizing public calls to improve the education system PISA also changed the stalemate among German education policymakers. The need for reforms stimulated a consensus for improvements. Speaking in terms of national transformation capacities, PISA circumvented the veto points and enforced a broad consensus for introducing secondary education reforms.

In contrast to the general agreement on outputs, reforms regarding school structures themselves were massively hindered by the national guiding principle of the tripartite structure and, moreover, varied from Land to Land. This finding illustrates that in the case of German secondary education the assumption that misfit between the international and national level facilitates change (see the Introductory chapter of this volume) does not hold true. The existence of opposing guiding principles regarding structural arrangements in secondary education prevented the adaptation of international models. In Bavaria, especially, the prevailing idea of separating and educating each student according to his or her abilities in different school types constitutes a major obstacle to altering the school system and introducing the comprehensive schools that were indirectly recommended by OECD surveys. To recapitulate, since the Land's administration is the highest authority in matters of secondary education it functions as a veto player against abolishing the tripartite system uniformly at the federal level. The "PISA winner," Bavaria, in particular, strongly opposed a dilution or even an abolition of tripartiteness. The political culture in Bavaria that strongly emphasizes autonomy is a prime obstacle for direct IO impact. In NRW, which did not perform very well in the PISA Study, the recommendations were adopted without the same degree of resistance as in Bavaria. The different assessments in different Länder made a uniform and overarching reform approach in secondary education impossible.

As regards the dimension of principles, the OECD had crucial influence on the understanding of the aims of education in Germany. Foremost, the OECD framed the discussion in terms of mobilizing human resources by providing better education; the interrelation between education and economic policy became a central focal point. This interpretation was contrary to the prior German noneconomic understanding of education. Present debates in Germany mostly accept the definition of education as an economic factor and the position that education and economics are not related has changed in recent years (Interviews GER07, GER02). In this context, the orientational framework of the IO was adapted on the national level and dissolved the preexisting misfit. Hence, the OECD had considerable success in disseminating its economic understanding of education and—regarding secondary education—it opened the corridor for integrating this understanding into further measures. PISA results also produced an ideational change, as the orientation toward basic competences has now become a focal point in education policymaking. The emphasis on aspired goals of excellent education for the gifted was eclipsed by a more fundamental understanding of the purpose of education. This more realistic attitude resulted in a new understanding that all students have to be educated equally well and weak students need special support in order to reduce the high disparities. In this regard a "pragmatization through internationalization" took place (Interview GER10).

German actors in secondary education did not change to a significant degree as a result of OECD influence. In particular, the composition of political stakeholders remains identical: the Länder governments are still the major authorities in governing secondary education. PISA did not foster the creation of an entire new structure in policymaking but, in accordance with the establishment of a culture of evaluation, it played a significant role in introducing new players on another level. As a result of the turn toward output orientation in education policy, political stakeholders increasingly consult scientific experts—such as the IQB and the KMK's "Scientific Advisory Body"—in order to identify the crucial problems and how to deal with them. The Länder authorities individually set up agencies for monitoring school performances to assure the quality of secondary education. In light of the PISA results, informal actors from the economic sector—such as interest groups and foundations—are also increasingly intervening in issues of education. They promote better education performance so that they can secure their economic competitiveness by hiring qualified employees (Interviews GER04, GER07, and GER09). By addressing the sensitive field of economic performance they gained influence on the process of education policymaking and thus produced a feedback loop on the guiding principles of German education.

The OECD essentially framed priorities for reforming secondary education by means of the PISA Study. By highlighting shortcomings and giving examples of best practices from other countries at the same time, the OECD successfully promoted its orientational framework in German secondary education through opinion formation and coordinative activities. In essence, the OECD not only promoted its orientational framework concerning education but also compelled Germany to adapt its instruments for the assessment of school performance. Furthermore, by means of PISA the OECD supported the existing efforts of the Länder to reform secondary education (Interview GER04). Planned reform schemes, which did not make it onto the political agenda, but were still in the pipeline, received increased attention after PISA and provided a basis for introducing reforms.

The Bologna Process, the European Union, and German higher education

Nearly all German reforms in higher education can be directly or indirectly explained in terms of the influence of the Bologna Process and the EU. Although the Bologna Process is an institution of its own, it cannot be understood except in the context of the EU (Reinalda 2008: 466). Thus, in assessing international influence on German higher education policy two dimensions can be separately taken into account: reforms directly related to the Bologna Process and the impact of the broader institutionalized EU framework.

At first glance the Bologna Process was primarily successful in implementing structural reforms (B.A./M.A., ECTS) by setting norms that were responsible for restructuring Germany's system of higher education. But beyond these agreements—as with secondary education—the new focus on the output dimension reflects a process that would not have been possible without Bologna because evaluation and quality assurance had not been major concerns in traditional German higher education policy (Interview GER08). The awareness that assuring the quality of higher education was necessary in order to compete at the international level was disseminated and gradually displaced the traditional German input orientation.

The implementation of B.A./M.A. study programs has to be interpreted in a twofold manner in the context of national guiding principles. On the one hand, it principally runs counter to traditional interpretations of higher education in terms of scientific education: one of the guiding principles of higher education in Germany is to enable students to boost their individual productivity, thus human capital, by imparting knowledge of scientific working methods. Hence, part of the teaching staff, especially from the nine Technical Universities, was not in favor of the restructuring of the educational modalities and hampered the transformation process. Acting as informal veto players, they feared the marginalization of the principle of unity of research and teaching (Interview GER09, GER12). On the other hand, the Bologna orientational framework which emphasizes the quality of teaching corresponds to the German guiding principle of the unity of research and teaching (Interview GER08). The enhanced focus on matters of teaching at the European level also reinforced the aspect of accounting for students' interests.

Although the Bologna Process was not established within the EU, the EU Commission accessed the process and influenced policymaking in higher education. Generally, the impact did not take place on the basis of a legal structure because pursuant to Articles 149 and 150 of the EU Treaty the EU is formally not entitled to govern matters of education. The role of the EU in influencing German higher education was more fine tuned and operated differently to Bologna. Although the EU norms were nonbinding and reflected a soft law approach of governance, they were of long-lasting significance on the national level. The direct influence of the EU on national higher education policymaking was limited because of its noncompetence in matters of education and because of the strong opposition of the Länder to allowing any formal EU influence. Even though the Directorate of Education of the EU Commission is a consultative member in the Bologna Process, which makes recommendations and initiates projects, its role can generally be interpreted as being the "BMBF on the European level" (Interview GER09): it provided financial incentives and disseminated its ideals. All interviewees evaluated the direct influence of the EU on higher education as only very rudimentary. The mechanism that exerted stronger influence was the parallel and related development of the Lisbon Process. Here, the EU basically incorporated the idea of economization and marketization, borrowed from the OECD, and promoted this ideal through its influence in the Lisbon Strategy (Interview GER11). The success of the EU in influencing higher education was caused by the incorporation of the concept of connecting education to economic performance and establishing benchmarks, which corresponds to this ideal. Member states were already sensitive to this approach as a result of the OECD initiatives and so the EU's efforts landed on fertile ground. Thus, the EU entered higher education policymaking through the back door and used the instruments of opinion formation, providing financial incentives,[14] and informal norm setting in shaping national higher education policy. The EU increasingly influenced policymaking in higher education by recommendations and other publications that worked as guidelines for reforming institutions of higher education (Interview GER06). Even without taking direct measures, the EU is passively involved in current developments in higher education. Making universities more autonomous has implications regarding binding EU law in the economic sphere, too. The more institutions of higher education become independent actors detached from the state and its resources, the less the state is able to provide them with financial support because this might affect EU market regulations that in turn restrict national intervention by private actors (Interview GER13). In reforming higher education the nation states have increasingly to account for EU law and need to act in accordance with EU legislation.

In German higher education the pattern of actors in policymaking remained stable. The primary responsibility for decisionmaking still lies at the level of the Länder. However, through the agreed standards of the Bologna Process institutions of accreditation were introduced.[15] In focusing on the output dimension of higher education institutions, councils were established in which representatives from social partners and the economy present their points of view on reforms needed to make higher education more effective.[16] Nonstate actors have also gained substantial influence on German education policymaking (see Nagel, Chapter 9 of this volume for a comparative perspective). First and foremost foundations like Bertelsmann, Hertie, Mercator, etc. have conducted empirical research on issues of education, launched programs, and offered detailed recommendations for reforming the education system for political stakeholders (Interviews GER01, GER08, and GER10). At the European level, the EU Commission has joined the established higher education policy process and indirectly exerts influence on the member states and shapes the area of European higher education without using the label of harmonization. However, it actually fosters harmonization (Interview GER05). The Commission strategically gained influence beyond its scope of competences without imposing unpopular harmonization measures on member states. By keeping its influence indirect and informal, the Commission has not been subject to the veto power of national stakeholders.

Although the Länder gained even more formal power in higher education after the Federalism Reform, they were marginalized by a constant growth in (nonbinding) norms stemming from the European level which they could not elude. Furthermore, resistance by the Länder to implementing an orientational framework that came from the European level was not successful because they were faced with pressure to modernize the higher education system and to adapt to challenges dealt with on the international level. Despite their competencies in higher education, the Länder did not respond to international higher education developments accordingly. In fact, international developments bypassed the autonomy of the Länder and exerted substantial influence on shaping national higher education.

Comparing the dimensions of IO influence on German education policymaking

Summing up, both IOs were very effective in promoting their orientational framework in Germany. The OECD had its primary influence in setting (agenda) priorities in education policy (Interview GER05) by using the instruments of opinion formation and coordinative activity. Since the OECD generally had no impact in terms of hard governance it notably affected German secondary education policy by influencing public debate and creating informal pressure to convert to its orientational framework. And since the OECD cannot govern through rules or financial means, other aspects like information exchange, creating knowledge, mutual learning, or pooling resources were at the center of its activities. The pressure for reforming secondary education triggered by PISA also bypassed the usual German veto points in advance and led to concordant efforts in reforming secondary education. By means of PISA, the impact of the OECD was even strong enough to transform some national guiding principles in accordance with the IO's orientational framework.

In higher education norm setting within the scope of Bologna fostered significant changes in the German system. In order to make the Bologna reforms work, this process was also supplemented by a readjustment of the fundamental guiding principles concerning higher education. The promotion of quality assurance, better employability, or the necessity to prepare universities for global competition, made changes possible and in a broader sense changed the perception of goals of higher education in Germany. This development illustrates that the emergence of new guiding principles—stemming from the IO level—was a fundamental precondition for the observed changes. This finding goes beyond the basic assumption that an existing misfit between the national and international levels promotes change (see the introduction chapter of this volume).

Bologna operated as a catalyst for developments in the German higher education system (Interview GER09). Although the concept of introducing consecutive study programs already existed, its implementation in the late 1990s was slow and rather tentative. The European initiatives boosted the development significantly. Again, German reforms in higher education were not deeply affected by formal German veto players. Since reforms were enacted in concordance with the most important veto players, namely the Länder, major obstacles for blocking reform undertakings had been removed in advance. Generally, while PISA basically bypassed the veto players, within the Bologna Process all veto players supported the reform approach. Only traditionalist informal veto players opposed the Bologna reforms and tried to influence their implementation. Regarding this rationale, the existing guiding principles in German higher education partly opposed the international efforts and caused barriers to implementing new structures in higher education.

Conclusion

Analyzing recent German reforms in secondary and higher education is not possible without referring to the impact IOs have had on this process. The initiatives of the OECD's PISA Study and the Bologna Process, as well as the involvement of the EU, substantially influenced the shape of the current education landscape in Germany. Generally speaking, from the mid-1990s education policy became a prominent issue on the political agenda because of developments on the international level. A structural change occurred in education policymaking that can be summarized in terms of an increase of the competences of the Länder and at the same time a decrease of the competences of the Federal Government, supplemented by emerging influence of IOs. Taking the underlying setting of Germany's ex-ante education system into account, the comprehensive impact of both IOs has to be emphasized. Despite the existence of multiple veto points and historically evolved guiding principles that were contrary to the orientational framework of PISA and Bologna, both IOs managed to overcome these obstacles and substantially influenced the German education system by applying IO governance instruments, such as opinion formation and coordinative activities. Additionally, (nonbinding) norm setting played a role in the context of higher education: the Bologna Process defined aims to be achieved in a certain time period.

A priori, it was expected that veto players would very strongly influence education policy in Germany. Overall, that was not the case. Further research is required to assess the detailed motives and driving forces behind this nonintervention of veto players. From the perspective of this chapter it can be taken that generally a high degree of agreement existed among political stakeholders regarding reforms in secondary and higher education. Furthermore, almost all veto points were to some extent circumvented in advance. The new developments did not only occur in the light of national guiding principles that were partially contrary to the international efforts. The IOs were able to alter the preexisting German guiding principles in general. Thus, as a result of the new interpretation of educational principles the implementation of IO-induced reforms was facilitated and opened a corridor for restructuring secondary and higher education. In this regard, delta-convergence has taken place: The German secondary and higher education systems successively moved closer to the orientational framework of the OECD/PISA and EU/Bologna.

Besides essential changes in policy, the politics of education were also altered to a certain degree through IO influence. In both secondary and higher education the empirical evaluation of outputs became a focal point in policymaking and consequently the process of policymaking altered in Germany. Furthermore, institutions providing empirical analyses increasingly became important actors in education policy and gained influence by making recommendations.

Assessing the developments in Germany's education policy reveals dynamics that can clearly be linked to the IO level. Whether this impact follows a general trend towards internationalized governance has to be analyzed in comparison to other countries studied here (see Windzio, Martens, and Nagel Chapter 11 in this volume). Are IOs becoming increasingly important in influencing national education policymaking? Are they fostering the harmonization of education systems in industrialized countries? Further research is needed to generalize observed patterns beyond the German case.

Notes

1. The European Commission's Education and Culture Directorate-General is the central actor within the EU context. The terms EU, European Commission, etc. are used interchangeable whereby the focus is foremost on the Commission.

2. The concept of delta convergence describes the decreasing gap of policies towards an exemplary model (Heichel et al. 2008: 83). Regarding education, delta convergence is present if German goals, instruments, and settings in this policy field approximate the orientational framework of IOs.
3. Depending on each Land, the individual names of the ministries for secondary education and higher education might differ.
4. De facto, this standard of equality is rather debatable.
5. Only the developments in the Federal Republic of Germany are described.
6. Starting with the establishment of the Federal Ministry for Nuclear Issues in 1955 the federal policy experienced another boost after the "Sputnik Shock" of 1957. The German administration forced development in sciences and geared its efforts to the example of U.S. promotional patterns (Krücken 2005: 17). Afterwards it continued to gain further competences and the BMBF was finally launched in 1994.
7. Overall, Germany was ranked (averaged) twentieth in PISA 2000, sixteenth in 2003, and twelfth in 2006.
8. All translations by the author.
9. The establishment of education standards also accompanied an increased implementation of comparative tests and evaluation aspects, like VERA or PISA-E, in schools.
10. In 2005 the Federal Government announced the creation of elite universities by supporting selected universities with a total amount of €1.9 billion over a four-year period. Universities have to develop an adequate concept for teaching and research in order to receive extra funding from federal agencies (for more details see, e.g. Hartmann 2006).
11. Since the Berlin Communiqué (2005) the two-cycle model has been amended by the inclusion of doctoral training.
12. The "Higher Education Pact 2020" is one example of this cooperative funding.
13. Additionally, the fundraising ability of higher education institutions shifted: a decision of the German Federal Constitutional Court in 2005 offered the opportunity to impose tuition fees (Carey 2008).
14. For example within the EU *Framework Programme for Research and Technological Development*.
15. At the European level the supervising European Quality Assurance Register for higher education was also founded (for more details see: EQAR 2009).
16. The new pattern in higher education is strongly related to the Anglo-American higher education system (Interview GER12).

References

Ammermüller, Andreas (2004) "PISA: What Makes the Difference?" *Diskussionspapiere der DFG-Forschergruppe* 04/07, 1–30.

Balzer, Carolin and Alessandra Rusconi (2007) "From the European Commission to the Member States and Back—a Comparison of the Bologna and the Copenhagen Process," in K. Martens, A. Rusconi, and K. Leuze, eds., *New Areas of Education Governance. The Impact of International Organizations and Markets on Educational Policy Making*, Houndmills, Basingstoke: Palgrave, 57–75.

Baumert, Jürgen, Cordula Artelt, Eckhardt Klieme, Michael Neubrand, Manfred Prenzel, Ulrich Schiefele, W. Schmieder, K.-J. Tilmann, and M. Weiß (2003) *Pisa 2000—Ein differenzierter Blick auf die Länder der Bundesrepublik Deutschland*, Opladen: Leske + Budrich.

Baumert, Jürgen, Petra Stanat, and Anke Demmrich (2001) "PISA 2000: Untersuchungsgegenstand, theoretische Grundlagen und Durchführung der Studie," in Deutsches PISA-Konsortium, ed., *PISA 2000—Basiskompetenzen von Schülerinnen und Schülern im internationalen Vergleich*, Opladen: Leske + Budrich, 15–68.

BMBF (2008) *Bericht zur Umsetzung des Bologna-Prozesses in Deutschland* (Online: http://www.bmbf.de/pub/umsetzung_bologna_prozess_2007_09.pdf, last access: June 15, 2009).

Carey, David (2008) "Improving Education Outcomes in Germany," OECD Economics Department Working Papers, 611.

EQAR, European Quality Assurance Register (2009) *European Quality Assurance Register—EQAR* (Online: http://www.eqar.eu/uploads/media/EQAR_Infodoc.pdf, last access: May 17, 2009).

Erk, Jan (2003) "Federal Germany and Its Non-Federal Society: Emergence of an All-German Educational Policy in a System of Exclusive Provincial Jurisdiction," *Canadian Journal of Political Science* 36 (2), 295–317.

Ertl, Hubert (2006) "Educational Standards and the Changing Discourses on Education: The Reception and Consequences of the PISA Study in Germany," *Oxford Review of Education* 32 (5), 619–34.

Ertl, Hubert and David Phillips (2000) "The Enduring Nature of the Tripartite System of Secondary Schooling in Germany: Some Explanations," *British Journal of Educational Studies* 48 (4), 391–412.

Führ, Christoph (1997) *Deutsches Bildungswesen seit 1945*, Kriftel, Neuwied: Luchterhand.

Gehrmann, Axel, Peter Massing, Einhard Rau, and Bernhard Muszynski (2003) *Bildungspolitik in der Bundesrepublik Deutschland—Eine Einführung*, Schwalbach, Taunus: Wochenschau Verlag.

Hahn, Karola (2004) *Die Internationalisierung der deutschen Hochschulen. Kontext, Kernprozesse, Konzepte und Strategien*, Wiesbaden: VS Verlag für Sozialwissenschaften.

Hartmann, Michael (2006) "Die Exzellenzinitiative—ein Paradigmenwechsel in der deutschen Hochschulpolitik," *Leviathan* 34 (4), 447–65.

Heichel, Stephan, Katharina Holzinger, Thomas Sommerer, Duncan Liefferink, Jessica Pape, and Sietske Veenman (2008) "Research Design, Variables and Data," in K. Holzinger, C. Knill, and B. Arts, eds., *Environmental Policy Convergence in Europe—the Impact of International Institutions and Trade*, Cambridge: Cambridge University Press, 64–97.

IQB, Institut zur Qualitätsentwicklung im Bildungswesen (2009) *Perspectives and Visions. The Standardization and Illustration of National Educational Standards in the Federal States of Germany. Introducing the IQB* (Online: http://www.iqb.hu-berlin.de/institut, last access: February 22, 2009).

Jakobi, Anja P. and Kerstin Martens (2007) "Diffusion durch internationale Organisationen: Die Bildungspolitik der OECD," in K. Holzinger, H. Jörgens, and C. Knill, eds., *Politische Vierteljahresschrift—Special Issue: Transfer, Diffusion und Konvergenz von Politiken*, 247–70.

Katzenstein, Peter (1987) *Policy and Politics in West Germany. The Growth of a Semisouvereign State*, Philadelphia, PA: Temple University Press.

Kiper, Hanna and Ulrich Kattmann (2003) "Basiskompetenzen im Vergleich—Überblick über Ergebnisse der PISA-Studie 2000," in B. Moschner, H. Kiper, and U. Kattmann, eds., *PISA 2000 als Herausforderung*, Baltmannweiler: Schneider Verlag Hohengehren, 15–37.

KMK (2001) *Strukturvorgaben für die Einführung von Bachelor-/Bakkalaureus und Master-/Magisterstudiengängen* (Online: http://www.hrk.de/de/download/dateien/strukvor.pdf, last access: October 15, 2008).

KMK (2008) *The Education System of the Federal Republic of Germany 2006. A Description of the Responsibilities, Structures and Developments in Education Policy for the Exchange of Information in Europe* (edited by B. Lohmar and T. Eckhardt), Bonn: KMK.

KMK and BMBF (2008) *Ergebnisse von PIRLS/IGLU 2006-I und PISA-I: Gemeinsame Empfehlungen der Kultusministerkonferenz und des Bundesministeriums für Bildung und Forschung* (Online: http://www.kmk.org/fileadmin/pdf/dokumentation/BeschlKMK/Vereinbarungen__Erklaerungen/080306-pisa.pdf, last access: May 28, 2009).

Krücken, Boris (2005) "Hochschulen im Wettbewerb—Eine Untersuchung am Beispiel der Einführung von Bachelor- und Masterstudiengängen an deutschen Universitäten," *Endbericht des Lehrforschungsprojekt*, 1–36.

Künzel, Klaus (1982) "The State and Higher Education in the Federal Republic of Germany," *European Journal of Education* 17 (3), 243–57.

Loeber, Heinz-Dieter and Wolf-Dieter Scholz (2003) "Von der Bildungskatastrophe zum Bildungsschock—Zur Kontinuität sozialer Benachteiligung durch das deutsche Bildungssystem," in B. Moschner, H. Kiper, and U. Kattmann, eds., *PISA 2000 als Herausforderung*, Baltmannsweiler: Schneider Verlag Hohengehren, 241–85.

Maassen, Oliver T. (2004) *Die Bologna-Revolution: Auswirkungen der Hochschulreform in Deutschland*, Frankfurt am Main: Bankakad.-Verlag.

Martens, Kerstin (2007) "How to Become an Influential Actor—the 'Comparative Turn' in OECD Education Policy," in K. Martens, A. Rusconi, and K. Leuze, eds., *New Areas of Education Governance. The Impact of International Organizations and Markets on Educational Policy Making*, Houndmills, Basingstoke: Palgrave, 40–56.

Martens, Kerstin and Dennis Niemann (2009) "Governance by Comparison—How Ratings & Rankings Can Impact National Policy Making in Education," paper presented at the Conference "International Studies Association," New York City, New York, February 15–18.

Massing, Peter (2003) "Konjunkturen und Institutionen der Bildungspolitik," in P. Massing, *Bildungspolitik in der Bundesrepublik Deutschland*, Schwalbach: Wochenschau Verlag, 9–25.

Mayer, Karl Ulrich (2005) "Das Hochschulwesen," in K.S. Cortina, J. Baumert, A. Leschinsky, K.U. Mayer, and L. Trommer, eds., *Das Bildungswesen in der Bundesrepublik Deutschland. Strukturen und Entwicklungen im Überblick*, Reinbek: Rowohlt Taschenbuch Verlag, 581–624.

MIWFT—Ministerium für Innovation, Wissenschaft, Forschung und Technologie des Landes Nordrhein-Westfalen (2007) *Ziel- und Leistungsvereinbarungen 2007–2010. Hochschulen in Nordrhein-Westfalen* (Online: http://www.innovation.nrw.

de/objekt-pool/download_dateien/hochschulen_und_forschung/Broschuere_ZLV_2007.pdf, last access: May 25, 2009).

Müller-Böling, Detlef (2000) *Die entfesselte Hochschule*, Gütersloh: Bertelsmann Stiftung.

Müller-Böling, Detlef (2006) *Nach der Reform ist vor der Reform. Neue Herausforderungen für die entfesselte Hochschule*, Cologne: Josef Eul Verlag GmbH.

Mushaben, Joyce Marie (1984) "Reform in Three Phases: Judicial Action and the German Federal Framework Law for Higher Education of 1976," *Higher Education* 13 (4), 423–38.

Nieke, Wolfgang (2003) "Schulreform: Wie reagiert die Fachpolitik auf bildungswissenschaftliche Bestandsaufnahmen?" in T. Hansel, ed., *PISA—und die Folgen? Die Wirkung von Leistungsvergleichsstudien in der Schule*, Herbolzheim: Centaurus Verlag, 197–214.

Picht, Georg (1964) *Die deutsche Bildungskatastrophe. Analyse und Dokumentation*, Munich: Walter.

Prenzel, Manfred (2007) "PISA 2006: Die wichtigsten Ergebnisse im Überblick," in M. Prenzel, C. Artelt, J. Baumert, W. Blum, M. Hammann, E. Klieme, and R. Pekrun, *PISA 2006. Die Ergebnisse der internationalen Vergleichsstudie*, Münster, Munich: Waxmann, 13–30.

Prenzel, Manfred, Jürgen Baumert, Werner Blum, Rainer Lehmann, Detlev Leutner, Michael Neubrand, Reinhard Pekrun, Jürgen Rost, and Ulrich Schiefele (2005) *PISA 2003. Der zweite Vergleich der Länder in Deutschland—Was wissen und können Jugendliche?*, Münster, New York, Munich, Berlin: Waxmann.

Pritchard, Rosalind (2006) "Trends in the Restructuring of German Universities," *Comparative Education Review* 50 (1), 90–112.

Reinalda, Bob (2008) "The Bologna Process and Its Achievements in Europe 1999–2007," *Journal of Political Science Education* 4 (4), 463–76.

Rürup, Matthias (2007) *Innovationswege im deutschen Bildungssystem. Die Verbreitung der Idee "Schulautonomie" im Ländervergleich*, Wiesbaden: VS Verlag für Sozialwissenschaften.

Schramm, Jürgen (1980) "Development of Higher Education and Employment in the Federal Republic of Germany," *Higher Education* 9 (5), 605–17.

STMWFK—Bayerisches Staatsministerium für Wissenschaft, Forschung und Kunst (2005) *Gemeinsamer Leitfaden für den Abschluss von Zielvereinbarungen zwischen den Bayerischen Universitäten und dem Staatsministerium für Wissenschaft, Forschung und Kunst*, Munich: STMWFK.

STMWFK—Bayerisches Staatsministerium für Wissenschaft, Forschung und Kunst (2006) *Neues Hochschulrecht in Bayern* (Online: http://www.stmwfk.bayern.de/Hochschule/pdf/themenblaetter_hochschulrecht.pdf, last access: May 25, 2009).

Teichler, Ulrich (2005) *Hochschulstrukturen im Umbruch. Eine Bilanz der Reformdynamik seit vier Jahrzehnten*, Frankfurt, New York: Campus Verlag.

Wilde, Stephanie (2002) "Secondary Education in Germany 1990–2000: 'One Decade of Non-Reform in Unified German Education'?" *Oxford Review of Education* 28 (1), 39–51.

Wößmann, Ludger (2002) *Schooling and the Quality of Human Capital*, Berlin: Springer.

5
Playing the Multilevel Game in Education—the PISA Study and the Bologna Process Triggering Swiss Harmonization

Tonia Bieber

Since the acceleration of globalization in the 1980s, the adaptation to international developments and discourses in education policymaking has become inevitable for nearly all countries (Drezner 2001). At the international level, the aim of enhancing global competitiveness is the special focus of diverse educational initiatives furthered by international organizations (IOs), particularly the European Union (EU) and the Organisation for Economic Cooperation and Development (OECD). The most outstanding examples of international initiatives in education in the last decade run the risk of being confused with Italian cities: the "Programme for International Student Assessment" (PISA) is a survey on student performance in secondary education performed every three years by the OECD since 2000. The intergovernmental "Bologna Process" of 1999 aims at integrating European higher education systems and is supported by the European Commission (Bologna Declaration 1999; Hackl 2001; Martens and Weymann 2005).

In the last decade, the two-level game between the cantons and the Federation in the federalist country of Switzerland has become a multilevel game as a result of these new international actors in the field of education. Nevertheless, Switzerland takes a special position concerning the internationalization of education policy. On the one hand, as a founding member of the OECD and participant in diverse OECD education programs, we would expect a high level of influence for the PISA Study. On the other hand, Switzerland is not a formal EU member (Fischer, Nicolet, and Sciarini 2002; Sciarini, Fischer, and Nicolet 2004), but has taken part in the Bologna Process as a bottom-up initiative since its very beginning. Thus we would expect a weaker influence of Bologna in Switzerland than in EU countries because the EU is a key Bologna actor. However, institutional settings in Switzerland hardly encourage reforms (Bonoli and Mach 2000): direct democracy, federalism, and consociationalism not only prolong decisionmaking processes and involve many veto players in the domestic sphere but also handicap coordination with IOs and other countries. These facts make Switzerland a hard case for internationalization (Bieber 2009). Likewise, the two international initiatives are least likely candidates for changing the education policymaking of countries: they are voluntary, legally nonbinding initiatives and can be categorized as so-called "soft governance."

This chapter thus deals with how the PISA Study and the Bologna Process have influenced Swiss education policymaking. To identify the causal mechanisms, it draws on the theoretical framework as introduced in the introductory chapter of this volume. The main theoretical argument states that IOs exert influence through their governance instruments, which range from norm setting, opinion formation, financial means, and coordinative activities to consulting services. However, the degree to which a country will respond to these international stimuli is mediated by national transformation capacities: veto players and points as well as guiding principles of education. To investigate this multilevel game between the two IOs and Switzerland (Putnam 1988), the case study empirically draws on qualitative methods as explored in Chapter 2 of this volume. These include expert interviews with 23 Swiss education policymakers and staff of the Directorate-General for Education and Culture of the European Commission, document analysis, and secondary literature analysis.

In this chapter, I will show that despite reform-hindering conditions, core reforms in Swiss education policymaking were triggered by the emergence of a third, international policymaking level in the context of PISA and Bologna that entered the education political arena in the last decade. Because of the comparatively comprehensive adoption of the respective international policy models, Switzerland exhibited—in addition to altered patterns of actors—both a high adaptation to international aims, particularly in the case of Bologna, and a domestic unification of the heterogeneous cantonal policies and educational structures, notably in the context of PISA.

This chapter is organized as follows: In the next part, I will present the current Swiss education system including its German and French historical roots. In the third part, the empirical analysis demonstrates that Swiss education underwent remarkable changes, which were triggered by the PISA Study and the Bologna Process—despite reform-hindering domestic settings responsible for the backlog of reforms in the 1980s and 1990s. In the fourth part, I evaluate the influence of IO governance instruments and national transformation capacities on reform processes in Swiss education policymaking and show how the international initiatives were able to impact on Switzerland and how they functioned as triggers for significant domestic change. The concluding part provides a final summary of main findings and points to subjects of further research.

Education policymaking in Switzerland

In Switzerland, there are 26 different cantonal education systems. However, because of intercantonal agreements, one can speak of one system. The complexity of joint decisionmaking (Scharpf 2006), competences, and legislative processes as well as of the pattern of actors and their roles in Swiss education policymaking reflects the political features of direct democracy, subsidiarity, and federalism (Scharpf 1988; Hega 2000). According to the Article 61a of the Constitution on the "Swiss Education Area" (Bundesverfassung 1999), the Federation, communities, and cantons, which constitute the main veto players, share responsibility for various parts of the system. Like the U.S., Switzerland is a federal state with substantial community power in education. Its highly heterogeneous education system is regionally influenced. The French-speaking *Suisse romande* is endowed with powerful cantonal departments with professional experts in education while German-speaking cantons rest on nonvocational or lay administrators at community and district level (Hega 2000). They try only to abolish differences in cantonal policies under joint supervision (negative integration), whereas the *Suisse romande* shifted policymaking from the communities to the higher authority. Each canton holds regulatory and financial power for compulsory schooling and the university located within its boundaries (Bundesverfassung 1999, Article 63). The primary responsibility for education and culture is held by cantonal education departments, which coordinate at the national level via the Swiss Conference of Cantonal Ministers of Education (EDK). The Federation has jurisdiction over the Federal Institutes of Technology (ETHs) and universities of applied sciences (FHs), supports cantonal universities, and encourages research. It bears the costs of ETHs and cantonal tertiary institutions and research. Uniquely, there is not one federal education authority, rather two: the State Secretariat for Education and Research (SBF) in the Federal Department of Home Affairs (EDI) is responsible for compulsory schooling and universities. In contrast, the Federal Office for Professional Education and Technology (BBT) in the Federal Department of Economic Affairs (EVD) is in charge of the FHs. The Federation and cantons jointly coordinate Swiss higher education and take account of the autonomy of the universities (Bundesverfassung 1999, Article 63a).

The structure of the education system

The levels of lower secondary and higher education are particularly affected by the international initiatives under study (see Figure 5.1). In the case of Swiss lower secondary education the structure is rather complex. It starts after primary school and forms the second and last part of compulsory schooling, until grade nine. Depending on the length of primary education that ranges from four to six years, lower secondary education consists of three to five years. In most cantons, there are school types with different requirements. Preprofessional schools

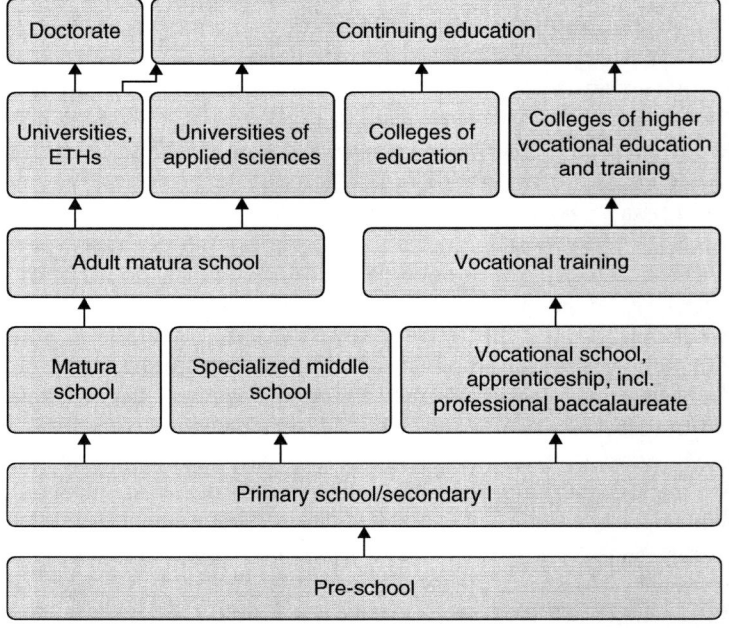

Figure 5.1 The Swiss education system

Source: Own account on basis of: http://www.sbf.admin.ch/htm/themen/bildung_en.html, last access: March 20, 2009.

recruit students who are more interested in manual jobs, and do not have any selection criteria for entry. They provide practical education to prepare pupils for basic vocational training. Pregymnasiums, types with higher requirements, aim to prepare students for grammar schools that deliver a Federal Matura (school leaving certificate). They include a selection for school entry, with the choice between science and literary streams. The third type of school does not have any selection based on student performance.

The dual Swiss higher education sector includes two types of institutions, with the same status but different philosophies. First, traditional universities—ten cantonal universities and two ETHs—center their instruction on basic research and teaching, applying an academic approach. ETHs are federally run universities involved in scientific and technical research. Having a high global reputation in providing research, teaching, and services of an advanced international standard, they provide technical subjects, in contrast to cantonal universities. To attend university, students must have a Matura from the four-year grammar school. There is no *numerus clausus* for subjects at university, except for medicine at German-speaking universities. Second, FHs have the same educational task as universities, combined with elements of general vocational education. In contrast to universities, they take a practice-oriented approach through a close link between teaching and applied research.

Historical and ideational background

Like other European education systems, the Swiss system has its origins in the nineteenth century. Its history is marked by a permanent struggle for educational competences between cantons and the Federation. After having been in the hands of the church for some centuries, the first federal public education law made schooling a state policy field during the Helvetic period from 1798–1803 (Hega 1999). The Constitution of 1848 transformed the loose federation of sovereign cantons into a federal state. However, the constitutional revision in 1874 left little political authority in the field to the Federation except in the areas of higher education and vocational training. After the Constitution and its revision, primary education in public schools was free, compulsory, state-controlled and secularized, and education policy the prerogative of cantonal governments. The struggle against federal influence over cantonal systems was finally successful when the "school bailiff" proposal was rejected in an 1882 referendum.

In the twentieth century, the education system lacked intercantonal and international cooperation. Although the EDK had been created in 1897 as a platform for coordination of cantonal school systems, the cantons took their own paths until the Second World War. Accordingly, no federal department for education was ever established (Hega 1999). Developments after the Second World War exhibit a phase of expansion and differentiation until the 1960s. The need for internal mobility increasingly required intercantonal—and later international—coordination, so that the EDK had to create four regional coordination areas. However, the conflict between unification and decentralization was also reflected in the new expansion period around 1970. This was stopped by economic depression, and school reformers tried to revise the system totally. As a result of the growing demand for education and mobility, a Concordance Treaty on School Coordination, or *Schulkonkordat*, was concluded in 1970 to coordinate the beginning of the school year,[1] school entrance age, and the length of time for compulsory schooling and gaining a school leaving examination (EDK 1970). However, this important legal instrument for unification was highly contested and did not lead to the establishment of a supracantonal or national authority (Hega 2000: 7).

Surprisingly, Switzerland developed from being a leader in educational expansion regarding student enrolment in primary schools in the late nineteenth century to a laggard 100 years later. By the 1970s, it fell behind all western European countries in student ratios in fulltime secondary schools and universities. OECD (1992) education statistics show that relatively low Swiss higher education entry and graduation rates in the 1970s and 1980s did not follow the pattern of expansion experienced in other OECD countries. The reason for expanding higher education cautiously was—and still is today—to sustain high quality and to match educational supply to the demand of the employment system. During expansion, the educational field changed, as new actors appeared and traditional players provided themselves with scientific staff to meet the demand for rational education politics (Osterwalder and Weber 2004). For example in higher education, the Federation created a scientific council in 1965 to enforce a harmonized policy vis-à-vis the cantons. The Federal Law on Higher Education Promotion of 1968 established a Swiss higher education area and transferred the coordination and harmonization of cantonal universities to the Federation. As in 1874, the attempt to empower the Federation failed again, as a constitutional amendment for education was rejected by the cantons in the 1973 referendum (Hega 1999). Even nowadays cantonal diversity and regional disparities in school systems, enrolment rates, and education opportunities are striking and cause problems for intra-Swiss mobility of students and teachers.

The historic development of the Swiss education system brought about specific guiding principles of education. They affect the impact of recent reform processes, but also may undergo processes of change themselves. Both the region and the phase of education determine guiding principles. As a result of the split education system following the German and French models, regional differences exist with regard to guiding principles of education. In the German part, the Swiss school system is tripartite as in Germany. Humboldt's ideal of unity of research and teaching as well as academic oligarchy is prevalent in Swiss higher education, as the German "institute universities" served as a model for their Swiss counterparts (Clark 1983: 50; Horvath, Weber, and Wicki 2000). In contrast, in French-speaking Switzerland the model of the all-day school is supposed to compensate social inequalities. In higher education, the state takes a more central role.

Moreover, guiding principles differ according to the educational level. The connotation of education in secondary education is rather political, in higher education it is economic. In secondary education, the performance principle was very strong in the nineteenth century, but its importance decreased with the development of the welfare state. Since Switzerland's foundation as a Federation in 1848, school has become a factor of societal cohesion and the focus is no longer placed on the individual. Education is considered a cultural good and civil liberty according to Dahrendorf (1965), and aims at equality of opportunities. As it was feared that competition would trigger performance variation and a loss of quality and equality of opportunities, the education system was kept in public hands and the free choice of school was not granted (Interview CH15, CH18). Another core function of the education system is social mobility, that is, overcoming formal societal barriers of sex, religion, and social background. In contrast, higher education is inspired by contradictory aims: there are macroeconomic principles, as education is considered the only resource for competing with other nations. Microeconomic principles aim to further human capital and stress a high selectivity by competition via performance. However, the German Humboldt model regards education as a form of self-realization. The publicly financed system with comparatively low study fees contributes to the aims of social mobility and accessibility (Interview CH03, CH05, CH13, CH15).

The context of internationalization

The Swiss education system is marked by a complex division of responsibilities between the cantons and the Federation as well as by historic guiding principles. However, in the last decade, novel international developments challenged these former patterns. Recent internationalization processes of Swiss education have been determined, in particular, by its participation in the PISA Study and the Bologna Process.

The PISA Study initiated in 2000 has become an influential and major constituent of the OECD's educational work (OECD 2008). PISA results did not meet Swiss expectations, although they were often significantly above the OECD average. Swiss children scored better in mathematics (in all three studies above OECD average) than in literacy and natural sciences (in PISA 2000 under OECD average, in 2003 and 2006 above). This revealed that some students were not prepared for entering work life, particularly those of immigrant families (EVD 2008). As in most OECD countries, economic, social, and cultural background is decisive for school performance. Accordingly, media attention on PISA in Switzerland was high (Stöckling 2005; Martens and Niemann 2009). As deficiencies in literacy are regarded as a relevant social problem and the illiterate are marginalized in society, the media proposed education measures—as realized in the reform project "HarmoS" elaborated on in the third part of this chapter—by referring to the example of the PISA "champion" Finland (SGB 2007).[2]

Switzerland has participated in the Bologna Process since its very beginning (Bologna Declaration 1999) in order to match its education system with the surrounding EU states. With regard to the introduction of Bachelor's and Master's (B.A./M.A.) structures, the implementation of Bologna[3] has made considerable progress in Switzerland: since fall 2006, all first-year university students enter B.A. programs. Presumably, in 2010/11 more than 95 percent of students will participate in B.A. and M.A. courses (SBF/BBT 2008). The European Credit Transfer System (ECTS) was introduced rapidly in all Swiss higher education institutions.[4] Officially, its implementation status is 100 percent of the total number of higher education programs. However, a national student survey revealed that there are still many differences between institutions or subjects regarding the use of ECTS and workload required per credit (SBF/BBT 2008). The reaction of Swiss actors to Bologna in the media was rather substantial and very positive. The criticism mostly concerned the manner of implementation in Switzerland, not the aims of Bologna, and depended on the class of actors: political and administrative actors in education were proponents, while students tended to have a critical position or stressed the need for improving implementation.

Latest reforms in Swiss education

The joint decision trap[5] of the federalist country (Scharpf 2006: 847) made the Swiss education system experience a backlog of reforms from the 1980s well into the 1990s. However, despite the high number of veto players, Switzerland has undergone various transformative processes in the last decade. While in secondary education, rearrangements concentrated on the HarmoS project, there were various areas of reform activity in higher education such as the establishment of the FHs, the Bologna implementation, and the "Swiss Higher Education Landscape" project.

The domestic harmonization of Swiss secondary education

One of the core reforms in Swiss secondary education is the revision of the educational constitution: by harmonizing cantonal education systems, it aims to enhance the international competitiveness of Switzerland and intra-Swiss mobility. In May 2006, the population and the cantons agreed by large majority to the new articles on education in the Constitution (Aprentas 2006). Surprisingly, veto players did not hinder reforms in this case, but even paved the way for far-reaching change. Although responsibilities in the system did not change and for primary school still lie within the cantons, the article 61a introduces the joint steering of higher education by Federation and cantons. Likewise, the cantons themselves have to coordinate as they are obligated to regulate structural indicators unitarily. Most recently, the Federation has another means to generate pressure for domestic harmonization as it can declare a concordat, which is an intercantonal agreement, as nationally binding if cantons do not reach an intercantonal solution. This harmonization is intended to enhance the effectiveness of compulsory schooling.

In order to implement the constitutional article and as an indirect reaction to PISA, the most outstanding reform project of the last decades was introduced in August 2009: the school concordat HarmoS for the harmonization of compulsory schooling[6] (Maradan and Mangold 2005; EDK 2007). Although the intention to harmonize was not new, the attempt to enhance intra-Swiss mobility and quality by harmonization was successful for the first time. HarmoS goes beyond the school concordat of 1970 (EDK 1970) that did not suffice to further harmonization and even hindered reforms. After coordination failed in the 1990s, the EDK created the basis for far-reaching harmonization of core indicators, such as school entrance age, length of compulsory schooling, aims, and transitions of educational phases. HarmoS has diverse instruments to this end (see Table 5.1). First, it introduces superordinate basic education aims for compulsory schooling in five subjects: languages, mathematics and natural sciences, social sciences and humanities, music and art, and sports and health. To develop competence levels for these subjects, Switzerland draws on international activities produced in the context of PISA (EDK 2004). HarmoS postulates for compulsory schooling a local standard language and competences in a second Swiss language and another foreign language. Second, structural benchmark figures determine the length of educational phases and increase the number of years for compulsory schooling from nine years to 11 to enhance early learning: eight years for primary school including two years basic level or Kindergarten—depending on the canton—from age four, and three years for upper secondary education. The transition to upper secondary education is planned for vocational education after the eleventh school year, and for Matura at a Gymnasium after the tenth school year. These regulations require some cantons to change their school system, which has increased costs and caused some opposition. Third, for quality assurance, the introduction of the instrument of national education standards is designed to reduce diversity and harmonize the aims of the single educational phases. The standards have been introduced, in particular, because of the results of PISA 2000 (EDK 2004). Instead of being decided at the cantonal level, curricula and teaching material will now be developed on a language-regional level. HarmoS also involves scientific education statistics and monitoring as an instrument for planning and politics: as a pilot scheme, the educational report of 2006 provides

Table 5.1 The instruments of the reform project "HarmoS"

1. Subordinate aims of compulsory schooling	Basic education aims Language teaching
2. Structural benchmark figures	School enrolment Length of levels of education
3. Instruments of system development and quality assurance	Educational standards Curricula, teaching aids and evaluation instruments Portfolios Educational Monitoring
4. Organization of the school day	Basic schedule and day structures

Source: Own account based on the Intercantonal Agreement on the Harmonization of Compulsory Schooling (EDK 2007).

data on all educational levels of Switzerland. The first regular report to be published in 2010 will assess the performance of the education system in terms of the three criteria of effectiveness, efficiency, and equity (SKBF 2006). Finally, the organization of instruction during schooldays is structured in blocks and there is an offer of optional daycare tailored to market needs.

Because of the developments in the new educational constitution and of HarmoS, the roles of the EDK and of the cantons have changed. The EDK has been established as an important steering body above the cantonal level (Criblez 2008: 286). At a new political level in the Swiss system, the EDK has emerged, a result of the complex horizontal and vertical "joint decision making" (Scharpf 2006) in education. Its function is to prevent federal solutions in the competence area of the cantons, but simultaneously to push the cantons into harmonization under the increasing pressure for coordination (Criblez 2008: 286). The EDK has been strengthened by the new educational constitution as it has become the most important actor in harmonization—in contrast to the Federation, which comes last, that is, only if coordination between cantons has failed.

In no other policy field is cooperative federalism as well developed as in education. This development has substantially constrained the educational autonomy of cantons that is not valid any more for the single cantons but only for the collectivity of cantons (Criblez 2008: 292–95). The individual cantons no longer determine education politics, rather they do so together in the EDK. It has become increasingly difficult for cantons to opt out of harmonized policies. The pressure for adaptation to HarmoS guidelines is high because nonconforming cantons run the risk of being blamed for the imposition of a federal solution. In the future, no canton can evade new intercantonal agreements. If it does so, it can be coerced by the Federation to obey them (Criblez 2008).

The international harmonization of Swiss higher education

The 1980s were in general marked by a phase of lack of reform in Swiss higher education. Then, in the run-up to the referendum on accession to the European Economic Area in 1992, the structural problems within Swiss higher education became apparent: the conditions for international comparability and foreign recognition of Swiss degrees were not met. In order for Switzerland to be able to operate internationally, structural changes and adaptations toward international developments had to be introduced (Criblez 2008). Therefore, Parliament passed a law in 1995 that created FHs and colleges of education, with FHs functioning as type of higher education institution in addition to universities (Fachhochschulgesetz 1995). Previously, only polytechnics and higher commercial or administration colleges, etc. had provided professional education. This tertiarization of higher vocational education upgraded them to a status comparable to that of universities.

The goals of the Bologna Declaration of 1999[7] were comparatively quickly and comprehensively implemented in Switzerland in the following years (SBF/BBT 2008), so it was called a "poster child."[8] Shortly after 1999, Swiss higher education institutions recognized the significance of this reform, initiated Bologna-related legislative reforms, and established project organizations. Bologna concerns many actors in Switzerland and requires national regimentation for guaranteeing uniform and coordinated implementation of reform. Toward this aim, the "Bologna Directives," which are legally binding on universities (SUK 2003) and FHs (EDK 2002), were adopted. The directives state that the implementation of new structures will be completed by the end of 2010 (SBF/BBT 2008). Although leaving sufficient leeway for the cantons, they fix a uniform framework for the introduction of new study structures and ECTS, admission to Master's studies, the title awards, and reform implementation. They are based upon the 2000 convention on the cooperation in higher education institutions between the Federation and cantons with universities. Moreover, to counteract the problem of changing studies between universities and FHs, in 2008 the Rectors' Conferences came to an agreement on permeability between the different types of higher education institutions that enables transition on condition of some supplementary performance records. The cantons with universities have consequently adapted their legislation. The FHs have undergone a parallel Bologna reform: the Federal Act on Universities of Applied Sciences was partially revised in 2005[9] in accordance with the new study structures to enhance national and international compatibility and competitiveness of degrees. This provided the legal foundation for the introduction of B.A. and M.A. studies that started in the falls of 2005 and 2008, respectively, and established quality and accreditation systems. Moreover, in addition to technology, economics, and design, the act put the areas of health, social matters, and arts under the guidance of the Federation.

The Bologna Process modified the Swiss pattern of actors in three areas. First, particularly against the background of financial shortfalls, Bologna changed the balance of power in favor of the executive at the expense of the legislative. The federal government gained power by providing financial means and having clear competences, as universities alone never would have been able to introduce Bologna (Interview CH07, CH14). Second, the cooperative federalism of Switzerland was enhanced as the establishment of the Swiss University Conference (SUK) in 2001 strengthened the cooperation between the Federation and the cantons: the SUK consists of representatives of both. It received financial and policymaking powers, and its directives became binding framework regulations. This guaranteed the feasibility and bindingness of Bologna. For the first time, guidelines could be fixed that are binding on all universities, while formerly the SUK had only been able to make recommendations (Interview CH02). Moreover, the federal government made the Rectors' Conference of the Swiss Universities (CRUS) responsible for Bologna coordination in universities in 2000. The government itself would not have been able to take on this task because the cantons would have rejected this as an intervention in their field of competence (Interview CH02). In the case of the FHs, the Rectors' Conference of the Swiss Universities of Applied Sciences (KFH) has gained weight by cooperating with federal and cantonal authorities and acting as the coordinating body for the Bologna implementation in the FHs. Thus, these three higher education institutions—SUK, CRUS and KFH—have become the most important players in the area through Bologna and its successful implementation (Interview CH14). Third, the increased autonomy of higher education institutions required new quality assurance mechanisms, so the actors responsible for quality assurance also changed: While formerly the Federation had been responsible, since 2001, the independent agency-like "Center of Accreditation and Quality Assurance of the Swiss Universities" (OAQ) has set requirements related to quality assurance, prepared the decisions for accreditation and regularly checked compliance.

The last substantial higher education reforms came into action in order to harmonize cantonal systems in the face of the rising cross-cantonal and international need for coordination. The revision of the Constitution (Article 63a on higher education) stated that the Federation and the cantons should enhance their cooperation to jointly steer higher education institutions and guarantee quality in Swiss higher education via contracts and transfer of competences to common organs—without fundamentally changing the existing division of competences (Interview CH13). It created the necessary preconditions for a strong all-Swiss steering of the whole higher education area, transparent financing orienting on performance and results, strategic planning, and better sharing of tasks among higher education institutions.[10] In May 2006, the people and the cantons approved this revision in a referendum by a substantial majority.

To fulfill this constitutional requirement for simplified steering of higher education, new legislative foundations were created for both the Federation and the cantons. The draft of the Federal Law on Promotion and Coordination of Higher Education Institutions (HFKG) produced great interest during its consultation process, as it will establish a unitary Swiss Higher Education Landscape after its expected coming into force in 2012.[11] It is intended to guarantee quality, competitiveness, coherence, and efficiency of the system. Toward this aim, it replaces the federal decrees for universities and FHs, and thus will be the only legal basis for the Federation regarding the financial promotion of cantonal universities and FHs, and concerning the political steering of the whole Swiss higher education area in concert with the cantons. This facilitated steering helps to regulate the entire higher education sector uniformly. Parallel to, and based on, the federal law, a concordat on higher education is prepared by the EDK. It will include intercantonal financing that is now regulated by two agreements for universities and FHs. The EDK issued this concordat in consultation at the beginning of 2009.

Summarizing the changing dimensions of education policymaking

This section set out to provide a picture of the political changes in Swiss secondary and higher education since the 1990s and brought to notice certain evidence that an unusually high number of comprehensive reforms have been introduced. In the field of secondary education, the most striking changes concerned policy, and the least were with regard to politics: policies changed with reforms, particularly with the intercantonal HarmoS concordat aimed at the harmonization of compulsory schooling through harmonizing structural benchmarks and establishing education standards and language-based regionally unitary curricula. According to the new educational constitution, it is not only the Federation and the cantons that are forced to cooperate, but also the cantons among themselves. Of course, such changes in polity also involved changes in politics. Although responsibilities in the system did not change, the Federation was given more far-reaching competences in cases in which the cantons do not reach a solution between themselves.

Likewise, in higher education, the changes in policy were the greatest, in polity the least. Bologna-related reforms mainly consisted in the introduction of the two-tier study system, the ECTS, and a quality assurance system in all cantons. Interestingly, while aimed at international harmonization, the international initiatives also led to domestic harmonization: a more unitary Swiss education system has come into being. For polity, the new constitutional article on higher education aims to improve cooperation between the Federation and cantons by committing them to joint steering of colleges and universities. Politics changed as new actors entered the scene, as a result of the establishment of the OAQ and the FHs, along with the KFH and the FH Council.

PISA and Bologna played a central role in the enactment of substantial reforms in Switzerland at the turn of the century (Aprentas 2006). The international imperative toward harmonization was furthered by intra-Swiss developments that expressed the increasing need for cross-cantonal coordination in such issues as mobility. Interestingly, the contents of the reforms in the two educational sectors point in a similar direction. HarmoS and reforms implementing Bologna aim at harmonization of education standards, structures such as the length of study or schooling, and quality assurance in the cantonal education systems. Consequently, Swiss education is becoming more unitary in both sectors. The trend toward domestic harmonization was even reflected in the reception of the educational constitution of 2006 by the cantons and the people.

While the period from the 1980s well into the 1990s was determined by few changes, the amount and intensity of Swiss education reforms has increased dramatically in the last decade. Consequently, reform activities can be divided into two periods, a rather passive and a highly active one. The dividing lines are the PISA Study since 2000 and the Bologna Process of 1999, which reveal the important role of international initiatives as catalysts of Swiss reforms.

International initiatives as triggers of change

Even in a policy field, like education, that is skeptically defended against exogenous invasions, the voluntary informal methods of IOs can be successful in influencing the national level: the impact of IO governance instruments—used in the context of PISA and Bologna—on Switzerland was actually very high. These instruments do not directly change domestic policymaking, but are mediated by national transformation capacities such as veto players and nationally rooted guiding principles.

The influence of PISA on Swiss secondary education

PISA played a vital role in the introduction of the latest Swiss secondary education reforms. Lacking authority over education, the OECD cannot enforce its aims but it has various soft governance instruments at hand to influence member states. The IO governance instrument of norm setting in its soft form recommends certain behaviors and concrete objectives. By providing comparative data, benchmarks, and rankings PISA enhances competition and performance orientation, and creates a normative pressure. The introduction of education standards to monitor outcomes was furthered by PISA and institutionalized by regular education reports. For example, PISA brought forward the issue of enhancing social mobility and integrating immigrants so that, in the context of HarmoS, the length of compulsory schooling was extended to include the kindergarten level. In addition, reducing the number of years in grammar schools was discussed, with a view to prolonging the number of years spent together by pupils of all tiers.

PISA is said to have had the strongest form of influence through forming opinions, namely by means of conferences on PISA, HarmoS, or of the OECD's "Centre for Educational Research and Innovation" (Interview CH08). This brought education back to the political agenda and put some topics in a new light, such as equity of chances, fairness, and the possibilities of participation, which in turn changed national guiding principles. PISA triggered HarmoS by changing the historically evolved guiding principle of "being the best" into a more critical self-perception (Interview CH07, CH17), as well as towards more equality and equal opportunities in education. Social discrimination has turned out to be very high (Zahner et al. 2002), and one's position in the education system is still to a large extent "inherited" because of the selective system. Thus, PISA helped to implement the principle of equal opportunity that is constitutionally guaranteed in Switzerland (Bundesverfassung 1999). Moreover, the economic rationale for education was introduced by PISA. Thus, the principles are based more on education as human capital than as a civil right (Interview CH05). As the international sphere started to influence Swiss principles, the old Swiss principle of performance returned, although it competes with various historic principles such as the myth of public schooling, equivalence of all teachers, and no free school choice. Thus, there is a medium degree of misfit between Swiss principles and the orientational framework of the OECD. However, nowadays the individual has become more important and both competition and free choice of school have become topics of discussion (Interview CH15).

IO governance through coordinative activities is the precondition for providing comparative PISA results. By organizing expert conferences on PISA, the OECD shows best practices and rankings, and recommends measures to overcome national problems. Competition between countries was enhanced by the PISA ranking (Interview CH05). Acting as agenda setters, PISA and the referenda on HarmoS increased the significance of the education system in the national public perception and reestablished education as a topic on the political agenda (Interview CH08, CH18). International comparison, as well as the fear of federal intervention, led to HarmoS. The idea was, given rising mobility in Europe, to abolish sectionalism, and to understand education as federal task. In contrast, HarmoS was created because the EDK refused to make the task of education federal. This has indirectly to do with PISA; because Switzerland scored worse than expected the pressure was enhanced. Nevertheless, the actual pressure emerges because of a desire to avoid the federal solution (Interview CH6). The instrument of the consulting services of the OECD has gained in importance: "The OECD influence is comparable with a consultancy that is called to corroborate decisions from abroad that were already made" (Interview CH18). In contrast, the IO governance instrument of financial means does not play a decisive role in the context of the PISA Study, because countries have to pay for the studies themselves and there is no desire for the OECD to make concrete corresponding demands to the countries.

The strongest veto player concerning HarmoS—the core reform inspired by PISA—is the Swiss People's Party, which is still intensively trying to hinder HarmoS by coordinating referenda against it. It accuses the EDK—the traditional guardian of the diversity of the Swiss education system—of centralization of compulsory schooling and intervention into cantonal responsibilities. The main criticism is the lower school entrance age of four years and extracurricular day care. Nevertheless, its referenda are not likely to be successful, as reforms are strongly needed (Interview CH13).

In sum, "PISA was considered a salvation by most policy actors" (Interview CH07), as it was highly responsible for the Swiss reforms in secondary education because of its demonstration of the improvements needed in the system and provision of examples of best practice of other countries. The OECD was able to further its interests effectively by disseminating ideas, setting norms, and providing advice. Its recommendations affected not only educational policymaking, but indirectly social policy, too, for example by stressing the need for support for immigrant students. Although some reforms triggered by PISA had already been discussed for a long time, it was the PISA impetus that triggered the breakthrough.

The influence of the Bologna Process on Swiss higher education

In Switzerland, Bologna is perceived as "the biggest reform since Humboldt" (Interview CH02), particularly as a result of its ability to foster simultaneously both international and intra-Swiss harmonization of structures and goals. Its power cannot be explained without referring to the European Commission. The international actor had to enter the "forbidden" area of national higher education very delicately or "crabwise," as it does not have any legal competences or coercive mechanisms in education towards the signatory states of Bologna. Moreover, Switzerland as a non-EU member would have repelled direct intrusion in this domain. Hence, the Commission, as a Bologna Follow-Up Group (BFUG) member, exerted indirect influence via soft governance instruments to trigger transformations in the Bologna countries that would build the European Higher Education Area (Borrás and Conzelmann 2007).

As a voting member in the BFUG, the Commission contributed to the Bologna Stocktaking exercise through the contributions of the Eurydice network, producing country analyses and comparative overviews. Through Bologna, the Commission provides a platform for international and national discussion of educational topics, thus spreading international policy models via transnational communication and policy learning in the Bologna countries. The Bologna seminars, in particular, reveal the importance of this opinion-forming instrument. By making diverse recommendations and circulating publications that were used as terms of reference for the reconstruction of the Swiss higher education system, the Commission influenced domestic policymaking. For instance, it disseminated the idea of stressing competition and the economic effects of education, so that focus was placed on quality assurance. The implementation of the aim of employability was realized by introducing the new study structures. Bologna spread consciousness of the importance of quality assurance and for education as a means for reaching economic aims, particularly regarding labor market issues and employability. The EU's orientational framework in the context of Bologna is primarily economic (Ciccone and de la Fuente 2002) and conceptualizes education as "wealth of nations" or "human capital." Education is regarded as a means to further the labor market and labor mobility. The Swiss principles did not completely match this framework, as explored earlier. Informal veto players were the student associations that feared a potential higher impact of employer associations, while professors regarded the aim of employability positively. However, Swiss principles were finally made compatible by the EU through the use of the opinion-forming instrument to enable the spreading of their aims. This paved the way for the integration of Bologna aims into Swiss tradition, and led to far-reaching reforms.

Via Bologna, the Commission participates in norm setting that establishes a definite set of aims for higher education, based on which the Swiss system has been transformed, such as the B.A./M.A. structure, quality standards, mobility enhancement, modularization, ECTS, and mutual recognition of study degrees. For quality assurance, the "European Standards and Guidelines for Quality Assurance" were adopted and specific European trends were discussed (ENQA 2005). The Bologna ideal of enhancing employability and the quality of higher education institutions by accreditation and evaluation reveals a greater focus on the labor market and international competitiveness than on education as a cultural asset. Hence, it does not match the Swiss guiding principle of Humboldt's ideal of unity of teaching and research, and thus provides potential for change. The new evaluation of teaching may change the role of actors and enhance the power of "customers," here students (Interview CH04, CH06).

The European Commission, as a Bologna member, was successful in creating benchmarks. This is a case of the IO governance instrument of coordinative activities through executive surveillance, and is particularly significant in Switzerland because of the country's low involvement with the EU. The use of the Bologna reports as a means of voluntary and legally nonbinding benchmarking increased the importance of the EU in Swiss higher education. In general, the role of the Commission was central, because without its coordination, and financing, Bologna would not have "survived." However, the importance of the provision of financial means and consulting services does not particularly apply to Switzerland.

Switzerland's cooperation with international actors dealing with Bologna is complicated by a high number of veto players such as the people and cantons, resulting from federalism, direct democracy, and consociationalism. How can the low resistance of veto players to the strong penetration of Bologna into the domestic education system be explained, and why did Swiss guiding principles, which do not totally fit those of the EU, not hinder change? First, pressure stems from the broad participation of the surrounding EU countries, in particular because Switzerland is isolated as a non-EU member (Riklin 1995). Thus, veto players regarded a high degree of adaptation to Bologna as necessary to make the Swiss education system compatible with those of other European countries (Interview CH06, CH14). Moreover, there is a strong need for reforms in universities. Bologna was strategically exploited by domestic actors as a vehicle for implementing other reforms that were controversial or overdue, such as the reform of teaching, in order to overcome the gridlock of the 1980s and 1990s (Interview CH07). Education political actors used the "international argument" of Bologna (Gonon 1998) as a reference point for legitimizing policymaking initiatives (Moravcsik 1999). Second, a moderate degree of misfit is indispensable for the possibility of change. This has also been the case in Switzerland, where the traditional guiding principles of education exhibit the ideals of Humboldt rather than the competitive worldview of the EU. However, reforms were made possible by the EU's instrument of norm setting that penetrated Swiss principles so that an attitude in favor of change in higher education was triggered.

Comparing governance instruments of the EU and the OECD

With the diverse governance instruments used in the context of PISA and Bologna, the OECD and the EU have triggered a wave of reforms in Swiss secondary and higher education in the last decade. Parallels in both educational sectors exist with regard to these instruments: of all IO governance instruments, opinion formation by establishing ideas and knowledge, and educational norm setting influenced Swiss policymaking the most. Coordinative activities and consulting services are also quite important, while the impact of financial means was found to be rather negligible.

PISA and Bologna provide a platform for international and national discussion and opinion formation on educational issues. International best practice models are spread in the participating countries by means of policy learning and transnational communication. In secondary education, PISA is part of a program of indicators which provides OECD countries with periodically comparative data on resources and the performance of their education systems. This implies that internationally comparative studies and identification of best practice may trigger transnational collective learning processes, such as in PISA and HarmoS seminars, and thus may enhance national education steering and provision. In higher education, the creation of educational guidelines through opinion formation is reflected mainly in Bologna seminars, which are viewed by interviewees as a central driving force for the Swiss implementation of Bologna. The instrument of norm setting with its dominant function of prescribing behavior, such as OECD benchmarks in the case of PISA, proved to be highly influential on the Swiss secondary education reform process. In higher education, informal standards through the regulation of behavior were set via Bologna and its follow-up conferences by the European Commission, to be achieved by 2010. For instance, in the FH sector, Switzerland adapted to the "European Standards and Guidelines for Quality Assurance" completely (ENQA 2005). The IO governance instrument of coordinative activities through executive surveillance is a decisive driving factor, for example in the OECD peer reviewing process. The European Commission plays a central role for Switzerland in coordinating Bologna as a result of the country's rather weak contacts with EU countries in educational matters. Consulting services as an IO governance instrument are of medium importance; the OECD, especially, is regarded as helpful because of its provision of peer reviews and country reports. As Swiss support structures are very sophisticated, the governance instrument of financial means through transfer payments does not play a big role in secondary and higher education. Switzerland itself finances the implementation of PISA-induced reforms, and provides the organization and data collection for the respective PISA Study. In higher education, the governance instrument of financial incentives in form of transfer payments, such as EU project financing, was found to be rather indecisive. However, the financing of Bologna by the European Commission has been indispensable for the progress of the European Higher Education Area.

In both sectors, the strong impact of these IO governance instruments succeeded in prevailing over Swiss reform-hindering transformation capacities in two regards. First, domestic veto players expected greater advantages from introducing reforms than from making use of their veto power because the adaptation to Bologna and PISA is highly relevant to the Swiss labor market and yields advantages for this small open economy surrounded by the EU market. Moreover, to overcome the long-standing reform backlog, veto players used the international initiatives strategically and justified domestic reforms by referring to international requirements. Second, the participation in the international initiatives converted domestic guiding principles toward the orientational frameworks of the IOs, which facilitated the implementation of the initiatives. Because of this special pattern of national and exogenous factors, a multitude of decisive reforms ended the backlog. Today, reforms induced by PISA and Bologna account for the majority of all Swiss education reforms since the late 1990s.

Conclusion

Despite its reform-obstructing institutional settings and its comparatively low level of involvement with IOs, Switzerland has exhibited a high degree of policy change induced by the international initiatives in the last decade. The core educational reforms were heavily inspired by the Bologna Process and the PISA Study that provoked the use of quality assurance measures and educational standards, and increased the autonomy of educational institutions. This not only led to a high degree of adaptation by Switzerland to the international models, but indirectly even to an intra-Swiss harmonization of education policies and structures.

Internationalization has altered the education politics, in particular the relationship between the Federation and cantons, and triggered far-reaching reforms in Swiss education policymaking, which had been relatively stable for a long time. Thus, the international initiatives have played an unparalleled role in triggering overdue and controversial reforms. The PISA results led to the core reform project "HarmoS," which reveals that PISA insights are particularly important for a multicultural country like Switzerland. A recent OECD report on economic development in Switzerland underlines the special demographic and sociocultural situation of Switzerland, whose students are comparatively heterogeneous concerning language and culture, and often have a migrant background (OECD 2007). Thus, PISA information on Swiss student performance may help to foster the integration of students into the labor market at the end of their compulsory schooling. Likewise, the impact of EU instruments used in Bologna was enormous: Bologna and the European Commission together were important forces driving education reforms in Switzerland even though it is not an EU member. EU influence on Bologna is high as it codetermines—as its main financial contributor—its goals and thus exerts indirect influence on Switzerland via Bologna. As demonstrated by the ideal implementation of Bologna in Switzerland, the participation in the European Higher Education Area is highly relevant to the country in terms of international mobility, competitiveness, and scientific exchange. Thus, the European integration of Swiss education constitutes the basis for integration in other policy fields, such as economics and labor (Armingeon 1999): Bologna membership is the ticket to the EU labor market.

The two IOs were successful in furthering their aims in education: the impact of soft IO governance instruments outstripped the conservative effects of national transformation capacities. For two reasons, the latter did not hinder far-reaching developments in Swiss education policy. First, this was the result of the high interrelation of introduced reforms with global labor market exigencies. Despite not being an EU member, Switzerland depends on the compatibility of its education system with those of the EU members. Moreover, the cooperation of veto players resulted from the long backlog of reforms. They were convinced of the need for change or did not want to be blamed for hindering necessary reforms. Thus, the results do not confirm the assumption of the theoretical framework in the introductory chapter of this volume that argues that veto players lower the possibility of domestic reform. Second, as hypothesized in the introductory chapter, there is a nonlinear relationship between misfit and change: a medium misfit maximizes the chance for change while a total fit or a misfit do not promote reforms. Swiss change was furthered by the moderate degree of misfit between the IOs' orientational frameworks and domestic guiding principles (Börzel 2003: 6).

In sum, the results of the empirical study on the internationalization processes of Swiss education policymaking are rather inconsistent with the theoretical framework presented in the introductory chapter of this volume. Further research should focus here on the underlying motives for the passiveness of veto players. The country case revealed that structural and ideational factors were not completely able to hinder the high degree of change. In contrast, Switzerland's small size in combination with transnational communication and economic pressure proved to make it very adaptive to the international scene (Katzenstein 1993; Kux 1998). Therefore, further research on Swiss policy change triggered by international models may apply convergence theory (Knill 2005) as well as research on small open economies (Starke, Obinger, and Castles 2008).

Notes

1. This aim only was reached in 1985 after a popular referendum.
2. Online: http://www.presseportal.ch/de/pm/100003695/100550715/schweizerischer_gewerkschaftsbund_sgb, last access: May 24, 2009.
3. The implementation is coordinated by a steering committee of delegates of federal offices, the EDK, and the three types of higher education institutions. At the institutional level, the implementation of the legal framework is overseen by the three executive bodies, the Rectors' Conferences.
4. Online: http://www.sbf.admin.ch/htm/themen/uni/universitaeten_en.html, last access: March 20, 2009.
5. Scharpf (2006) describes the trap as a situation in which the contribution of institutional settings to the considerable shortcomings of joint policymaking is related to two requirements: decisions of the central government depend on the approval of constituent governments whose agreement must be (nearly) unanimous.

6. After the formal procedure of consulting cantons, German- and French-speaking teacher associations, and parent organizations, and subsequent revision the EDK passed the concordat in June 2007. Since fall 2007, the ratification decision has been made either, by the cantonal parliament, or in a referendum. The necessary number of ten cantons was reached in April 2009, so that the EDK decided to put the concordat into force in August 2009. From then on, the concordat was valid for the ratifying cantons that have to make legal adjustments within six years. Online: http://www.edk.ch/dyn/14901.php, last access: May 26, 2009.
7. Regarding Bologna coordination during the period 2008–11, the SUK will effect a monitoring project considering all core Bologna characteristics (Ryhn 2009: 190).
8. Online: http://www.studienreform.uzh.ch/bologna-uzh/national/080915_Bolognatagung_Bericht.pdf, last access: June 11, 2009.
9. Online: http://www.bbt.admin.ch/themen/hochschulen/00213/00222/index.html?lang=de, last access: May 20, 2009.
10. Online: http://www.sbf.admin.ch/htm/dokumentation/publikationen/grundlagen/factsheets/FS01_Hochschulsystem_e_2008.pdf, last access: 20/03/2009 and http://www.sbf.admin.ch/htm/themen/uni/hls_de.html, last access: March 20, 2009.
11. Online: http://www.sbf.admin.ch/htm/themen/uni_en.html, last access: March 25, 2009.

References

Aprentas (2006) Die Bildungsverfassung ist revidiert—und nun? *Harmonisierung des schweizerischen Bildungssystems*, Jahresbericht 2006, Basel: Aprentas.

Armingeon, Klaus (1999) "Swiss Labour Market Policy in Comparative Perspective," in U. Klöti and K. Yorimoto, eds., *Institutional Change and Public Policy in Japan and Switzerland*, Zürich: IPZ, 179–94.

Bieber, Tonia (2010) *The Internationalization of Education Policy-Making in Switzerland*, TranState Working Papers, Bremen: CRC 597.

Bologna Declaration (1999) *Joint Declaration of the European Ministers of Education*, June 19, 1999 (Online: yogm.meb.gov.tr/TheBolognaDeclaration.doc, last access: June 18, 2009).

Bonoli, Giuliano and André Mach (2000) "Switzerland: Adjustment Politics within Institutional Constraints," in F.W. Scharpf and V. Schmidt, eds., *Welfare and Work in the Open Economy*, New York: Oxford University Press, 131–74.

Borrás, Susana and Thomas Conzelmann (2007) "Democracy, Legitimacy and Soft Modes of Governance in the EU: The Empirical Turn," *European Integration* 29 (5), 531–48.

Börzel, Tanja A. (2003) "How the European Union Interacts with Its Member States," *Political Science Series* 93, 1–22.

Bundesverfassung der Schweizerischen Eidgenossenschaft, April 18, 1999.

Ciccone, Antonia and Angel de la Fuente (2002) *Human Capital and Growth in a Global and Knowledge-Based Economy*, Brussels: Final Report for the European Commission.

Clark, Burton R. (1983) *The Higher Education System: Academic Organization in Cross-National Perspective*, Berkeley, Los Angeles, and London: University of California Press.

Criblez, Lucien (2008) "Die neue Bildungsverfassung und die Harmonisierung des Bildungswesens," in L. Criblez, ed., *Bildungsraum Schweiz: historische Entwicklung und aktuelle Herausforderungen*, Bern: Haupt Verlag, 277–99.

Dahrendorf, Ralf (1965) *Bildung ist Bürgerrecht. Plädoyer für eine aktive Bildungspolitik*, Hamburg: Nannen.

Drezner, Daniel W. (2001) "Globalization and Policy Convergence," *International Studies Review* 3 (1), 53–78.

EDK (1970) "Konkordat über die Schulkoordination vom 29. Oktober 1970," in EDK, ed., *Interkantonale Zusammenarbeit im Bildungswesen. Rechtsgrundlagen*, Bern: EDK, 91–4.

EDK (2002) *Bologna Directives*, Bern: Eidgenössische Direktorenkonferenz.

EDK (2004) *HarmoS. Zielsetzungen und Konzeption*, Bern: Schweizerische Konferenz der kantonalen Erziehungsdirektoren.

EDK (2007) *Interkantonale Vereinbarung über die Harmonisierung der obligatorischen Schule [HarmoS-Konkordat] vom 14. Juni 2007* (Online: http://www.edk.ch/d/EDK/Geschaefte/framesets/mainHarmoS_d.htm, last access: June 1, 2009).

Eidgenössisches Volkswirtschaftsdepartment (2008) *Wachstumsbericht 2008* (Online: http://www.news-service.admin.ch/NSBSubscriber/message/attachments/11639.pdf, last access: March 31, 2008).

ENQA (2005) *Standards and Guidelines for Quality Assurance in the European Higher Education Area*, Helsinki: European Association for Quality Assurance.

EVD (2008) "Wachstumsbericht 2008" (Online: http://www.news-service.admin.ch/NSBSubscriber/message/attachments/11639.pdf, last access: March 31, 2008).

Fachhochschulgesetz (Bundesgesetz über die Fachhochschulen), October 06, 1995.

Fischer, Alex, Sarah Nicolet, and Pascal Sciarini (2002) "Europeanisation of a Non-EU Country: The Case of Swiss Immigration Policy," *West European Politics* 25 (4), 143–70.

Gonon, Philipp (1998) *Das internationale Argument in der Bildungsreform. Die Rolle internationaler Bezüge in den bildungspolitischen Debatten zur schweizerischen Berufsbildung und zur englischen Reform der Sekundarstufe II*, Bern, Berlin: Peter Lang.

Hackl, Elsa (2001) *Towards a European Area of Higher Education*, EUI Working Paper 09/2001, San Domenico (FI): European University Institute.

Hega, Gunther M. (1999) *Consensus Democracy? Swiss Education Policy between Federalism and Subsidiarity*, New York: Peter Lang.

Hega, Gunther M. (2000) "Federalism, Subsidiarity and Education Policy in Switzerland," *Regional and Federal Studies* 10 (1), 1–35.

Horvath, Franz, Karl Weber, and Martin Wicki (2000) "International Research Orientation of Swiss Universities: Self-regulated or Politically Imposed?" *Higher Education* 40 (4), 389–408.

Katzenstein, Peter J. (1993) *Small States in World Markets: Industrial Policy in Europe*, Ithaca, NY: Cornell University Press.

Knill, Christoph (2005) "Cross-National Policy Convergence," *Journal of European Public Policy: Special Issue* 12 (5), 765–67.

Kux, Stephan (1998) "Switzerland: Adjustment Despite Deadlock," in K. Hanf and B. Soetendorf, eds., *Adapting to European Integration: Small States and the European Union*, Reading, MA: Addison-Wesley, 167–85.

Maradan, Olivier and Max Mangold (2005) "Bildungsstandards in der Schweiz. Das Projekt HarmoS," *PH Akzente* 2005 (2), 23–27.

Martens, Kerstin and Ansgar Weymann (2005) "Bildungspolitik durch internationale Organisationen—Entwicklung, Strategien und Bedeutung der OECD," *Österreichische Zeitschrift für Soziologie* 30 (4), 68–86.

Martens, Kerstin and Dennis Niemann (2009) "Governance by Comparison—How Ratings & Rankings Can Impact National Policy Making in Education," paper presented at the "International Studies Association" meeting, New York City, New York, U.S.A., February 15–18, 2009.

Moravcsik, Andrew (1999) *The Choice for Europe. Social Purpose and State Power from Messina to Maastricht*, London: Cornell University Press.

OECD (1992) *Education at a Glance. OECD Indicators*, Paris: OECD.

OECD (2007) *Economic Survey of Switzerland* (Online: http://www.oecd.org/document/1/0,3343,en_2649_33733_39566053_1_1_1_1,00.html, last access: June 11, 2009).

OECD (2008) *Kompetenzmessung bei 15-Jährigen. Piloterhebung für den vierten Zyklus*, Neuchatel: Bundesamt für Statistik.

Osterwalder, Fritz and Karl Weber (2004) "Die Internationalisierung der föderalistischen Bildungspolitik," *Schweizerische Zeitschrift für Bildungswissenschaften* 26 (1), 11–32.

Putnam, Robert (1988) "Diplomacy and Domestic Politics: The Logic of Two Level Games," *International Organization* 42 (3), 427–60.

Riklin, Alois (1995) "Isolierte Schweiz. Eine europa- und innenpolitische Lagebeurteilung," *Swiss Political Science Review* 1 (2–3), 1–26.

Ryhn, Heinz (2009) "Evaluation im Bildungsbereich in der Schweiz," in T. Widmer, W. Beywl and C. Fabian, eds., *Evaluation. Ein systematisches Handbuch*, Wiesbaden: VS Verlag, 182–92.

SBF and BBT (2008) *Bologna Process. National Report 2005–2007. Switzerland*.

Scharpf, Fritz W. (1988) "The Joint Decision Trap. Lessons from German Federalism and European Integration," *Public Administration* 66 (3), 239–78.

Scharpf, Fritz W. (2006) "The Joint-Decision Trap Revisited," *Journal of Common Market Studies* 44 (4), 845–64.

SGB (2007) *PISA zum Dritten—Mathe topp, Lesen flop* (Online: http://www.presseportal.ch/de/pm/100003695/100550715/schweizeris, last access: June 19, 2009).

Sciarini, Pascal, Alex Fischer, and Sarah Nicolet (2004) "How Europe Hits Home: Evidence from the Swiss Case," *Journal of European Public Policy* 11 (3), 353–78.

SKBF (2006) *Bildungsbericht Schweiz 2006*, Aarau: SKBF.

Starke, Peter, Herbert Obinger, and Francis G. Castles (2008) "Convergence towards Where: In What Ways, If Any, Are Welfare States Becoming More Similar?" *Journal of European Public Policy* 15 (7), 975–1000.

Stöckling, Hans Ulrich (2005) "PISA und Benchmarking als Chance für die Bildungspolitik?" *Die Volkswirtschaft. Das Magazin für Wirtschaftspolitik* 2005 (4), 25–8.

SUK (2003) Directives for the Coordinated Renewal of Teaching at Swiss Universities Within the Framework of the Bologna Process (Bologna Directives), Bern: Schweizerische Universitätskonferenz.

Zahner, Claudia, Urs Moser, Claudia Brühwiler, Maja C. Vellacott, Maja Huber, Tina Malti, Erich Ramseier, Stefan C. Wolter, and Michael Zutavern (2002) *Für das Leben gerüstet? Die Grundkompetenzen der Jugendlichen—Nationaler Bericht der Erhebung PISA 2000*, Neuchatel, Bern: Bundesamt für Statistik, EDK.

6
What's England Got to Do with It? British Underestimation of International Initiatives in Education Policy

Philipp Knodel and Heiko Walkenhorst

The traditionally eurosceptic environment in the British Isles accounts for a political culture that is far less enthusiastic for international projects than in other countries on the continent. Over the years, this has contributed to the image of the United Kingdom (UK) as an "awkward partner" (George 1990). Among British academics and policymakers there are great reservations against wide-ranging cooperation in education or international harmonization. The government itself ignored Europe's attempts to create a common higher education area for a long time. And even though the UK was a signatory of the Sorbonne Declaration in 1999, it has always taken a rather critical and passive stance towards the Bologna Process. There was little interest regarding the Programme for International Student Assessment (PISA) since there had already been a number of tests and domestic comparisons in secondary education in the UK.

In this chapter we explore education reforms from the 1980s in the light of internationalization processes. We therefore address the question if and how far international organizations (IOs) like the European Union (EU) and the Organisation for Economic Cooperation and Development (OECD) have influenced education policymaking. Because of the absence of direct implementation or sanction power, we refer to a broad set of governance instruments, as for instance opinion formation or financial means (see the Introduction of this volume). IO activity can be blocked, redirected or even reinforced through national transformation capacities. We conceptualize both veto players and points as well as guiding principles of education as mediating factors which influence the direction and the degree of change. In our research framework England represents a country which is exposed to IO governance as a result of the UK being a member of the EU and the OECD. What is more, with its centralized education system, England exhibits a small number of formal veto players. According to our theoretical framework we thus expect distinct changes in education policymaking due to the degree of exposure to IOs and the veto patterns. The qualitative data originates from 15 semi-standardized interviews we conducted with education stakeholders and policymakers in England (see Nagel et al., Chapter 2 in this volume). However, as we show in the following, the case of education in England differs from our theoretical assumptions.

Similar to New Zealand (see Dobbins, Chapter 7 in this volume), the education system in the UK was radically reformed in the 1980s and 1990s. Owing to these reforms, the UK successfully managed to transform its traditionalist, fragmented, and ponderous system into a modern and flexible form of interlocking sectors that has become a model for many governments in the world. With its institutional stability and the relative congruence between national guiding principles and orientational frameworks of IOs, the education system appeared to be well prepared for any sort of international comparison. As we discuss in this chapter, these processes were for a long time ignored by Whitehall as being irrelevant to the British system. Apparently, the government did not anticipate that signing and participating in nonbinding international cooperation agreements could affect its education policy. There is, however, evidence that both the British government and education policy stakeholders underestimated the soft power of international agreements and organizations alike. Compared to other European countries, the influence of IOs on English education policymaking is certainly rather small (see Niemann and Bieber in Chapters 4 and 5 in this volume). However, because of a lack of awareness or deliberate back turning, many political actors were taken by surprise when realizing the dynamics that the PISA Study and the Bologna Process unfolded.

To explore the question of IO governance in English education, we will proceed as follows. First, we provide a brief overview of education policy in England and particularly focus on veto players and national guiding principles of education. After outlining the participation in international initiatives, namely the PISA Study and the Bologna Process, we discuss the main reforms in secondary and higher education from 1980 onward. In a third step, we assess the influence of IOs on education policymaking in England by accounting for transformation capacities there as mediators of change. Finally, the empirical findings are summarized and discussed referring to the theoretical framework of this volume.

Education policy in England[1]

The structure of the British education system has always been institutionally diverse and rather fragmented (Green 1990: 314). Before the devolution of power in 1999, the UK government was directly responsible for education policy in Wales and Northern Ireland.[2] Although the central government is formally responsible for determining education policy, there are numerous actors at both national and local levels sharing responsibility for the administration, funding, and delivery of education. At the very centre of education policymaking in England are the ministries.[3] The Department for Children, Schools and Families (DCSF) is currently responsible for secondary education and the Department for Innovation, Universities and Skills (DIUS) for the tertiary sector. The Secretaries of State are commonly supported by two or three pairs of junior ministers—the Ministers of State—and Parliamentary Under-Secretaries of State. The ministers responsible for education can appoint so called advisory or expert committees. Group representatives or individual experts invited by the committees provide evidence, expertise, and advice on a certain topic as to facilitate major policy decisions (Birch 1993: 112). Most of the reports that led to education policy reforms were drafted by committees. Among these is the National Committee of Inquiry into Higher Education, which prepared the Dearing Report in 1996. This report marks a "big shift" in UK education as it radically reviewed the higher education structure (Interview ENG13; see further below).

Full-time education in England is compulsory for all children aged between 5 and 16. In most areas, compulsory education is divided into primary and secondary education. Many secondary schools also provide for postcompulsory study through sixth forms, and there are also separate sixth form colleges. All school types enjoy a large degree of financial and managerial autonomy from the local authority. Schools control their own budget and head teachers have considerable autonomy in the way they manage their schools (Johnson 2004: 179). The principal academic qualification available to students between 16 and 18 years is the A-Level. The A-Level, once the "gold standard" of the UK education system, has been the subject of controversy in recent years over the issue of alleged grade inflation (Richardson 2007). Nevertheless, it remains the principal qualification and the basis on which students are admitted to universities.

Most students enter university at the age of 18 or 19 and study for an academic degree. The typical first degree offered by English universities is the Bachelor's (B.A.) degree, which takes full-time students three or four years to complete. Postgraduate students are typically divided into those taking taught Master's (M.A.) degrees and those undertaking research degrees. A taught Master requires one year of full-time study, while a Doctorate, the standard research degree, takes at least three years to complete. Undergraduate education is largely state financed whereas postgraduate study is not automatically funded by the state. In contrast to Scotland, where university education is still free, English students have had to contribute to their tuition fees since 1998. Starting 2006, a new scheme was established, known informally as "top-up fees." Tuition fees were increased to a maximum index-linked £3000 per year, repayable after graduation once the student attained a certain level of income. Students are also generally entitled to student loans for maintenance.

Actors and guiding principles in England

When it comes to power in British politics, the cabinet, ministries, and parliament have the strongest positions. Like in most western democracies, the number and variety of consultative actors, such as agencies, professional associations, interest groups, unions, and other bodies has increased. These actors, however, do not represent a major factor in determining education policymaking (Interview ENG06, ENG12). Education policy in England is a prime example of "quango governance," that is, the involvement of hybrid organizations with both public and private sector legislative functions. Since the 1980s, there is a visible trend toward outsourcing and delegating administrative governmental functions toward newly established quasi-autonomous bodies (see Flinders and Smith 1999).[4] These agencies work closely together with the policymakers in the ministries and public administrations on the one hand, and with the policy receivers like schools and universities on the other (Interview ENG06). They can thus be seen as "kind of a buffer body at arm's length of the government" (Interview ENG04) operating in a grey zone. With regard to veto players, however, there is no clear-cut line of division in education policy. There are instead changing and temporary coalitions with overlapping functional interests. In UK policymaking there is also significant congruence between party and opposition aims, as there are hardly distinct differences between party manifestos or between party positions in day-to-day politics. It is therefore not surprising that former Prime Minister Blair's education policy principally followed that of his conservative predecessors (see Power and Whitty 1999).

Organized education has a long history and developed through a process of gradual evolution. Generally speaking, the notion of a liberal education has predominated in England (Miller 2007: 185). Pupils and students are taught a curriculum of subject disciplines to cultivate the self. The philosophy, famously espoused by John Henry Newman, was "self-justifying, an end in itself" (Sanderson 1993: 189): a liberally educated mind, trained in an abstract discipline, could apply itself to any subject matter. Moreover, during the late nineteenth and early twentieth centuries a liberal education was associated with the institutions of government and accorded with views about social class. These "Victorian liberal education values enshrined in the ancient Universities, public schools and Civil Service were transmitted to and through the 20th century" (ibid.: 190).

Ideas about justice and equality have also infused education practice. The 1944 Butler Act was an integral part of the post-1945 welfare state settlement that intended to prevent England and Wales returning to "the stagnant, class-ridden depressing society of the 1930s" (Simon 1991: 35). As another commentator noted earlier, the defense of the new system was to provide both equal opportunity and to nurture an intellectual elite (Quandt 1960: 91). The Robbins Report of 1963 provided a clear communitarian philosophy for higher education in England, Wales and Scotland, emphasizing the role of public institutions in promoting social development and strong communities (Baber and Lindsay 2006: 151). On the one hand, the report justified higher education in economic terms, in that economic growth required a well educated society in which individuals could develop their talents and abilities. On the other hand, it justified higher education on the basis that it provided opportunities for citizens to be informed participants in a democratic society (Bligh 1990).

Government tended to assume a "hands-off" role (Interview ENG03) in education, framing the basic system but devolving operational responsibility to local government and especially the schools and universities. Under the 1944 Butler Act system, schools and teachers had great autonomy, and the majority of local education authorities in England failed "to exercise even a nominal control over the curriculum and related policies of their primary and secondary schools" (Chitty 2002: 263).

During the 1970s, however, concerns grew about the state of the UK's education system and the autonomy given to teachers (Woods 2002: 121). A picture emerged that was "one of incompetent, unaccountable and often 'trendy-Lefty' teachers, delivering an increasingly irrelevant curriculum to bored teenagers who were poorly motivated, illiterate and innumerate" (Chitty 2005: 58). In response to these concerns, the then Labour prime Minister James Callaghan made a famous speech at Ruskin College, Oxford, in 1976, in which he set out a number of key ideas that would resonate in education policy over the next decades. Callaghan emphasized the need to question teacher autonomy, the importance of value-for-money in education expenditure, and, perhaps most significantly, the need for central government to play a greater role in the provision of education and in setting the curriculum (Kelly 2004: 174–76).

Obviously, the old British education system was built on general principles such as democracy and liberalism. Because of widespread acceptance of these guiding principles they play only a hidden role in English education policymaking today. To put it in another way, both secondary and tertiary education are characterized by institutional autonomy and competitiveness. Among more general categories of transformation capacities, education in England mainly builds upon the notion of "human capital," that is, education as a means of boosting individual productivity. Thus, the focus of education policy in England is "opportunity rather than education as a quality or education for society" (Interview ENG01; for a more detailed historical elaboration see Weymann, Chapter 3 in this volume).

England's participation in the PISA Study and the Bologna Process

As a full member of the OECD (since 1961) and the European Communities (since 1973) the UK has participated in all important international and European programs and assessments. Except for schools in Wales in 2000, separate surveys have been conducted in England, Northern Ireland, and Scotland in all three rounds of the PISA Study. In 2000, the response rate among the schools initially selected for the English survey fell below the 65 percent level required by the OECD, but further analysis showed no evidence of any bias. The OECD thus accepted the data as having met the required technical standards (Office for National Statistics 2001). In 2003, however, the English PISA results were not published. Despite of a lack of evidence, the British government argued that the response rate had fallen even further short of the pre-agreed school-level and pupil-level response rates. Consequently, Whitehall convinced the OECD that the data could not be compared reliably with other countries or with the performance scores for England from the study of 2000 (see further below). The response rate in 2006 was sufficient again for the English scores to be compared to other national-level data. Compared to the first PISA round, the average reading scores dropped in 2006. While England's scores in science were still above OECD average, the results in math fell below it. Overall, this latest survey confirms the decline of England's PISA performance (see OECD 2006; Smithers 2007).

Together with France, Germany, and Italy, the UK was one of four signatories to the Sorbonne Declaration in 1998, which aimed at the "harmonisation of the architecture of the European higher education system" (Sorbonne Declaration 1998). For the French and German ministers in particular this initiative was an attempt to use "Europe as a kind of group mechanism by which you could actually kick-start domestic reform agendas" (Interview ENG03). The UK's role in this quartet, however, was rather vague: "We can obviously fall in with this because we did already. We already have a three-stage structure of higher education" (Interview ENG08). The Bologna members agreed to implement a comparable three-cycle degree structure, divided into Bachelor, Master, and Doctorate degrees, a Europe-wide structure for quality assurance in higher education, and the recognition of foreign degrees and other higher education qualifications. Since the ministerial conference in Berlin 2003 the Bologna Process has been linked to the EU's Lisbon Agenda of making the EU "the most dynamic and competitive knowledge-based economy in the world" by 2010 (Berlin Communiqué of Ministers 2003: 2).

Educational reforms in England since the 1980s

The period 1980–2007 is quite distinct as it brought about a significant system change in the UK. This change, however, did not happen overnight; it was neither a revolution nor an ad hoc shock-therapy. It was rather a continuous stream of successive reform policies (for a comprehensive overview see European Commission 2007). More than a dozen pieces of groundbreaking legislation were implemented over the years, affecting all sectors of the system.[5] In contrast to its European neighbors the UK central government was able to introduce radical reforms without being caught in, or even stopped by, any ideological struggle or power games among stakeholders. Probably more than in any other industrialized country prime ministers have been successfully using education policy as a testing ground for new ideas, processes and operations (Klein 2006: 151).

The 1980s were a turning point for the UK's ineffective and strike-ridden economy. In the previous decades, the country had suffered from low productivity, slow growth, and insufficient trade margins. At the end of the 1970s the high oil price and the overvalued pound resulted in an economic crisis. The new economic strategy was to strengthen the service sector, which would heavily rely on "human resources," that is, cohorts of well educated young men and women. But the education system was not built for that. Comprehensive secondary education was generally poor and higher education was still designed to produce the country's elite. In order to meet the new challenges of the knowledge economy the system required a complete overhaul. To improve the standards in primary and secondary education, a system of quality assurance was set in place alongside new schemes for teacher training and school management. Turning the hitherto elite university sector into a system that could educate millions of new students required an even bigger effort. As a result, the infrastructure for tertiary education became a major building site. The organization, management, and financing of universities were changed. New operational procedures were put in place and new legislation produced to regulate the new system (see Jones 2003; Lawton 1994). Thus, modernizing British education became a project of national importance. Despite the fact that almost all important actors in the field welcomed this reform, it was anything but harmonious.

Reforms in secondary education

For a couple of years education experts worked on a comprehensive national strategy. The results, the Education (No. 2) Act (1986) and the Education Reform Act (1988), are still regarded as milestones of education policy reforms as they changed the whole secondary education system. First, the national curriculum was introduced, which set minimal standards for skills and content. Under the National Curriculum, pupils are tested at four points in their education, known as Key Stage National Curriculum Tests (SATS). The final Key Stage 4 tests occur at the end of compulsory education and are incorporated into General Certificate of Secondary Education (GCSE) examinations, the standard qualification taken by students aged between 15 and 16. In the 1980s, a number of schools were failing badly. Because there was no tool to measure this failure, testing was brought back in by the Conservative government (Interview ENG12). Most importantly for the public impact of the reform, the School Act allowed the publication of SATS test results. Often referred to as league tables, the statistics appear annually in the national newspapers, becoming the major measure for teaching quality. Under the old system parents were required to send their children to the local school. The new regulations allowed them to choose the institution of their liking. Unsurprisingly, the SATS score of a particular institution primarily determined parent's choice. The consequence was that school headteachers were suddenly not only competing for good exam results but also for pupils. Thus, a school with insufficient student numbers would simply be closed, making staff and administration redundant. Linking enrolment numbers to government funding proved to be a harsh but effective policy tool to generate a new generation of business-oriented principals who could run a school successfully.

The 1988 Education Reform Act increased the institutional variety in secondary schooling. New school types were created, such as grant-maintained schools and city colleges, thereby answering the demands of the newly emerged education market (see Taylor 2002). The implications were far-reaching and manifold. Opening up the public monopoly on education toward socioeconomic self-regulation triggered dynamics not only within the education sector itself but also in adjacent areas. For instance, free school choice led to sudden house price increases in the proximity of popular schools, so-called "catchment areas." This created a financial barrier between those families who could afford to live in these areas opposed to those who lacked the necessary financial means. The 1992 Education Act additionally triggered a process that disadvantaged schools in deprived areas. Over the years the new system manifested social divides within communities with "good schools" in upmarket neighborhoods and "bad schools" in lower income areas (Bradley et al. 2000).

After the period of the conservative government, further adjustments in secondary education were made. The new government showed a high level of activity in the field of education, thereby underlining Blair's claim "education, education, education." New Labour immediately abolished some policies of the Tories, such as the Assisted Places Scheme in 1997 (see Phillips 2001 for an overview). The "Every Child Matters" scheme reflected what was then labeled as Labour's personalization approach in education (Department for Children Schools and Families 2003). It offered parents support in upbringing and educating their children and also allowed the state to interfere with education at a much earlier age. These actions were based upon the fear that the social divide in education would widen further. As a former government official put it, the attempt was "to narrow the gap between those who have high levels of achievement and those who do not do very well" (Interview ENG08). With hindsight, the reforms of New Labour represent continuity with the ideas and policies of the 1980s and 1990s (Power and Whitty 1999; Phillips 2001; Whitty 2008).

Reforms in higher education

The Further and Higher Education Reform Act was passed in 1992 under the new Major government. It introduced and enforced competition and standardization in higher education. First and foremost, the act established the Funding Councils. The councils obtained the statutory responsibility for the assessment of the quality of publicly funded higher education. Serving as buffer bodies between institutions and the government, they prohibit the executive from directly regulating university matters. The result of this kind of academic autonomy was inter-institutional competition. Via the Research Councils the government introduced a "carrot and stick" instrument, the Research Assessment Exercise (RAE). Next to teaching quality all universities were graded upon their research activities on a scale from 1–4 (since 1996 to 5 and 5*). The exercises were held in 1992, 1996, 2001, and 2008. The time-consuming RAEs were increasingly feared by the universities as the rating determined government funding. The second major change of the 1992 Act was the transformation of many polytechnics into universities. These primarily vocational institutions had served as the second tier in UK postsecondary education. The reason for abolishing what had been referred to as "binary divide" in tertiary education was the desire to have a larger and uniform higher education sector which could accommodate for the growing cohorts of students.

The rapid massification of higher education posed more problems for the sector than it could handle at a time. Between 1989 and 1995 student numbers in higher education increased by almost 70 percent. Instead of one in six, now one in three young people in the UK entered higher education (Eurydice 2000: 492). Over the same period funding per student was halved in real terms (Greenaway and Haynes 2003). Thus, the question of how to finance the expansion of higher education became the focus of the mid-1990s debate. The government asked Lord Dearing to review the system in the light of recent reforms and to suggest solutions for the pressing question of underfunded universities. Dearing's report recommended further growth and widening participation toward disadvantaged groups, more emphasis on teaching quality and staff training monitored by a national agency, increased higher education spending, modernized university governance, and the introduction of tuition fees (National Committee of Enquiry into Higher Education 1997). The report had been commissioned under the Conservatives but was published in 1997 when Tony Blair had already assumed office. Dearing's answer to the funding question was simple but controversial: those who benefit from tertiary education should contribute to its costs, rather than the taxpayer. Consequently, in 1998 tuition fees became applicable for domestic students.

As a result, social cohesion in education became a central issue for the Blair government. The bottom line of the "New Labour" party ideology was basically that it turned away from its original egalitarianism. Liberalizing the education system and introducing market instruments like competition and choice fitted the Third Way (Giddens 1998, 1999) ideology. Increasing frictions in Parliament and within the Labour Party itself culminated in 2004 when the Blair government pushed the "Higher Education Act," which allows universities to charge variable (and higher) tuition fees, through Parliament. Yet, the parliamentary vote brought the Labour government close to a political collapse. Despite its comfortable majority of 161 seats in the lower chamber the bill passed by a majority of only five votes (BBC 2004). As a consequence, improved countermeasures were put in place for better student support. Grants became more generous, more grants were offered and deferred fees were introduced, so that no student would have to pay tuition fees upfront. Repayment of the fees is interest free and starts when the student's earnings reach a specific amount (Department for Education and Skills 2004). The Office for Fair Access (OFFA) was brought in as the new institution to administer this quite complicated study grants regime and further encourage wider participation in higher education.

Summary: Education reforms in England and IO governance

Summing up, the 1980s and 1990s are characterized by fundamental changes in education polity, policy, and politics. Both secondary and tertiary education have been radically reformed without external impulses. In fact, with its competitive orientation, quality assurance, and tuition fees, the English education system rather served as a blueprint for current processes in Europe. During the last 20 years the guiding principles of education have not changed. On the contrary, they were rather reinforced by increasing global competition. Nevertheless, the interplay between England's partially Bologna-compliant higher education structure, as well as distinct shortcomings in secondary education revealed by the PISA Study did not leave the country unaffected.

The purpose of the following is to examine subsequently the influence of IO governance on both secondary and tertiary education in England.

The influence of international organizations and national transformation capacities on education policymaking

After four rounds of PISA evaluations and consistent middle-range results for the UK, can England's response to PISA still be considered as "relaxed" (Grek 2009: 34)? With the development of the Bologna Process towards a European Higher Education Area, do its political actors still think Bologna is no more than a city in Northern Italy (Interview ENG08)? In this section we analyze the influence of IO governance on education policy in England. The aim is to learn if and how IOs influence the domestic education policy routine and to elucidate how the established policy frameworks in return mediate or filter IO influence. Thus, in the following we focus particularly on veto players and points as well as on nationally rooted guiding principles.

England's pick and choose PISA strategy

Despite the fact that England scored very low marks in some parts of the PISA Study, a public "PISA shock" as in other countries, namely Germany, did not occur (see Niemann, Chapter 4 in this volume). There is no doubt among Westminster's policymakers that international education assessments like PISA can have a significant impact on domestic policy shaping. As one official of a nonministerial organization put it, political actors in Britain have become aware of that: "we are starting to compare ourselves more seriously with the results obtained in other countries and that is a fairly recent development.... This is one of the ways in which OECD sort of comes into the picture" (Interview ENG05). In recent years it has become evident that international comparisons are a relatively new but broadening phenomenon in English education politics. Indeed, the awareness of the impact of international comparisons did not change overnight; it has been more about a "gradual progressive realization" (Interview ENG06).

Considering that English schools have been using testing systems for a long time, PISA did not bring about anything completely new. Yet participation in the PISA Study for many is just another burden: "We do the PISA, another morning off, we do another test" (Interview ENG09). And despite the fact that the PISA Study requires a considerable amount of institutional preparation and organization, the study itself did not lead to the institutionalization of new bodies, agencies, or actors as happened in, for example, Germany. PISA, however, did initiate a political discourse which has led to an increasing attention to education policy outside the country. The English political dialogue, which has never been very outward looking, is recently changing "because of the concern to be world class" (Interview ENG06). Political actors in England have started looking at other countries which scored higher in terms of participation and performance, as for instance Finland (Interview ENG12). In doing so, their intention is to understand the reasons for the success of other countries, and at best, to import them into domestic education policy: "What are these countries doing that is different from us?" (Interview ENG11). And even though there are still some critical voices regarding the influence of the OECD, none of the interviewees totally rejected it. In fact, we observed a trend toward rather functional arguments. For British politicians one reason to engage with multinational bodies is "to find out what others are doing and learn from it" (Interview ENG03).

In recent years, English educational performance with its competitive orientation has increasingly been challenged by PISA. The major function and governance mechanism of the OECD appears to be the provision of information. Certainly, the capability of the OECD to influence education policymaking in England is limited because of a traditional skepticism regarding international activities. By publishing the PISA Study the OECD exerts its capacity to initiate and influence debates on policy issues. In addition to the government many other education organizations regularly make references to data and information provided in OECD reports (Interview ENG02). Since there was already a testing regime in England, governance by opinion formation has to a lesser extent than in other countries generated new ideas. What has changed is the attitude of political actors toward the work of the OECD: nowadays, these "OECD kinds of studies of educational performance are taken quite seriously. They do have an impact" (Interview ENG08). As one member of a government department emphasized, PISA has become a "brand" in England, well marketed by the OECD (Interview ENG12). The PISA Study revealed and named other countries who turned causal beliefs of education into action more efficiently. What is more, the causal beliefs of these challengers are similar to the English ones. Putting it in more general terms, the English understanding of education has been challenged by the orientational framework of an international organization, namely the OECD.

Clearly, with regard to the PISA Study and international comparisons, the British government employs a *pick and choose* strategy. Descriptions about the reception of the three PISA survey rounds have already demonstrated that the executive uses positive results as proof for good governance, while ignoring or trying to ignore failing results. An example of this application of PISA is reflected in how the government handled the results of the first two rounds. While the UK did well in 2000 and published the results despite a very low response rate, the situation changed in the second round. The results in 2003 were much worse and the response rate only marginally lower. This time, the government insisted on being left out, ironically with reference to the low response rate (The *Economist* 2004). As this example shows, prominent actors in England tried to exert an influence in blocking, or at least controlling, international impulses. This interpretation is in line with the results gained in the chapter on policy networks for the case of England and can thus be characterized as "crowding out" or "active exclusion" (see Nagel, Chapter 9 of this volume).

The strategy of *pick and choose* combined with the declining results in PISA 2006 nevertheless generated an increasing media attention in England (Interview ENG12, ENG02; see also Grek 2008). However, the slowly growing pressure "has not actually translated into a thoughtful and constructive analysis of what" to do. Political actors are beginning to outline concepts to improve England's performance in the PISA Study (Interview ENG11). For instance, regarding attitudes toward science, English teenagers were performing well below the OECD average in 2006. Most of the students tested stated that they did not want to be involved in science in their future lives (Department for Children Schools and Families 2007). In consequence of the PISA score, political actors have begun to adapt their strategies, as a DCSF official put it: "we are incorporating that into our policies" (Interview ENG12). This evidence certainly should not be overestimated since there have as yet been no concrete initiatives in English secondary education resulting from PISA. Additionally, compared to the position in other European countries the influence of the PISA Study and the OECD on education policymaking is rather small. At the same time, however, a discourse in England has emerged that could be interpreted as a preliminary stage of change. It is obvious that because of the congruence between the OECD understanding of education and the current English secondary education structure small-scale adjustments are more likely than fundamental reforms.

Bologna and English competitiveness

As a full member of the Bologna Process, the UK has been involved in various international meetings and conferences. As outlined above,

British interests in international education processes are that they should affect the domestic sector as little as possible. The subsequent attitude in the early Bologna years was basically that of a permissive consensus, that is, it is welcome as long as it does not threaten the autonomy of national policymaking. Hence, the position in international initiatives is a rather blocking one. In the European University Association (EUA), for instance, the UK is notorious for its inactive and unsupportive role. As has often been reported, the government sends a delegation that consists only of Scottish higher education experts who cannot make any credible commitments for the entire UK sector (Interview ENG04). It is worth emphasizing that the Bologna Process did not "lead to a need for fundamental reform of the UK higher education structures" (Department for Education and Skills 2005: 9). When the Bologna Declaration was signed in 1999, the general perception among UK policymakers was that the Bologna objectives had already been met in principle. There "were not any sort of details to be worried about," neither with regard to degrees nor to the length of time that they occupied (Interview ENG08).

The government's view of the future of higher education is documented in a 2003 White Paper (Department for Education and Skills 2003). The primary goals include expanding participation, teaching and research excellence, higher education and business connections, fair access, and funding. References are made to OECD statistics, but the Bologna Process and the European Higher Education Area are not mentioned at all. In some of these cases the report distinctly proposes the use of American practices (e.g. private funding). Even though the U.S. does not serve as a blueprint, policy actors in England "will be looking over their shoulders" sometimes (Interview ENG05). In short, the European Higher Education Area was perceived to be a reform project that transformed continental higher education into an English style system—England's position being that of a *primus inter pares*.

In the meantime, however, the Bologna Process revealed some implications which did not match perfectly with the higher education structure in England. In particular, the discussion about the English one-year Master turned out to be difficult and there is still a lot of "jiggery-pokery" going on about it (Interview ENG01). Within about ten months, students undergo a dense learning schedule that is finished with a Master dissertation. This scheme is particularly attractive for overseas students who want to benefit from the reputation of an English university degree but cannot afford two full study years abroad. The one-year Master is a major reason for the economic success of English higher education

(Cemmell and Bekhradnia 2008). However important it may be, it did not fulfill the Bologna guidelines and was thus awarded only with limited ECTS credits (Witte 2006: 138–39). While there are still open questions regarding the one-year Master, this debate shows the impact of the Bologna Process. The hitherto successful higher education structure is no longer unaffected. With further development of the Bologna Process it is increasingly "jeopardized" and under pressure (Interview ENG13).

Particularly with regard to foreign universities (e.g. in France) now offering Bachelor and Master courses conducted in English, the Bologna Process has increased the competition for the UK (Interview ENG07). As a result even hitherto critics or opponents of the Bologna Process are becoming alarmed. A member of parliament put it as follows: "If we went to see that the French have a system of doing things better I would be in favor" (Interview ENG14). Thus, the English education system has shown slight institutional changes since 2003. Perhaps the most obvious institutional adaption of the Bologna Process was the formation of the Europe Unit in 2004. The Europe Unit works closely with education ministries and cooperates with the large number of UK organizations.[6] It fulfills the triple role of monitoring the Bologna Process, informing institutions, and coordinating strategic responses (UK Higher Education Europe Unit 2004: 29). In doing so, the Europe Unit keeps guard over British interests, be it as a blocking lobbyist or as an advocate of ideas originating from the EU or the OECD (Interview ENG02).

The ministers responsible for higher education have constantly confirmed the objective of developing a cohesive European Higher Education Area by 2010 (Ministers responsible for Higher Education 2007). As this target date approaches, political actors in England have recognized the magnitude of the undertaking and possible negative effects that might result from missing the Bologna train. The most important policy document on the Bologna Process was produced in the preparation of the Ministerial conference in London (House of Commons 2007). In this report the British government raised critical but crucial questions about the advantages of being a full Bologna member (ibid.: 4). Moreover, since there was not a genuine Bologna debate in England until 2003, this report provided the information base for the government's higher education strategy. Among English education experts, Bologna has become a desirable label because of its international recognition. The Bologna critical Higher Education Policy Institute (HEPI) explains why it nevertheless advocates the membership: "...if the Bologna brand were to become well-established, and if the UK was seen not to be 'Bologna-compliant'..., then that could damage the UK's attractiveness to international students" (Cemmell and Bekhradnia 2008: 8).

With its focus on education as human capital, English higher education has been dominated by the political culture of autonomy, individualism, and, most notably, competition. More than in other Bologna member states, participation for UK is an economic cost-benefit analysis. For the government, the Bologna Process and the European Higher Education Area are not goals in themselves. As the former Education Minister Bill Rammell emphasized after the ministerial conference in London, "Bologna must remain a process that enables institutions to play to its strengths and overcome its weakness through collaboration" (Rammell 2007: 13). The processes have been seen as instrumental for further domestic achievement, which is to increase academic excellence, to retain European leadership, and to compete globally. As with PISA and English secondary education, there is already a great congruence between Bologna guidelines and the higher education structure. Fundamental changes thus are unlikely and unnecessary. Yet in spite of similar starting positions, political actors in England are "pretty well aware of what is going on, and doing the rationale for it" (Interview ENG03). The threat of EU harmonization notwithstanding, global competitiveness as guiding principle of higher education in England has increasingly been challenged (Interview ENG13, ENG14).

Conclusion: What's England Got to Do with It?

For a long time England had nothing to do with international initiatives on education policy. Because of its entrepreneurial autonomy, both secondary and tertiary institutions are much more market-oriented than for instance universities in Germany. The main policy shift towards marketization happened in the 1980s and did not coincide with the PISA Study or the Bologna Process. In this way, the influence of IO governance in education policymaking is far less felt in England than in the rest of Europe. By analyzing the internationalization of education policy, our study provided some fruitful results. First, despite the fact that there is only a small number of veto players, the English education system did not change significantly. There have certainly been some institutional adaptations in education politics, for instance with the establishment of the Europe Unit. With regard to our theoretical framework, the veto pattern appears not to be a key explanatory determinant of change in education policymaking. Second, the case under research highlighted the relevance of deeply rooted ideas in national cultures in the context of education policy. With its competitive orientation and institutional autonomy the English understanding of education has already complied with many of the models promoted by the PISA Study and the Bologna Process. In terms of the underlying theoretical framework there has already been a distinct overlap between national guiding principles of education and orientational frameworks proposed by IOs. Thus, the impact of IO governance on education policymaking in England has been largely neutralized for a certain time. Things changed, however, as it became clear that there are other countries doing things better. Finally and crucially, the analysis brought about evidence that political actors in England have in the meantime begun to recognize that the international dimension cannot be ignored. The traditionally inward-looking attitude has gradually opened towards international trends and processes. Hence, from a qualitative perspective there is evidence that IOs incrementally enter the political discourse in England (for a network-analytical validation see Nagel, Chapter 9 in this volume). The status of implementation of the Bologna Process in 2010 and England's performance in further PISA studies notwithstanding, one thing has become clear: political actors underestimated the influence of international initiatives on domestic policymaking. It seems, however, that the question of how England deals with these new conditions of education policymaking, that is, conforming to international pressure closely or not, requires further analysis at a later date.

Notes

1. This part mainly builds on the Eurydice Report on education structures in the UK (Eurydice 2006).
2. When we discuss reforms before 1999, the term UK is short-hand for England, Northern Ireland, and Wales.
3. Contrary to the common perception the education ministries are not a fixed point in education policy. They have been restructured and renamed no fewer than four times in the last ten years. In 2001 the "Department for Education and Employment," was changed into "Department for Education and Skills (DfES) & Department for Work and Pensions." It then became the "Department for Education and Skills" (DES). This was divided in 2007 into two departments, interestingly, neither of them with the term "Education" in the title.
4. Prime examples of nonministerial organizations in English education are the Higher Education Funding Council for England (HEFCE), the Office for Standards in Education, Children's Services and Skills (OFSTED), the Qualifications and Curriculum Authority (QCA), the Quality Assurance Agency for Higher Education (QAA), and UK NARIC.

150 Transformation of Education Policy

5. Education Acts 1 (1981) and 2 (1986), Education Reform Act 1988, Further and Higher Education Act 1992, School Standards and Framework Act 1998, Teaching and Higher Education Act 1998, Learning and Skills Act 2000, Education Act 2002, Higher Education Act 2004, Children Act 2004, Education Act 2005, Education and Inspections Act 2006, Childcare Act 2006, Further Education and Training Act 2007, Education and Skills Bill 2007, and Children and Young Persons Bill 2007. For a detailed analysis of Higher Education Reforms in England since 1998 see Witte (2006).
6. For example, European Officers (HEURO), UK Research Office (UKRO), British Council, UK Higher Education International Unit, Welsh Higher Education Brussels (WHEB), University and College Union (UCU), National Union of Students (NUS), and the British Academy.

References

Baber, Lorenzo Dubois and Beverly Lindsay (2006) "Analytical Reflections on Access in English Higher Education: Transnational Lessons across the Pond," *Research in Comparative and International Education* 1 (2), 146–55.

BBC (2004) *Blair Wins Key Top-up Fees Vote* (Online: http://news.bbc.co.uk/1/hi/uk_politics/3434329.stm, last access: June, 25 2009).

Berlin Communiqué of Ministers (2003) *Realising the European Higher Education Area. Communiqué of the Conference of Ministers Responsible for Higher Education in Berlin* (Online: http://www.bologna-bergen2005.no/Docs/00-Main_doc/030919Berlin_Communique.PDF, last access: June 25, 2009).

Birch, Anthony H. (1993) *The British System of Government*, London and New York: Routledge.

Bligh, Donald (1990) *Higher Education*, London: Cassell.

Bradley, Steve, Jim Taylor, Jim Millington, and Robert Crouchley (2000) "Testing for Quasi-Market Forces in Secondary Education," *Oxford Bulletin of Economics and Statistics* 62 (3), 357–90.

Cemmell, James and Bahram Bekhradnia (2008) *The Bologna Process and the UK's International Student Market* (Online: http://www.hepi.ac.uk/downloads/36Bolognaprocessfull.pdf, last access: June 25, 2009).

Chitty, C. (2002) "The Role and Status of LEAs: Post-war Pride and fin de siecle Uncertainty," *Oxford Review of Education* 28 (2–3), 261–73.

Chitty, Clyde (2005) "Education Policy," in P. Dorey, ed., *Developments in British Public Policy*, London: SAGE, 46–66.

Department for Children Schools and Families (2003) *Every Child Matters* (Online: http://www.dcsf.gov.uk/everychildmatters/_download/?id=2674, last access: June 25, 2009).

Department for Children Schools and Families (2007) *Statement on PISA 2006* (Online: http://www.dcsf.gov.uk/rsgateway/DB/SFR/s000763/STATEMENT_ON_PISA_FINAL.pdf, last access: June 25, 2009).

Department for Education and Skills (2003) *White Paper on the Future of Higher Education* (Online: http://www.dcsf.gov.uk/hegateway/strategy/hestrategy/pdfs/DfES-HigherEducation.pdf, last access: June 25, 2009).

Department for Education and Skills (2004) *The Higher Education Bill, Bill 35*, London: HMSO.

Department for Education and Skills (2005) *UK National Report on the Implementation of the Bologna Process* (Online: http://www.bologna-berlin2003. de/pdf/UK.pdf, last access: June 25, 2009).
Economist, The (2004) *Bad Marks All Round—Education*, December 11, London: The *Economist*.
Eurydice (2000) *Two Decades of Reform in Higher Education in Europe: 1980 Onwards* (Online: http://eacea.ec.europa.eu/ressources/eurydice/pdf/0_integral/008EN. pdf, last access: June 25, 2009).
Eurydice (2006) *Structures of Education, Vocational Training and Adult Education Systems in Europe: United Kingdom* (Online: http://eacea.ec.europa.eu/ressources/ eurydice/pdf/041DN/041_UN_EN.pdf, last access: June 25, 2009).
European Commission (2007) *School Autonomy in Europe—Policies and Measures* (Online: http://www.eurydice.org/ressources/eurydice/pdf/0_integral/090EN. pdf, last access: June 25, 2009).
Flinders, Matthew V. and Martin J. Smith, eds. (1999) *Quangos, Accountability and Reform: The Politics of Quasi-Government*, Basingstoke: Macmillan.
George, Stephen (1990) *An Awkward Partner: Britain in the European Community*, Oxford: Oxford University Press.
Giddens, Anthony (1998) *The Third Way: The Renewal of Social Democracy*, Cambridge: Polity Press.
Giddens, Anthony (1999) *The Third Way and Its Critics*, Cambridge: Polity Press.
Green, Andy (1990) *Education and State Formation: The Rise of Education Systems in England, France and the USA*, Houndmills, Basingstoke: Palgrave Macmillan.
Greenaway, David and Michelle Haynes (2003) "Funding Higher Education in the UK: The Role of Fees and Loans," *The Economic Journal* 113, 150–66.
Grek, Sotiria (2008) "PISA in the British Media: Leaning Tower or Robust Testing Tool?" CES Briefing No. 45, Edinburgh: Centre for Educational Sociology.
Grek, Sotiria (2009) "Governing by Number: The PISA 'Effect' in Europe," *Journal of Education Policy* 24 (1), 23–37.
House of Commons, Education and Skills Committee (2007) *The Bologna Process. Fourth Report of Session 2006–07* (Online: http://www.publications.parliament. uk/pa/cm200607/cmselect/cmeduski/205/205.pdf, last access: June 25, 2009).
Johnson, Paul (2004) "Education Policy in England," *Oxford Review of Economic Policy* 20 (2), 173–97.
Jones, Ken (2003) *Education in Britain: 1944 to the Present*, Cambridge: Polity Press.
Kelly, Albert Victor (2004) *The Curriculum: Theory and Practice*, 5th ed., London: Sage.
Klein, Rudolf (2006) *The New Politics of the National Health Service*, 5th ed., Harlow and others: Pearson Education and others.
Lawton, Dennis (1994) *The Tory Mind on Education*, London: The Falmer Press.
Miller, A. (2007) "Rhetoric, Paideia and the Old Idea of a Liberal Education," *Journal of Philosophy of Education* 41 (2), 183–206.
Ministers responsible for Higher Education (2007) *London Communiqué* (Online: http://www.dfes.gov.uk/londonbologna/uploads/documents/ LondonCommuniquefinalwithLondonlogo.pdf, last access: June 25, 2009).
National Committee of Enquiry into Higher Education (1997) *Higher Education and the Learning Society: Report of the National Committee of Enquiry into Higher Education*, London: HMSO.

OECD (2006) *Education at a Glance 2006—Briefing Note for the United Kingdom* (Online: http://www.oecd.org/dataoecd/32/50/37392956.pdf, last access: June 25, 2009).

Office for National Statistics (2001) *First Release: International Student Assessment* (Online: http://www.statistics.gov.uk/pdfdir/isae1201.pdf, last access: June 25, 2009).

Phillips, Robert (2001) "Education, the State and the Politics of Reform: The Historical Context, 1976–2001," in Philipps, Robert and John Furlong (ed.) *Education, Reform and the State: Twenty Five Years of Politics, Policy and Practice*, London and New York: Routledge, 12–29.

Power, Sally and Geoff Whitty (1999) "New Labour's Education Policy: First, Second or Third Way?" *Journal of Education Policy* 14 (5), 535–46.

Quandt, Jean B. (1960) "Philosophy and Educational Debate in England," *International Review of Education* 6 (1), 91–98.

Rammell, Bill (2007) *Speech at the Bologna HE Europe Unit. UUK Conference, 19 June* (Online: http://www.europeunit.ac.uk/sites/europe_unit2/resources/Bill%20Rammell's%20speech%20FINAL.doc, last access: June 25, 2009).

Richardson, William (2007) "Public Policy Failure and Fiasco in Education: Perspectives on the British Examinations Crises of 2000–2002 and Other Episodes Since 1975," *Oxford Review of Education* 33 (2), 143–60.

Sanderson, Michael (1993) "Vocational and Liberal Education: A Historian's View," *European Journal of Education* 28 (2), 189–96.

Simon, Brian (1991) *Education and the Social Order, 1940–1990*, London: Lawrence & Wishart.

Smithers, Alan (2007) *Blairs Education. An International Perspective*, London: Trust Sutton.

Sorbonne Declaration (1998) *Sorbonne Joint Declaration. Joint Declaration on Harmonisation of the Architecture of the European Higher Education System, May 25* (Online: http://www.bologna-bergen2005.no/Docs/00-Main_doc/980525SORBONNE_DECLARATION.PDF, last access: June 25, 2009).

Taylor, Chris (2002) *Geography of the "New" Education Market: Secondary School Choice in England and Wales*, Burlington: Ashgate.

UK Higher Education Europe Unit (2004) *Annual Report 2003–4* (Online: http://www.europeunit.ac.uk/sites/europe_unit2/resources/Annual%20Report%2003–04%20web.pdf, last access: June 25, 2009).

Whitty, Geoff (2008) "Twenty Years of Progress? English Education Policy 1988 to Present," *Educational Management Administration & Leadership* 36 (2), 165–84.

Witte, Johanna (2006) *Change of Degrees and Degrees of Change: Comparing Adaptations of European Higher Education Systems in the Context of the Bologna Process*, Enschede: CHEPS (Center for Higher Education Policy Studies).

Woods, Philipp A. (2002) "Space for Idealism? Politics and Education in the United Kingdom," *Educational Policy* 16 (1), 118–38.

7
Education Policy in New Zealand—Successfully Navigating the International Market for Education

Michael Dobbins

Studying New Zealand's education system is an interesting endeavor for various reasons and this analysis sheds light on the policy process and outcomes in this country of 4.1 million. First, the analysis highlights that geographical distances can easily be overcome during the spread of international best practice. New Zealand's policymakers demonstrate a unique willingness to engage in international cooperation and also have influenced the development of education policy in the Organisation for Economic Cooperation and Development (OECD). Second, New Zealand education has undergone radical changes over the past 25 years. The sweeping changes in the public sector spilled over to the education system, making New Zealand an early reformer, forerunner, and education "experimenter." Third, New Zealand education is strongly impacted by its key role in the global education market. The government has actively facilitated the liberalization of education through the General Agreement on Trade and Services (GATS) framework (Codd 2003; Martens and Starke 2008), making the "export" of tertiary and secondary education to foreign students a core national industry. Fourth, as a result of the parameters set in the 1980s, New Zealand currently finds itself in an arguably more favorable situation than many European countries and therefore perhaps offers a preview of what is to come for European education systems. Unlike in Germany (see Niemann, Chapter 4 in this volume), the past 15 years have not been characterized by transformation, but rather by efforts to optimize education in symbiosis with both national and international demands. Hence, New Zealand has consistently aligned itself with internationally promoted policies to balance effectively underlying education philosophies (broad participation, equity, return on investment).

Unlike other countries in this research framework, New Zealand is not a signatory to the Bologna Process. Nevertheless, it is actively involved in various transnational education regimes, often as an initiator and facilitator. New Zealand has a long tradition of cooperation with the OECD, dating back to the first OECD Review of New Zealand's Education Policies in 1983 (OECD 1983).This has intensified in the past 15 years, foremost as a result of changes in the OECD's working methods toward comparative assessment (Martens 2007) and New Zealand's participation in the Thematic Review of Tertiary Education. In 2007 New Zealand provided the OECD with a fresh Country Background Report as part of the Thematic Review of Education.

Drawing on the concept of *IO governance* (see the introductory chapter of this volume), this chapter outlines the domestic and external factors shaping reform in New Zealand education. Under what conditions do international organizations (IOs) stimulate domestic change—for example, in governance, quantitative-structural developments, or funding? As for secondary education, particular emphasis is placed on the PISA Study (Programme for International Student Assessment). For higher education, the impact of New Zealand's involvement in various international and multilateral education initiatives within the OECD framework will be scrutinized. Although New Zealand is not a Bologna Process member, the analysis will examine whether this European cooperative platform has influenced policy in any way.

Theoretical focus is placed on national transformation capacities, which encompass national veto players and historically rooted guiding principles of the role and function of education (see introductory chapter to this volume). As a result of the low number of institutional veto players and the relative flexibility and pragmatism in New Zealand education, there are favorable conditions for policy change and high potential for convergence towards education models, instruments, and principles advocated by international organizations, and thus delta-convergence (see Heichel, Pape, and Sommerer 2005). This chapter draws on qualitative data from various sources, including OECD datasets and 14 interviews conducted in New Zealand with ministerial employees, representatives of quasi-governmental qualifications authorities, teachers' unions, and academic lobbies. I first provide a concise historical overview of New Zealand education, before examining what I call the "big bang" in education in the 1980s. Subsequently, I focus on the impact of IOs on education policy, politics, and polity in New Zealand. Emphasis is placed on how IO governance has guided and facilitated the "phase of stabilization and optimization" since the drastic reform of the 1980s. Particular attention is dedicated to how New Zealand has managed tensions between various guiding principles on education, for example, human capital vs. human right, and the potential impact of IOs. The conclusion offers a summarizing analysis of the findings through the prism of state transformation capacity and international stimuli for policy change.

Education policymaking in New Zealand—historical developments and transnational context

This section briefly[1] addresses the historical development of New Zealand education, its core features, and the context of internationalization. I then address the "big bang" phase in the 1980s. This phase is crucial for understanding the subsequent reforms of the 1990s and present decade and because of its magnitude must be treated separately from the later reforms. It also explains the different starting position of New Zealand as compared to most European countries with regard to the internationalization of education in the past two decades.

A historical overview of New Zealand's education system

The Education Act of 1877 established the first free national system of primary education, while free secondary education only gained traction after the Education Act of 1914. Schooling was based on the egalitarian ideas of early policymakers aimed at providing students with a common set of values and knowledge (Olssen and Morris Matthews 1997). By 1917 more than one-third of the population went to secondary school. A further impetus for the expansion of secondary education was the Thomas Report of 1944, which introduced a core academic and practical curriculum for all children. Tertiary education also emerged in the late 1800s with the establishment of the University of New Zealand which spanned several campuses. The 1961 Universities Act granted individual campuses university status, leading to the emergence of eight separate universities.[2]

New Zealand education is characterized by a series of guiding principles which complement each other and offer possible explanations for the success of the system. The main guiding principles of postwar secondary education were comparable quality of schooling and equity (Gordon 1997: 66). Unlike in other colonial societies, social distinctions did not consolidate into a class-based system (OECD 1983: 21). Tertiary education has also traditionally been characterized by openness and equity (Interview NZ07). Partially as a result of this, New Zealand is not tied to one single historically embedded education philosophy, for example, Humboldtism in Germany or étatism in France (Interview NZ01; see Neave 2003). Nevertheless, an orientation toward British traditions is obvious, but not as trivial as one may think. In New Zealand a distinction between English and Scottish education traditions comes to bear. While the English tradition viewed the task of the university as the diffusion of knowledge to create a class of "gentlemen" well equipped for public functions (Neave 2003), the Scottish tradition is primarily based on accessibility and equality (Interview NZ07). Both of these philosophies are reflected in New Zealand's strong tradition of community stakeholdership, openness, and accessibility.

Nonetheless, New Zealand witnessed a rise of market philosophy over the 1990s (Gordon 1997; Olssen and Morris Matthews 1997) and is increasingly characterized by funding diversification, strengthened university management, tight private sector interlinkages, and a fortified entrepreneurial spirit. In short, New Zealand education policy is driven by efforts to balance the notion of education as a human right and education as human capital, complemented by the conviction that education is essential for survival in the knowledge economy (Fitzsimmons 1997).

Several key features of secondary education stand out. New Zealand boasts a very high number of schools per capita, offering compulsory education for students between age six and 16, while citizens have a right to education until the end of the calendar year of their nineteenth birthday. The country operates various types of secondary schools, comprising private, state, and state-integrated schools, with the latter two being government funded. The private schools, by contrast, are only state funded at a rate of approximately 25 percent. Before 1990, New Zealand had a well differentiated tertiary system consisting of universities, polytechnics, and colleges of education (Codling and Meek 2003). However, the Education Amendment Act altered this pattern by redefining these institutions and introducing a fourth institution known as *wananga* to cater to the Māori community.[3] There are currently eight universities, 23 polytechnics, four colleges of education and four *wananga*. Hence, higher or tertiary (as it is referred to in New Zealand) education spans a larger spectrum of institutions than the general OECD definition, comprising all postsecondary education including industrial training, adult and community education, and postgraduate qualifications (OECD 2006). New Zealand is unique among OECD countries in that it guarantees entry to university for a first degree to mature age students (usually 20 years), without regard to qualifications already held (OECD 1997: 9).[4] And for polytechnics and colleges of education there are no national minimum entry requirements, as they are set exclusively by the individual institutions.

As a result of this open access regime and government policies supporting increased participation, tertiary education has been characterized by unprecedented expansion and diversification since about 1979. Even by the mid-1990s, nearly half of all school graduates were continuing to some form of tertiary education (OECD 1997: 9). By 2004 nearly 60 percent of all New Zealanders had tertiary qualifications, while the number of students completing certificate and diploma qualifications more than doubled (Ministry of Education 2006: 15).[5]

Context of internationalization

Because of its geographic isolation, New Zealand has proven extremely open to international markets of students and ideas and has made education a fundamental component of its export-driven economy (see Martens and Starke 2008). Over the last 15 years, the government—allied with quasi-governmental bodies (quangos) and private sector institutions—has devised a comprehensive strategy to export New Zealand education to fee-paying foreign secondary (see Lewis 2005) and tertiary students. The commitment to education export has been reinforced by a long-term strategy known as the 2004 International Education Framework, which reflects the widespread consensus on the benefits of internationalization and the macroeconomic significance of the education industry (see OECD 2006). Thus, New Zealand has consistently pressed for international mutual recognition of qualifications and actively encouraged transnational partnerships between tertiary institutions and international businesses. Subsequently, education policymakers demonstrate a keen awareness of how their system is perceived by the outside world (Interviews NZ02, NZ12).

Changes in education policymaking since the 1980s—the first wave of reforms

New Zealand embarked on a reform package 20 years ago which has enabled the country to position itself in the global education market. In this phase, *IO governance* does not come to bear. As Martens and Jakobi argue, OECD education activities were limited until the 1990s, as the organization primarily responded to national priorities, while refraining from imposing its perspective on individual countries (Martens and Jakobi 2007: 248). Thus, the main thrust for reform emerged from within New Zealand and from extreme socioeconomic problem pressure. However, many of the reforms undertaken account for the uniqueness of New Zealand education, in particular with regard to its role in and receptiveness to IO governance as well as its national transformation capacities.

The "big bang" in secondary education in New Zealand

Secondary education reform could best be described as the "big bang." New Zealand was a welfare state marked by protectionism and interventionist government. It suffered from low productivity and growth, high deficits and unemployment, and overdependence on the UK, which under Margaret Thatcher embarked on mass deregulation and shifted its economic focus to the European Union. With the Thatcher reforms as a point of reference (Interview NZ10), the New Zealand Labour government embarked on arguably the most extensive economic liberalization and deregulation program ever undertaken by a stable democracy (Interview NZ10; see Fitzsimmons, Peters, and Roberts1999). At the same time, the Treasury emerged as a key policymaker, enabling the diffusion of human capital theory to wide segments of society (see Fitzsimmons 1997). These circumstances led to extreme pressure for New Zealand education, which was increasingly perceived as a costly burden, instead of a revenue-generating force (Codd 2003: 24). Subsequently, in 1988 a mandated taskforce drew up the report *Administering for Excellence: Effective Administration in Education*, also known as the Picot Report (see McKenzie 1997). While the economy was in fundamental transition, the taskforce overwhelmingly supported the spillover of the reforms to secondary education. The Department of Education concluded that "merely massaging present administrative structures would be both ineffective and time-wasting because urgently needed reform would not be achieved" (Department of Education of New Zealand, 1988: vii). So the Department sought to revamp secondary education on the basis of the 1989 Reform of Education Act and the "Tomorrow's Schools" initiative (see Wylie 1989).

This had philosophical, policy-oriented, and institutional (polity) ramifications. Philosophically, the previous understanding of education based on equality and opportunity was soon overshadowed by principles of "efficiency," "choice," "competition," and "accountability" (Olssen and Morris Matthews 1997: 18). The new approach drew on Transaction Cost Economics, which aims at restructuring schools to reduce costs of quality control, professional development, institutional arrangements, and information provision (see Olssen 2001: 22). The Department of

Education was not only downsized into a significantly smaller Ministry of Education, but also "deregionalized" with the abolition of regional Education Boards.[6] The Act turned schools into self-managing entities, resulting in the creation of boards of trustees for each school consisting of community representatives and stakeholders (Interview NZ03).

Moreover, bulk-funding was introduced, which meant that each school is granted a lump sum to spend at will on teaching staff. Purported advantages are increased staffing flexibility, financial advantages, and improvements in student-teacher ratios (LaRocque 2005). The government also introduced a national certificate of education achievements and simultaneously undertook measures to establish greater educational opportunities for disadvantaged groups, in particular Māori and children from low-income homes. According to Olssen and Morris Matthews (1997: 19) "Tomorrow's Schools" resulted in the following fundamental changes: transfer of personnel and coordination responsibility to elected boards; associations, and councils; transfer of management of assets, property, and money to institution-based boards; increased emphasis on "choice"; and greater state control over essential educational services in the form of curriculum guidelines and assessment procedures.

In fact, Hirsch goes so far as to speak of New Zealand "abolishing its education" system, while creating a "series of virtually autonomous providers of education" (Hirsch 1995: 6). New Zealand indeed shifted toward a quasi-market scheme based on local enterprise and school choice. However, the quality of education provision was bolstered and monitored by a series of quangos. This was reflected in the National Qualifications Framework, a unifying approach to qualifications with a strong outcome focus. The New Zealand Qualifications Authority (NZQA) was entrusted with assisting industrial partners and other parties to develop qualifications. On these foundations, the quality assurance of providers was achieved through processes of registration and accreditation, while standards were set with which providers must comply before becoming eligible for funding or awarding credits (Eppel 2007). Nevertheless, the OECD has identified New Zealand as one of the countries with the highest proportion of decisions made directly at the secondary school level (OECD 2008b: 485).

The early marketization of tertiary education

Following a more moderate approach than in the secondary sector, the Ministry also veered tertiary education towards greater institutional autonomy and competitiveness, leading to mass increases in participation (see OECD 1997). The most significant government-mandated document was the Hawke Report[7] (1988), which framed tertiary reform within the "Learning for Life" strategy (Department of Education of New Zealand 1988; see Codling and Meek 2003; Lange and Goff 1989), which sought to foster a culture of "fluidity" between secondary and tertiary education and the labor market (Eppel 2007). The proposals in the Hawke Report (financial autonomy, accountability) were later codified in the 1990 Education Amendment Act, which fostered a series of reforms to structure, funding, and governance. Contrary to previous formula-based funding devolved via the University Grants Commission (UGC), funding was now attached to student numbers. The government subsequently reduced its funding share to less than half of university budgets, enabling the introduction of tuition fees, contract-based research and consultancy, and start-up companies.

The reform essentially endeavored to marketize and diversify the funding system, while sustaining a strong equity component (Interview NZ05).[8] The government provides "teaching and learning" funding and operates a student loans scheme, while students pay tuition fees averaging €2500–€3000 per semester. An additional vital source of funding comes from foreign fee-paying (FFP) students, who are cited as contributing approx. 1.7 billion NZ$ to the national economy annually (Codd 2003: 21). Despite this financial diversification, tertiary education operates within an integrated funding framework, enabling the government to steer the system in line with its Tertiary Education Strategy (TES). In other words, the government uses the funding scheme to maintain leverage over the otherwise highly autonomous institutions to ensure that they operate in a flexible and accountable manner.

The changing education playing field 1985–95

Despite the increase of tuition fees, New Zealand experienced a massive increase in the number of providers and tertiary participation rates, so that it is now well above the OECD average (Ministry of Education 2006: 28). The reforms also drastically reshaped and diversified the policy arena. However, with regard to institutional diversification, secondary and tertiary education pursued different paths. In secondary education, the new actors were essentially the now highly autonomous schools themselves. Detached from state control, they were now influenced by greater local stakeholder engagement. In tertiary education, stakeholder engagement was assured through institutional diversification, beginning with institutional reforms at the state level. First, the

Ministry of Education replaced the Department of Education as the policymaking nucleus. Second, unique to New Zealand is the strong leverage of the Treasury over education policymaking. More than just a "banker" for the government, the Treasury has authority and veto power over issues with funding implications (Interview NZ10). Yet the most significant developments arguably took place at the intermediate level, with the establishment of various stakeholder bodies. First, the New Zealand Vice-Chancellors' Committee (NZVCC) inherited various functions of the UGC including academic program approval, accreditation, and moderation procedures. Thus, universities seeking to offer new qualifications must consult the NZVCC, which then evaluates proposals by peer review. Second, the University Academic Audit Unit, an independent body established by the NZVCC, provides support to universities in achieving standards of research and teaching excellence (NZVCC 2008). The NZVCC also assumed a fundamental role in policy advocacy for universities vis-à-vis the state (Interview NZ13).

As an independent and impartial expert organization, the New Zealand Qualifications Authority (NZQA) was entrusted with the administration of quality assurance of national qualifications. The Ministry appoints NZQA's Statutory Board, which must reflect community, industry, and education interests. The board sets the strategic direction of NZQA in consultation with the competent ministers, while the NZQA as a whole bears responsibility for implementing the National Qualifications Framework. However, NZQA is not responsible for university qualifications, rather only nonuniversity secondary and tertiary providers. The "Tomorrow's Schools" reforms also recognized that the greater the level of self-management and diversity, the more difficult it was for the state to keep a grip on the system (Interview NZ10). In consequence, the Education Review Office (ERO) was set up as a state audit body for schools and childhood centers.

The reforms also gave rise to policy think tanks. The New Zealand Business Roundtable (NZBRT) advocated the notion that education is a marketable commodity (Olssen 2001: 26) and the "Education Forum" arose from the NZBRT as a promarket think tank involved in the dissemination of market-friendly views (e.g. tuition burden-sharing, school choice). It had a major impact in fostering a "culture of international comparison" in education by disseminating information and international analyses (Interview NZ10). The introduction of tuition fees also led to a more assertive role of the Union of Students' Associations (NZUSA). Previously, New Zealand students lacked a history of strong activism (Interview NZ13). Yet the reform package enabled them to take positions on decisionmaking bodies, thus reinforcing the corporatist nature of policymaking (Interview NZ06).

Altogether, education was heavily impacted by what is known as the "New Zealand experiment," characterized by the emergence of market philosophy, the broadening of the policy arena, and institutional diversification. Even earlier than in other western democracies, the number of consultative actors and quangos multiplied (on this point see Knodel and Walkenhorst, Chapter 6 in this volume). As expected, IO governance did not play a significant role because the activities of IOs, in particular the OECD, were limited in this phase. However, one must emphasize the willingness of the government to draw on scientific and academic advice (e.g. the Hawke and Picot reports) and conduct in-depth analysis of foreign practice. Before giving a more extensive account, it should also be noted that institutional veto points were not an obstacle—as expected for the case of New Zealand. After all, the reform package was enforced by the center-left Labour Party (see Shaw and Eichbaum 2006) and embraced by the promarket, center-right National Party (Interview NZ05). Potential academic veto players were also willing to "come on board" because of diverse incentives (self-management, diversified funding). Moreover, the self-managed schools are cited as fitting well with New Zealand culture, which is driven by small municipalities and community and parental involvement (Interview NZ04). However, it is critical to note that the reforms actually created more potential informal veto points due to the shift to "quango governance."

The second wave of reforms—1995 to the present

By the mid-1990s New Zealand had already converged on the market-oriented paradigm of tertiary education governance (see Dobbins 2009). The government also actively promoted institutional diversification, reflected in increased autonomy for polytechnics and the emergence of Māori *wananga*. Secondary education witnessed a rapid shift toward school autonomy and performance optimization. As a result, various new challenges were on the horizon, in particular balancing autonomy with management capacity. Moreover, the recruitment and assimilation of international students also placed additional burdens on tertiary (and some secondary) school managers (Ministry of Education 2007: 22; see Lewis 2005).

Tertiary education reforms

Considering that New Zealand had already adopted a wide array of internationally promoted policies, the question arises of whether IO governance and the OECD, in particular, have affected New Zealand education at all. Referring back to the theoretical framework of this volume, it should be stressed, however, that New Zealand is a country with a high capacity for policy change as a result of its low number of veto players and flexible political system. In addition, as the previous section showed, policymakers were able relatively swiftly to topple previously existing guiding principles of education.

The OECD asserts that New Zealand is a country that is reforming again and again (OECD 1997: 3). However, upon closer analysis, it appears that New Zealand is engaged in small-scale policy adjustment within the already established *grandes lignes* (Interview NZ10). Essentially, the second reform phase can be characterized by three concurring phenomena: internationalization through education export, the optimization of resources, and quality assurance enhancements. The ensuing policies have been tailor-made to the long-term goals of internationalization, expansion, equity/inclusion, and cost-sharing, all of which coincide with OECD-promoted principles (see OECD 2008a).

Once again, the main impetus for reform came from the ministry in its so-called Green Paper (Tertiary Education Review) of 1997 and White Paper of 1998. Guided by the themes "accountability," "responsiveness," and "transparency," the policy documents aimed to foster improvements to student tuition schemes, research funding, quality assurance, and university governance (Olssen 2001: 29). The resulting ministerial activism can be viewed in two different ways. On the one hand, the role of the state was transformed from control and oversight to what Neave deemed the "evaluative state" (1998), which seeks to ensure quality and accountability. On the other hand, the modified framework is indicative of more state steering (Interview NZ04). For example, Olssen (2001: 29) asserts that "state-centrist tendencies are indeed evident...in all tertiary education policies since 1990, a trend highly contradictory of the anti-statist ideology one would assume from a neo-liberal approach."

This explains the initial academic resistance to the Hawke Report proposals implemented in the late 1990s: the increased separation of research and teaching, private funding, the fixed-term appointments of business executives to university councils, and increased auditing and performance monitoring. However, academia has been able to fend off overzealous state intervention by creating institutional buffers. This is reflected, first, in the more proactive role of university management. According to one ministerial interviewee (Interview NZ04), tertiary education management moved away from being a mere academic community and is now "run much like businesses or academic enterprises." Strategic planning is conducted foremost by vice-chancellors whose role, in a nutshell, is to "keep senior academics happy, while also meeting business objectives" (Interview NZ04).

The relationship with the ministry also changed with the establishment of the Tertiary Education Commission (TEC) in 2001, which was born out of the dissatisfaction among tertiary providers with ministerial intervention (Interview NZ05). Conceived as an intermediary body, the TEC assumed responsibilities for administering state funding and shaping policy and strategy in symbiosis with the ministry. Contrary to Olssen's fear of increasing state-centeredness, the establishment of the TEC fortified the corporatist nature of policymaking, with the TEC now functioning as a strong advocate of academia and advisor to the government. Thus, the NZVCC bears responsibility for quality assurance, while the TEC is entrusted with the allocation of government funding and planning matters. As a result, "system design" and quality monitoring are now vested in these two intermediate bodies with strong academic representation.

External stakeholder representation is guaranteed within both the TEC and tertiary management structures, most frequently known as councils. A council usually consists of about 20 members—a chancellor, vice-chancellor, but also employer, union, academic staff, and student representatives. As a rule of thumb, the university council has about 50 percent internal representation and four or five government appointees (Interview NZ05). The TEC commissioners and executive board are also characterized by their mixture of academic and management experience, and various high-ranking members have even been employed directly by the OECD.[9]

Also striking is the shift toward performance-based funding. Previously, state funding was pegged to student numbers, which automatically compelled institutions to increase enrolment (Interview NZ13). However, New Zealand has recently moved toward a quality-based system. The evidence indicates that international policy developments, but not necessarily the OECD, influenced the "Performance Based Research Fund" (PBRF) (Boston 2006: 12). The main driving force behind its introduction was the broad perception that state funding in tertiary education was too low. In particular the British Research Assessment Exercise provided a substantial anchor point (Interview NZ05) for the new system, which aimed at increasing performance accountability and granting universities incentives to procure additional research funds.

However, the PBRF has not been without controversy, as a broad array of academics regards it as an intrusion on institutional autonomy (Interview NZ13) because it gives the government greater traction over the focus and content of research. Thus, we are witnessing a more assertive role of the state in setting targets, steering the system, and ensuring education accountability for the sake of national economic benefit. At the same time though, tertiary providers themselves are now actively engaged in self-assessment and benchmarking themselves with similar institutions overseas (Interview NZ13). Hence, New Zealand can now boast a "multipolar" quality assurance system. The ministry seeks to ensure quality and accountability through evaluation and review, combined with the PBRF, while universities now have multiple incentives for performance optimization. The most important is the targeted recruitment of foreign fee-paying students (see Martens and Starke 2008), meaning that institutions compete with domestic and, above all, Australian institutions to attract foreign students and thus foreign capital. This in turn has ramifications for the quality assurance system, which must ensure clear and transparent qualifications for incoming and outgoing students. This automatically compels policymakers to match up national qualifications with international best practice (Interview NZ12, NZ02).

Figure 7.1 depicts the relationship between key actors in the New Zealand tertiary education systems.

Secondary education reforms

Like the tertiary sector, secondary education has not radically changed recently. The past 10–15 years have instead been characterized by a mixture of policy "roll-back" and "build-up," with the "build-up" component largely driven by IO governance. The "roll-back" affected, foremost, the system of bulk-funding implemented after 1989. The 1990s witnessed a more assertive role for teachers, resulting in the consolidation of various teachers' unions into the New Zealand Education Institute Te Rui Roa. They succeeded in dismantling some of the perceived more burdensome and less practicable aspects of self-management, above all the bulk-funding system. Unions asserted several fears with regard to bulk-funding—that it would (1) lead to lower teacher salaries, (2) impose excessive burdens on management capacities of urban schools and (3) widen the gap between rich and poor schools (LaRocque 2005). Under pressure

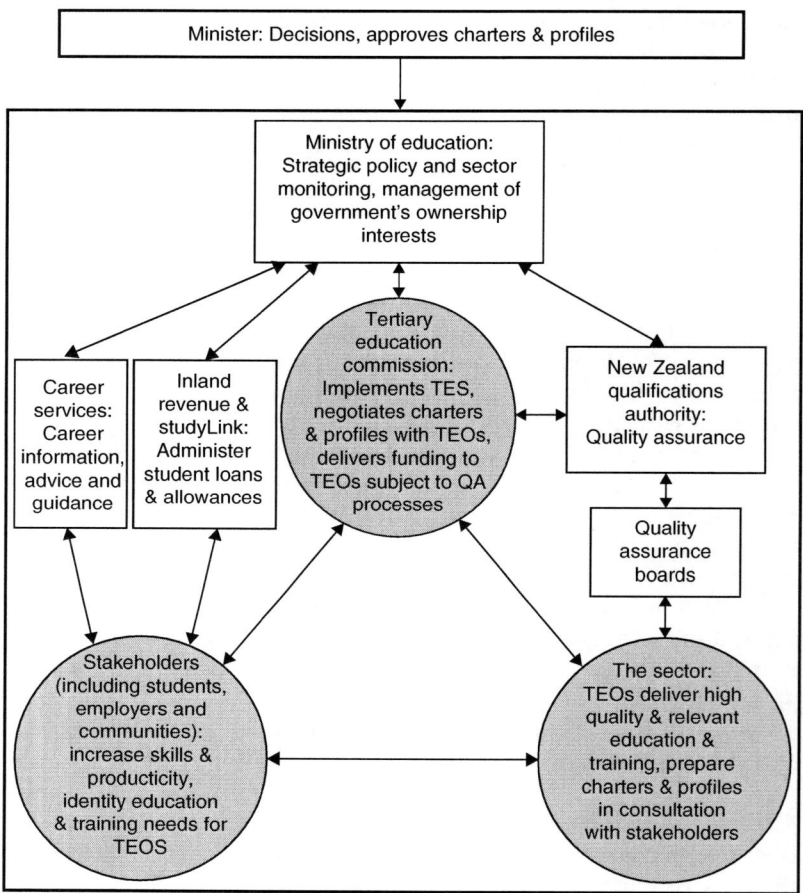

Figure 7.1 Relationships between key actors in the tertiary education system
Source: Ministry of Education (2006).

from teachers' unions, the Labour government reintroduced a more formula-based funding method, thus slightly reducing the degree of school self-management.

A partial roll-back is also reflected in school enrolment schemes and zoning policy. Following the "Tomorrow's Schools" reforms, enrolment provisions were loosened in 1989 and 1991. This meant that schools determined and approved their enrolment schemes and that pupils did not have an absolute right to attend local schools (LaRocque 2005). In other words, schools were authorized to enroll "out-of-zone" children to fill in vacancies. This open policy was amended under the Labour government in 2000–2001, giving the Secretary of Education more authority over enrolments and decreasing school discretion. As a consequence, the reintroduction of school zoning, that is, the geographical assignment of pupils to schools, has led to a decrease in school choice.

Despite this policy roll-back, the devolution of self-management authority to schools changed the playing field to the extent that it is difficult for the state to promote overarching innovation and change vis-à-vis highly autonomous schools (Interview NZ08). However, the ministry has increasingly engaged in policy "build-up" to increase its steering capacity in reaction to various ascertained weaknesses in the system. It is here that the PISA Study has played a decisive role. New Zealand had inherited a largely British system, which assumed that some pupils would perform well and others would not (Interview NZ08). However, it has recently departed from that philosophy and pursued a strategy which, in short, raises achievement while reducing disparity. It has designed a series of measures aimed at:

- raising expectations for all students;
- focusing on outcomes;
- improving teachers' qualities and capabilities through professional development, support tools, good practice examples, and supplementary funding;
- strengthening family engagement;
- improving the knowledge and information available to decisionmakers to ensure that teaching, management, and policy review are up-to-date, focused, and effective;
- improving schools' flexibility over property-related decisions, and encouraging resource usage through collaboration (Ministry of Education 2008).

One of the main reform pillars since 2000 has been the assessment of the qualifications at secondary schools. New Zealand has established a multipolar assessment regime with a strong focus on the learning content, which in turn facilitates economic transformation and innovation through knowledge, skills, and research (Ministry of Education 2008; Interview NZ08). For example, the Education Standards Act 2001 instituted a mandatory self-review procedure for individual schools in addition to ERO audits. This is intended to ensure greater correlation between guiding principles of the twenty-first-century knowledge economy and curriculum (Interview NZ12).

Besides greater pressures for accountability and performance optimization, the past five to ten years have also been marked by greater ministerial activism, flanked significantly by the PISA Study. Previous PISA rounds revealed that New Zealand 15-year-olds significantly outperform the international average for math, science, and reading. This very high performance was also highlighted by recent results (September 2008), in which New Zealand excelled in all categories. As a result of these consistently high rankings, PISA has not triggered extensive media coverage and thrown the *raison d'être* of the system into question. In fact, the PISA Study has only been addressed by an average of one or two articles annually in the leading daily, the *New Zealand Herald*. However:

> The PISA results have been very important..., because they have given us some benchmarks,...being able to see what distinguishes us...; not just our average results but also...the size of our underachievement. Despite a good proportion of high achievement there are too many down at the bottom. It has been a cause to improve teaching and learning and to work with principals in these self-managing schools. (Interview NZ12)

Each round of PISA has revealed that despite the overall high average achievement, there are significant performance disparities, with key population groups (e.g. Māori and Pasifika students) overrepresented among the low achievers. In other words, the best students performed very well, while New Zealand has a disproportionate number of students who fare very poorly. Thus, PISA has revealed that certain groups are not meeting expectations, which is particularly problematic in a society that values equality (Interview NZ08).

PISA has thus been an ice-breaker in addressing the "long tail of underachievers" (Interview NZ13). This has prompted the ministry to undertake concrete measures to decrease disparities (Interview NZ03):

> The results of PISA have had a huge impact on policy in really attending to what are we going to do with this large group of people who aren't doing so well, particularly when you are trying to build up a knowledge-based economy. (Interview NZ14)

This is reflected in the latest Māori education strategy and *Schools Plus* strategy, which assume that the traditional school format is not suited to all pupils and must be adapted to individual needs (Interview NZ08). The most current Māori strategy advocates a shift in philosophy to overcome the severe achievement gap. This entails, for example, a greater emphasis on realizing potential instead of remedying deficits, investing in people and potential instead of government intervention, tailoring education to learners instead of targeting shortcomings, and focusing on Māori background as an asset and not a hindrance (Ministry of Education 2008).

The high performance gap revealed by PISA has also resulted in the *Schools Plus* framework, which addresses students who leave school without labor market qualifications. The state-funded program aims to keep struggling students in the education system, by opening up pathways beyond school (Ministry of Education 2008). Like the Māori strategy, Schools Plus emphasizes tailor-made learning, flexibility, and smooth transition to tertiary education or the working environment. The strategy also seeks to bring the labor market directly into classrooms. Examples are the Youth Apprentice Scheme, which enables pupils to accumulate career skills while still in school, and the Youth Training program, which provides preemployment training to children under 18 (Ministry of Education 2008). Finally, the Ministry has adapted its funding formula to support schools or classes with large numbers of Māori more generously (Interview NZ08).

Assessing the influence of IOs and national transformation capacities on New Zealand's education policymaking

As discussed in the introduction, New Zealand demonstrates favorable conditions for policy change because of its unicameral, nonfederal political system. Indeed, with its strong tradition of internationalization in education, it is expected to be highly receptive to transnational forces. This chapter will now briefly reexamine to what extent these expectations were fulfilled with regard to the OECD's education initiatives, while also briefly discussing the impact of the Bologna Process.

The PISA Study and secondary education

As demonstrated, New Zealand secondary education demonstrates an overarching commitment to the internationalization and economization of education. This is reflected in the embedding of goals of adapting to the knowledge economy and return on investment into all strata of policy. The evidence has revealed that the OECD is a potent actor in secondary education by virtue of the PISA Study, in particular through its coordinative and consultative activities which make performance comparable. By no means as influential in New Zealand as in Germany (see Niemann, Chapter 4 in this volume), PISA has, by identifying various system weaknesses, prompted the ministry to reassess learning and teaching methods aimed at students struggling with traditional learning formats. Pressures to compete in the twenty-first-century economy have increased the perception that large performance gaps between schoolchildren are no longer tolerable. Instead of contenting themselves with their outstanding performance by international standards, New Zealand policymakers have used the PISA Study as a springboard to alleviate the various shortcomings, such as preventing dropouts through vocational training in the classroom. In short, PISA has been an additional contributing factor to New Zealand's long-standing policy of inclusiveness.

The OECD, the Bologna Process and tertiary education

In order to understand the potential role of the Bologna Process in New Zealand it is helpful to take another look at the OECD. The frequent references to the OECD in the New Zealand Tertiary Education Strategy are particularly striking. In fact, it appears that outperforming other OECD countries (in particular Australia) is a constant policy aim. As a result, the strategy bears scattered assertions to the tune of "New Zealand now spends more of its national income on tertiary education than most OECD nations." Moreover, since the 1990s there have been striking correlations between New Zealand policies and the norms set by the OECD such as greater participation, tuition/diversified funding, inclusion of ethnic minorities, education export, internationalization, and a focus on the economic value of education. Core elements of the Tertiary Education Strategy are reflective of relative weaknesses of New Zealand in comparison to the U.S., UK, and Australia. Compared with the OECD average, the U.S. and UK, New Zealand has a lower participation rate in the youngest age group but higher participation rates thereafter. This comparative weakness was immediately addressed by the ministry, which sought to ensure that more New Zealanders complete tertiary education qualifications by age 25. Thus, OECD comparisons have set standards for New Zealand as to the level and allocation of expenditure (Interview NZ01).

On the one hand, New Zealand policymakers are very engaged in OECD policymaking and always have their "global antennae" out. As one TEC official states:

> Even back then New Zealand officials would go to meetings with the OECD...and other kinds of education experts. So I imagine it was an

awful lot of stuff in the wider international policy community that was drawn on. We are very globalised. I would say we are constantly running across every theory, constantly looking across our shoulders. (Interview NZ05)

On the other hand, it is difficult to disentangle the impact of the OECD from broader trends in international academic and economic policy networks. After all, the OECD is a conveyer of "modern" economic philosophy stemming primarily from Anglo-American countries. One could equally plausibly argue that New Zealand's participation in the international market for education services, combined with economic exigencies, has been the main driving force for change. In this vein, IO governance and the OECD in particular could be regarded as an additional anchor point to legitimize an already stabilized web of related policies. Hence, IO governance has a reinforcing and optimizing impact on the existing central policy pillars of secondary and tertiary education—broad participation, marketization, economic relevance, and inclusion. The impact of IO governance is also inseparable from New Zealand's policy of education export. However, education export is not a by-product of IO governance, as New Zealand had adopted this strategy long before it was promoted by the OECD. Instead, it is actually the OECD that continually points to New Zealand's success in this field in order to promote this policy goal internationally (OECD 2004). The same applies to life-long learning and related policies of expanding education, areas in which New Zealand has excelled because of the policies implemented in the late 1980s. Thus, in various ways New Zealand has become the "poster child" for the success of the education regime promoted by the OECD (Interview NZ09).

As a result, New Zealand has its international "antennae" out continuously to tap into transnational developments. The Bologna Process, which is geographically irrelevant to New Zealand, is an example of this. The establishment of a European Higher Education Area is perceived as a springboard for New Zealand to enhance its international interlinkages and thereby ensure that its graduates can access global academic and labor markets (Ministry of Education 2008). Although New Zealand is already fully compatible with the Bologna study-cycle model, the ministry strives to tap into approaches developed within the Bologna framework to promote the recognition of New Zealand qualifications. At the same time, various policymakers (Interviews NZ07, NZ04, and NZ01) explicitly state that Bologna provides a platform for New Zealand to build on its existing quality assurance framework. For example, it has joined the Lisbon Qualification Recognition Convention and is investigating the introduction of a diploma supplement (Ministry of Education 2008). According to the Ministry, "[a]t the same time as enhancing our engagement with Bologna, we have also focused on ensuring our tertiary education system relates to other education systems around the world and maintains its own individual characteristics" (ibid.). Bologna has additionally provided New Zealand an impetus to engage in the bilateral "synchronization" of qualifications and quality assurance instruments. This is reflected by cooperation between the NZVCC, NZQA, and the Republic of Ireland aimed at increasing the comparability of the NZ Register of Quality Assured Qualifications with the Irish National Framework of Qualifications (Interview NZ07).

Summary: IO governance and national transformation capacities

Now that the impact of IOs on the policymaking machinery and outcomes has been discussed, it is expedient to examine whether domestic institutions have impeded or facilitated their influence. In this regard, two aspects are crucial: first, formal and nonformal veto players and second, guiding principles on the role, purpose, and function of education.

On both fronts, New Zealand demonstrates a fertile basis for swift policy adjustment with its unicameral political system based on the Westminster model, which according to Tsebelis (1995) only knows one partisan veto player—the opposition party. The resulting high capacity for policy change is enhanced by the nonfederal structure.

> We have a unicameral parliament and no senate.... We do not have subnational government that you have to get on course to do things. We have a very centralized government, but decentralized governance. From the constitutional point of view there are few veto players...in the education system. (Interview NZ05)

Thus, New Zealand has high executive capacity, which means that the government has the legal authority to compel education providers to take action, whereas in Australia, for example, individual state governments have that authority (Interview NZ01). However, it would be careless to focus exclusively on formal veto players, as a system of "quango governance" has also emerged. As a result, education policy is designed and steered by a dense network of statutory and nonstatutory actors. This complexity is increased by strong community involvement and the breadth of tertiary education. However, as Tsebelis (1995) asserts, it is not the number of veto players which is decisive, rather their preference heterogeneity. Most education policymakers demonstrate remarkable congruence in terms of their policy aims—quality optimization, education export, internationalization, balancing equity with competition, and finding an equitable funding mix. It would, however, be an exaggeration to assert that education is not a conflict-ridden issue. Conflicts over academic autonomy in universities have frequently resurfaced, as the state has continually pushed for entrepreneurial management and external stakeholder participation. Such efforts have, however, been resisted by the NZVCC and university staff (Interview NZ05). Yet as one interviewee states, the "god-professor Humboldt model has been dead for 30 years now" (Interview NZ01), implying that the academic lobby is less potent than in continental Europe.

The relative weakness of veto players is also explained by the culture of consultation and moderation. The government has a strong capacity to assert itself, but has shied away from radical approaches. Even before the "big bang," the OECD made various key observations on the policymaking style:

> New Zealand is saved from many time-consuming and frequently unproductive arguments that beset societies elsewhere. The style of education policy-making...remains consensual and incremental, guided by a combination of individualism and tolerant conformity within what has been...a society characterized by common values to an unusual degree. (OECD 1983: 10)

This spirit of consensus, consultation, and community involvement still characterizes the policymaking style today, which helps neutralize potential veto players. This also holds for the parliamentary process, as coalition governments are forced to compromise on key policy issues (Interviews NZ07, NZ12). Once deals have been reached, the government—unconstrained by formal veto points—can push through its agenda.

The role of overarching education principles must also be considered when examining policy change. Unlike in some countries, the policy debate is not centered on the logic, function, and role of education. New Zealand has instead successfully balanced a series of principles viewed as complementary (broad participation, market proximity, return on investment, equality). The notion of education as an elite privilege vanished decades ago (Interview NZ01), which explains the promotion of inclusiveness and investment in lower-performing secondary students. Thus, the system has effectively catered to both guiding philosophies on education: education as a human right and as human capital. On the one hand, there is a perception that more education is better, resulting in open and flexible access and institutional diversity, for example, Māori *wananga*. On the other hand, market proximity ensures that education is aimed at generating human capital to help New Zealand to thrive in the twenty-first century.

Conclusion

Unlike much of western Europe, New Zealand education had already been radically transformed in the 1980s, leading to entrepreneurial self-management, extensive evaluation mechanisms, multistakeholdership, tuition, system diversification, etc. The ensuing phase was marked by smaller-scale reforms to optimize the interplay between accountability, market relevancy, quality, and equity. New Zealand policymakers have indeed dedicated great attention to policies promoted through IO governance. Unlike Germany, for example, though (see Niemann, Chapter 4 in this volume), this has not led to any noteworthy changes resulting from the relative congruence between "modern education ideas" promoted by the OECD and New Zealand education policy. Nevertheless, New Zealand has consistently drawn on the "international market of ideas" to promote policies based on equilibrium, balance, effectiveness, and accountability.

Geographically isolated New Zealand has also successfully drawn on the international market for academic services. The system of education export thrives on the widespread consensus on the advantages of internationalization for the national economy (see OECD 2006). The provision of education to foreign students has in turn affected the system of governance by granting university and school management greater financial authority and possibilities for strategic marketing. Moreover, policymakers must ensure transparency for incoming and outgoing students and thus match up national qualifications with international best practice.

The analysis highlighted that the relatively smooth introduction of various policy modifications was facilitated by factors addressed in the theoretical framework. Firstly, New Zealand can be attested a high transformation capacity, because of its unicameralism with few veto players. Once policies are agreed, the government is relatively unconstrained in implementing them. Perhaps more important, however, is the relative congruence among actors over education policy goals. Unlike the German case, where academic autonomy, competition, equity, and marketization are often seen as conflicting goals, New Zealand policymakers tend to view these as interdependent and pragmatically seek to reconcile them. Consequently, New Zealand has experimented with various unique policy approaches, while consistently avoiding more "radical" approaches (e.g. high tuition fees, extreme professorial autonomy, or school vouchers).

Finally, system reformability is enhanced by the deeply entrenched "culture of international comparison." As outlined, IO governance has not triggered a paradigmatic transformation of New Zealand education. Instead, international interlinkages with the OECD have reinforced and to a large extent optimized its main pillars—broad participation, marketization, economic relevance, and inclusion—all of which are promoted by the OECD (OECD 2008a). However, performance comparisons—combined with the "national pastime" of outperforming Australia—have starkly impacted public expenditure in secondary education and efforts to increase tertiary participation, policymakers have used the results of international comparisons to smoothen out the revealed weaknesses of the system.

Notes

1. For a more thorough account, see the Working Paper on New Zealand by the same author, University of Bremen, Collaborate Research Center 597.
2. Auckland University of Technology, Lincoln University (Canterbury), Massey University (Palmerston North, Auckland, Wellington), University of Auckland, University of Canterbury (Christchurch), University of Otago (Dunedin), University of Waikato (Hamilton), and Victoria University (Wellington).
3. It should be noted that New Zealand is a bicultural nation and multicultural society, with prominence given to its two founding cultures—indigenous Māori and English-speaking settlers from Great Britain and Europe (Pakeha). Moreover, New Zealand is an attractive destination for immigration and both biculturalism and multiculturalism have left their mark on the education system.
4. Specified courses may be subject to restrictions on the grounds of insufficient resources. Some programs (medicine, dentistry) automatically have restricted entry.
5. New Zealand has traditionally followed the three-cycle degree structure now promoted in Europe. The Register of Quality Assured Qualifications contains details on the qualifications and a credit-point system which defines common standards for different levels of qualifications. The national register comprises ten levels with 10 (doctoral degree) being the highest. Levels 1 to 4 pertain to the mentioned certificates, levels 5 and 6 are diplomas, while level 7 comprises Bachelor's (B.A.) degrees. Level 8 covers postgraduate diplomas

and B.A.s with honours and level 9 (OECD 2006: 119). The levels do not reflect the length or duration of study programs, rather the depth and complexity of learning involved to achieve the qualification.
6. To put this in perspective, each New Zealand school has its own school board which handles governance activities in cooperation with teachers, parents and local stakeholders. In the U.S.A., by contrast, school boards generally function as umbrella organizations for a conglomerate of several local schools.
7. Report of the Working Groups on Post-Compulsory Education and Training (Department of Education 1988).
8. The evidence reveals that New Zealand policymakers were inspired by foreign practice, even prior to increased OECD involvement. Faced with competing interests over a private or public loan scheme and calls for a stronger equity (Interview NZ05), governmental policymakers actively conducted an extensive analysis of experiences in North America and Europe. Specifically, policymakers sought to integrate elements of the Swedish model to offset the tuition burden on students with a stronger equity component. This resulted in student loan scheme, in which loans were granted on a noninterest basis—and exemptions from payback obligations were granted to students under a certain income level after tertiary education.
9. See TEC website—www.tec.govt.nz.

References

Boston, Jonathan (2006) "Rationale for the Performance-Based Research Fund: Personal Reflections," in Bakker, Leon, Boston, Jonathan, Campbell, Lesley, and Smyth, Roger (eds.) *Evaluating the Performance-Based Fund: Framing the Debate*. Wellington. Institute of Policy Studies.

Codd, John (2003) "Export Education and the Commercialisation of Public Education in New Zealand," in I. Livingstone, ed., *New Zealand Annual Review of Education*, 13, 21–41.

Codling, Andrew and Lynn V. Meek (2003) "The Impact of the State on Institutional Differentiation in New Zealand," *Higher Education Policy and Management* 15 (2), 83–98.

Department of Education of New Zealand (1988) *Administering for Excellence: Effective Administration in Education* (Picot Report), Wellington: Government Printer.

Dobbins, Michael (2009) "Comparing Higher Education Policies in Central and Eastern Europe," in A.P. Jakobi, K. Martens, and K.D. Wolf, eds., *Governance and Education—Discovering a Neglected Field for Political Science*, London and New York: Routledge.

Eppel, Elizabeth (2007) "World Bank—New Zealand and Australia—Vocational Education and Training," Presentation given at the World Bank Conference on "The Missing Link: Rethinking the Role of Technical Vocational Education in Upper Secondary Education," Tirana, Albania, October 24–27 (Online: http://siteresources.worldbank.org/EXTECAREGTOPEDUCATION/Resources/444607-1192636551820/New-zealand_%5Bre-formatted%5D.ppt, last access: June 24, 2009).

Fitzsimmons, Patrick (1997) "Human Capital Theory and Participation in Tertiary Education in New Zealand," in M. Olssen and K. Morris Matthews, eds., *Education Policy in New Zealand: The 1990s and Beyond*, Palmerston North: The Dunmore Press, 107–109.

Fitzsimmons, Patrick, Michael Peters, and Peter Roberts (1999) "Economics and the Educational Policy Process in New Zealand," *New Zealand Journal of Educational Studies* 34 (1), 35–44.

Gordon, Liz (1997) "Tomorrow's Schools Today: School Choice and the Education Quasi-Market," in M. Olssen and K. Morris Matthews, eds., *Education Policy in New Zealand: the 1990s and Beyond*, Palmerston North: The Dunmore Press, 65–82.

Hawke, Gary (1988) *Report of the Working Group on Post Compulsory Education and Training* (The Hawke Report), Cabinet Committee on Social Equity, Wellington: Government Printer.

Heichel, Stephan, Jessica Pape, and Thomas Sommerer (2005) "Is There Convergence in Convergence Research? An Overview of Empirical Studies in the Field of Policy Convergence," *Journal of European Public Policy* 12 (5), 817–40.

Hirsch, Donald (1995) "The Other School Choice: How Oversubscribed Schools Select Their Students," Paper presented in a public lecture at London Institute of Education, May 1995.

Lange, David and Phil Goff (1989) "Learning for Life. Education and Training beyond the Age of Fifteen," Wellington: Government Printer.

LaRocque, Norman (2005) "Bulk-Funding: Time to Get Back to the Future," *Otago Daily Times*, July 21, 2005.

Lewis, Nicolas (2005) "Code of Practice for the Pastoral Care of International Students: Making a Globalizing Industry in New Zealand," *Globalisation, Societies, and Education* 3 (1), March 2005, 5–47.

Martens, Kerstin (2007) "How to Become an Influential Actor—the 'Comparative Turn' in OECD Education Policy," in K. Martens, A. Rusconi, and K. Leuze, eds., *New Arenas of Education Governance—the Impact of International Organisations and Markets on Educational Policymaking*, Houndmills, Basingstoke: Palgrave, 40–56.

Martens, Kerstin and Anja P. Jakobi (2007) "Diffusion und Konvergenz durch Internationale Organisationen: Der Einfluss der OECD in der Bildungspolitik," in K. Holzinger, H. Jörgens, and C. Knill, eds., *Politische Vierteljahresschrift—Special Issue: Transfer, Diffusion und Konvergenz von Politiken* 38, 247–70.

Martens, Kerstin and Peter Starke (2008) "Small Country, Big Business? New Zealand as an Education Exporter," *Comperative Education* 44 (1), 3–19.

McKenzie, David (1997) "The Cult of Efficiency and Miseducation: Issues of Assessment in New Zealand Schools," in M. Olssen and K. Morris Matthews, eds., *Education Policy in New Zealand: The 1990s and Beyond*, Palmerston North: The Dunmore Press, 56–62.

Ministry of Education of New Zealand (1997) *A Future Tertiary Education Policy for New Zealand: Tertiary Education Review Green Paper*, Wellington: Ministry of Education.

Ministry of Education of New Zealand (2006) *OECD Thematic Review of Tertiary Education: New Zealand Country Background Report*, Wellington: Ministry of Education.

Ministry of Education of New Zealand (2008) *New Zealand and the Bologna Process* (Online: http://www.minedu.govt.nz/~/media/MinEdu/Files/EducationSectors/InternationalEducation/PolicyStrategy/NZandBologna.pdf, last access: June 16, 2009).

Neave, Guy (1998) "The Evaluative State Reconsidered," *European Journal of Education* 33 (3), 265–84.

Neave, Guy (2003) "The Bologna Declaration: Some of the Historic Dilemmas Posed by the Reconstruction of the Community in Europe's System of Higher Education," *Educational Policy* 17 (1), 141–64.

NZVCC (2008) *Website* (Online: http://www.nzvcc.ac.nz/, last access: June 20, 2009).

OECD (1983) Reviews of National Policies for Education: New Zealand. OECD Publications and Information Center. Washington, DC.

OECD (1997) Thematic Review of the First Years of Tertiary Education. Country Note: New Zealand), OECD, Paris.

OECD (2004) *Internationalisation and Trade in Higher Education. Opportunities and Challenges,* Paris: OECD.

OECD (2006) *Range of Rank on the PISA 2006 Science Scale* (Online: www.oecd.org/dataoecd/42/8/39700724.pdf, last access: June 13, 2009).

OECD (2008a) *Tertiary Education for the Knowledge Society—OECD Thematic Review of Tertiary Education: Synthesis Report,* Paris: OECD.

OECD (2008b) *Education at a Glance—OECD Indicators,* Paris: OECD.

Olssen, Mark (2001) *The Neo-Liberal Appropriation of Tertiary Education Policy in New Zealand: Accountability, Research and Academic Freedom. State-of-the-Art,* Monograph No. 8, New Zealand Association for Research in Education.

Olssen, Mark and Kay Morris Matthews (1997) *Education Policy in New Zealand: The 1990s and Beyond,* Palmerston North: The Dunmore Press.

Shaw, Richard and Chris Eichbaum (2006) "Labour in Government, Social Democracy and the Third Way: The New Zealand Experience," paper presented at the "British Political Studies Association Conference," Reading, UK, March 2006 (Online: http://www.psa.ac.uk/cps/cps.asp, last access: June 20, 2009).

Tsebelis, George (1995) "Decision Making in Political Systems: Veto Players in Presidentialism, Parliamentarism, Multi-Cameralism and Multipartyism," *British Journal of Political Science* 25 (3), 289–335.

Wylie, Cathy (1989) *The Impact of Tomorrow's Schools in Primary Schools and Intermediaries,* Wellington: New Zealand Council for Education Research.

8
A Contrasting Case—the U.S.A. and Its Weak Response to Internationalization Processes in Education Policy

Michael Dobbins and Kerstin Martens

The impact of internationalization processes in education policy varies across the participating member countries. As explored in the previous chapters on Germany, Switzerland, England and New Zealand, countries reacted differently as regards the influence of international organization (IO) governance on national policy, politics, and polity in the field of education. National transformation capacities have modified the responses of countries to the international initiatives in the field of education (see Introduction to this volume). In Germany and Switzerland, the Organisation for Economic Cooperation and Development's (OECD) Programme for International Student Assessment (PISA) Study and the European Bologna Process led to comprehensive political initiatives—despite their institutional settings, which are unfavorable to reforms. The misfit between nationally guiding principles of education and orientational frameworks promoted by the two international initiatives was high enough to facilitate reform processes in education. In contrast, England and New Zealand had already initiated educational reform in the 1980s, before processes of internationalization driven by the PISA Study and the Bologna Process. Nonetheless, both countries are now addressing PISA and Bologna to some extent. The UK, however, has underestimated both processes as regards the comparative political dimension while New Zealand has used the PISA results in order to adopt measures to decrease performance disparities.

These internationalization processes triggered by the PISA Study and the Bologna Process are not necessarily of global reach. PISA is conducted in 66 countries, while the Bologna Process only applies to the European region, including some countries at the Asian fringe. However, both processes have triggered interest on a global scale. Since the first PISA round in 2000, more and more countries have taken part in this survey. By 2009, more nonmembers than OECD members took part in the survey. Also, Finland as one of the best performers in PISA is now frequently visited by delegations from around the world wishing to learn from the Finnish system. Perhaps even more importantly, observers from all continents are monitoring the Bologna Process with great interest, trying to determine what influence the changes introduced in Europe may have for their own education systems. Thus, the Bologna Process is having a global impact: Latin American and African states have expressed interest in emulating the Bologna Process for their continents, while Australia is heading an initiative similar to the Bologna model for the Asian-Pacific region (which has become known as the Brisbane Communiqué).

However, the responses in countries taking part in these international initiatives vary significantly. In many other industrialized countries, the PISA results remain unheard of in general and have triggered no public discussion or any reforms in education policy—even though these countries fared poorly. For example, in Norway, Canada, New Zealand, Great Britain, or Poland, the media has paid almost no attention to the OECD's survey and their country's results in the international comparative ranking—regardless of whether these are good or bad (Martens and Niemann 2009). The Bologna Process has had a moderate to massive impact on study structures, quality assurance measures, and governance in participating countries. In Germany and Switzerland, the establishment of a European dimension in higher education has helped policy-makers to introduce a series of policy innovations which run counter to historical education traditions. In Balkan countries such as Romania and Bulgaria, the Bologna Process has helped to redefine the role and function of universities and facilitated a visible shift towards market-based governance mechanisms (see Dobbins and Knill 2009).

In this chapter, we explore the U.S.A. as a contrasting case to the previous chapters. Unlike other countries explored in this volume, the country's reactions to these internationalization processes in education policy are rather insignificant. This is astonishing in the sense that the U.S.A. is a prime destination for international students. However, its education system is very decentralized, at both secondary and tertiary levels, and a national policy for education is almost nonexistent. As a result, dealing with education policy as an internationalized field of policy presents a problem to the U.S.A. Although the U.S.A. finds itself at the lower end of the PISA rankings, there has been little discussion about improving the quality of schools or teaching after such disastrous results. The European Bologna Process, however, is increasingly attracting the interest of, and posing new problems for, policymakers. The paradox is therefore that the U.S.A. has taken little notice of the large-scale PISA Study in which it has taken part, while the geographically irrelevant Bologna Process is increasingly attracting the attention of the affected policy community and has already inspired some U.S. states to harmonize their qualifications frameworks better.

How the U.S.A. disregards its PISA results[1]

The U.S.A. stands out for its particularly weak public and political responses to the OECD's PISA Study. The different cycles of the PISA Study since 2000 and their results have remained almost unheard among the general public. To put it simply, PISA is just not an issue in the U.S.A.; for example, of eight major U.S. daily and weekly newspapers, only eight articles over the period between 2001 and 2008 covered the OECD's PISA Study at all, and of these eight articles only three deal with the poor results of U.S. students.[2] (During the same period a *single* German daily newspaper, namely the *Süddeutsche Zeitung*, published 253 articles mentioning PISA.) Thus, the American media have taken little notice of this study and its results—even though their country performed badly, being ranked below the average of all the participating countries. For example, the U.S.A. scored worse in the 2006 study than it did in the previous two studies: in this third PISA Study it ranked only twenty-fourth in math among the 30 OECD member states. However, despite these poor results, reactions among the broader public or politicians were sparse. Unlike other countries in this study, the U.S.A. somehow ignored its comparatively poor performance results. Why did PISA not trigger an education shock in the U.S.A. as a result of this low ranking? Part of the answer is 1) that the country's *poor school results* as exposed by the PISA Study *were already known* in the U.S.A. and 2) that the *decentralized secondary school system* hindered nationwide standards for a long time.

First, *poor school results* are no news for the U.S.A. The country has been exposed to them (or perceived them as such) since the Soviet Union launched the first satellite in 1957: Sputnik put secondary education policy on the political agenda in the U.S.A. and even today no speaker on education policy would fail to make a reference to Sputnik (Interview USA12). From the U.S. perspective, Sputnik proved the Soviet Union's technological superiority or at least its equality with the U.S.A.

in this area. This technological capacity challenged the West's previous sense of technological preeminence. The reasons for this western "lag" were mainly identified in the education system: according to experts the main problem was the prevailing circumstances in schools which excluded too many people from participating in the social progress.

The launch of Sputnik triggered a crisis in the self-image of Americans who had naturally considered themselves inhabitants of the technologically most progressive nation. In this context, democracy and capitalism had also been widely considered as natural competitive advantages accounting for the U.S.A.'s technological superiority. The fact that the communist Soviet Union with its planned economy was one step ahead of the U.S.A. in space-related issues deeply shocked the Americans and led to a comprehensive reform of the American education system. In particular, critics pointed to the deficiencies of American students in math and the natural sciences since the Soviet Union trained two or even three times as many engineers as the U.S.A. For this reason, in 1957 the "Federal-Aid-to-Education-Program" was launched to finance the reform of the education system over a period of four years.

With these measures new emphasis was placed on the inclusion of underprivileged classes in the hope of discovering new resources for the education system. New school buses were put on the road to integrate children from remote areas into the education system. Further, curricula were restructured and courses which had previously dealt with housekeeping or direct vocational education were substituted by math, physics, and chemistry. However, the advancement of the humanities, such as political science, history, and languages, was also part of the program. These measures were aimed at producing wise leaders who could apply the technological achievements for the collective good of the American nation. Television education programs were promoted as well as the end-to-end integration of education institutions and libraries in order to grant better accessibility to education. In the 1960s, the "New-Math-Program" aimed at familiarizing children with abstract math from very early on.

In the early 1980s, the U.S. Government enlisted a national commission to conduct a study of the American educational system 25 years after Sputnik in order to review the progress made since. The resulting report of 1983 "A Nation at Risk: Imperatives for Educational Reforms" found devastating outcomes: with 23 million adults and 17 percent of juveniles illiterate, the American educational system was abysmal. Written in very dramatic language, the report triggered a broad public concern about the quality of education, identifying the need for the monitoring of schools, standards, and teachers. It resulted in a "Great

School Debate" (Gross and Gross 1985): during the height of the Cold War, political stakeholders considered this state of affairs a national security risk and made school reform a first priority. In the years to follow, education matters have been at the top of each presidential administration's list of reforms.

The U.S.A. thus had its "education shock" decades before PISA. Thus, unlike Germany, for example, the shock was triggered not by an international organization, such as the OECD, but by a comparison with its direct enemy, the Soviet Union. Again, since the 1980s, a series of educational reforms aiming at creating standards, providing for accountability, enabling school choice, and improving the quality of teaching have been initiated and implemented. Most importantly, these reforms have led to outcome-oriented types of educational teaching, based on the belief that setting high standards and establishing measurable goals can improve individual results in education (Interviews USA03, USA06, USA10).

The latest of these reforms is the current No Child Left Behind Act (NCLB) of 2001.[3] The law reauthorized a number of federal programs aimed at improving the performance of U.S. primary and secondary schools by increasing the standards of accountability for states, school districts, and schools, as well as providing parents with more flexibility in choosing which schools their children will attend. The Act requires states wishing to receive federal funding for schools to develop assessments in basic skills that are to be conveyed to all students in certain grades.[4] However, NCLB does not assert a national achievement standard; instead, standards are set by each individual state, in line with the schools' principle of local control.

Second, such standardization was necessary because the U.S. system is historically *decentralized* as regards its secondary school system (Interview USA03). The country has a very long history of local control. "And that really means a local school district is in charge of running the school. They have a hard time even giving up authority to the state, but if you look at the constitution the states are charged with the responsibility of education. Education is not actually in the United States Federal Constitution" (Interview USA06).[5] In a way, NCLB is almost a revolution: "to figure out what material you are going to study in what grade and in what degree of detail—that was radical for American schools. [...] This reform is going to change practice" (Interview USA03). Such explicit standards are necessary in order to provide American teachers with a clear and common vision and prevent students from receiving inconsistent and incoherent instruction (Interview USA06).

The initiative for this law came from governors (Interviews USA03, 06) and this was the first time that the standardization of education was addressed at the federal level. Before NCLB, federal policy had mainly been concerned with giving more resources and money to pool schools, but without asking for any evaluation results in return. Only the late 1980s and early 1990s did a few key states press for common standards. The federal government caught on to this idea and promoted the Improving America's Schools Act in 1994, which, for the first time, stated that standards, assessments, and accountability are in fact a must if states want to receive federal money. However, states did not really take it seriously until the No Child Left Behind Act of 2001: NCLB provided them with well-defined standards and specific directions (Interview USA06).

Unusual for American politics, NCLB was primarily a bipartisan project of the Democrats and Republicans and therefore influenced by both ideologies. For example, the Democrats pushed for additional funding for schools, while the Republicans strongly supported greater accountability and provisions for school choice. However, there has also been convergence of the two parties' ideas. For example, both Democrats and Republicans agreed on the need to set common standards with regard to what students should know and be able to do, and to hold schools accountable for meeting these standards (Interview USA06).

However, the various reforms have so far only had marginal success: "the standards are pretty low level. For example, even if a student was to meet the standards, that would not necessarily mean that he/she is prepared for college" (Interview USA06); one of the reasons being that teaching itself has not changed: "If you looked at what has happened in classrooms over 30 years, then you will actually see very little change. So the system, the structures, the policy and the funding and all the stuff surrounding the classroom may have changed but the class room itself largely looks the same" (Interview USA03). In a way, there is a sense of resignation in the U.S.A. about how to reform the system so that the outcome (better educated pupils) really improves. In fact, the 2004 and 2008 presidential elections were the first since the 1980s where other issues, in particular the war against terrorism and the state of the economy, outrank education in terms of importance. However, education was also ignored because candidates from both sides were unable to provide new convincing concepts as to how to improve education standards in the U.S.A.

Thus, within the domestic sphere, the U.S.A. has taken a path to more standardization and comparative evaluations, but international comparisons such as the PISA Study did not provoke any reactions. While ratings and rankings within the U.S.A. play a decisive role today as regards the choice of school, the international standing of the U.S.A. as a whole has not drawn significant attention. The irony, however, is that it was in fact the U.S.A. that gave the incentive for the PISA Study, and this then impacted far more on other countries' education policies than on America's own (see Niemann on Germany and Bieber on Switzerland, Chapters 4 and 5 in this volume). When "A Nation at Risk" hit the U.S.A., the Reagan administration not only initiated domestic reforms, it also demanded international comparative data on the state of education in the industrialized world in general. The idea of an international comparative study was then brought to the OECD. Being the major financial contributor to the OECD's budget for education, the U.S.A. pushed the IO to significantly change its activities in education and to compile internationally comparable statistical data. In response to tremendous pressure from the U.S.A., the International Indicators of Educational Systems (INES) project was established in 1988. It began to produce regular publications on education indicators—of which the PISA Study is the latest offspring.[6]

All in all, IOs such as the OECD have not had any significant direct impact on the national education system (Interview USA03). As the U.S.A. sees itself from a paradigm of "American exceptionalism," it has been assumed that it cannot really learn from other systems (Interview USA03)—unlike for example New Zealand, which seeks to learn from best practices (see Dobbins, Chapter 7 in this volume). The image predominates that the U.S.A. is somehow different from the rest of the world and that is why it is not fair or reasonable to compare it to other countries (Interview USA06). The PISA results are known by an elite, by policymakers and education groups in the USA, but they constitute only one of a variety of tests in which the country takes part (Interview USA06). Thus, despite the reforms of the last 25 years since "A Nation at Risk" was published, schools in the U.S.A. have improved only to a limited extent. The various low PISA scores for the U.S.A. did not generate a shock, since it is essentially a well-known fact that the U.S. education system still needs improvement. As expressed in an interview: "every few years [...] PISA, TIMSS—we have been hearing for 25 years the study drumbeat of news that the rest of the world is doing better than us; this doesn't come as any surprise" (Interview USA03). In a way, it would have instead been a positive shock for the Americans, if they had achieved better results in the PISA Study (Interview USA01).

"What are we going to do about Bologna?"

As was the case with PISA, the U.S. higher education community for a long time paid little attention to the Bologna Process. From a U.S. perspective, the Bologna Declaration aims to create a *European* university space to promote mobility, transparency, labor market qualifications, and the harmonization of the overarching architecture of the extremely diverse European higher education systems. From a technical standpoint, Bologna promotes a higher education structure based on two main cycles (B.A./M.A.). Coinciding in part with the American B.A. degree, the first degree lasts three years at least. In addition, the Bologna Process calls for a diploma supplement stating exactly what skills and qualifications were acquired by graduates from a given program. Moreover, participating countries are also aiming to fortify a "European dimension in quality assurance based on comparable criteria and methods." (Bologna Declaration 1999) The European Commission, which only emerged as a key player in 2001, has also expressed a clear vision of the future of European higher education, which may be interpreted as convergence on American practice and a stronger market orientation (European Commission 2003).

Thus, the Bologna Process at first sight may appear to be a concerted effort to emulate the Anglo-American model of higher education. After all, the U.S. system would hypothetically comply fully with major aspects of the Bologna guidelines. Indeed a survey of American higher education experts within the framework of the project "National conditions of cross-national policy convergence in the context of the Bologna-Process" has revealed that Bologna has not had an impact on any significant aspect of American higher education, for example, study structures, quality assurance, or governance (see Vögtle, Knill and Dobbins 2009). In other words, the overwhelming response is that Bologna is a nonissue in the U.S.A.

However, the reality is becoming more complex and Bologna is bound to become more relevant for the U.S.A. In fact, there are reasons to believe that Bologna will eventually not only increasingly attract the attention of American policymakers, but may also have long-term ramifications for American higher education policy, both at the institutional and national level. Although geographically distant from the U.S.A., the Bologna Process is likely to affect American higher education in three distinct ways: (1) issues related to recognition *technicalities*, (2) increased *problem pressure* on individual institutions and the federal government, and (3) *emulation effects*, most likely at the decentralized institutional level.

There are indications that many international educators and higher education policymakers are currently asking themselves what should be done about the European Bologna Process (see Bell and Watkins 2006). Not surprisingly, Bologna has triggered a mixed bag of reactions from American higher education policymakers. These span from no reaction, to a moderate interest among higher education internationalization specialists, to recent ardent calls for action and changes in U.S. higher education at various levels.

In the case of the U.S.A., it is important to recall that higher education policy is not guided by a ministry of education or an overarching federal authority. Federal influence is primarily restricted to the federal student aid program. Contrary to the federal government, individual U.S. states can indeed considerably influence institutions which are part of state systems of higher education, but rarely become involved in academic policy issues (Thompson 2007). The U.S. higher education landscape is highly decentralized, even with regard to credit systems and credit transfer, which are administered solely at the institutional level. Thus, individual higher education providers are granted a supreme degree of autonomy with regard to admissions, substantive and procedural issues, and finances. This has resulted in a nearly unfathomable diversity of higher education providers catering to highly diverse demands, without the guidance of an overarching authority.

This diversity is likely to be reflected in the diverse responses to *technical issues* for U.S. universities raised by the Bologna Process. The European convergence process surrounding diploma structures has put U.S. higher education providers in an awkward situation with regard to the recognition of the new European-style three-year B.A. degrees. On the one hand, the new European diploma supplements are cited as being of inestimable value to U.S. international admission officers and credentials evaluators. On the other hand, American admissions policymakers have traditionally weighed educational achievements on the basis of quantitative models, that is, years of study, and not necessarily by examining documented students skills and qualifications (Bell and Watkins 2006: 71). Graduate schools usually have required four years of B.A.-level study for entry, terms with which the new Bologna-based three-year degrees do not comply. Thus, the recruitment and admission of graduate students from the Bologna region have imposed a new range of issues on international credentials assessors. Because of the lack of an overarching nationwide policy, university admissions officers have adopted varied approaches to the recognition of three-year European B.A. degrees. According to Bell and Watkins (2006: 71) some universities have pursued an "all-or-nothing" approach and insist on four-year Bachelor degrees. Other providers have opted to admit to American graduate programs only those students who have completed a Bologna-based B.A. degree, while excluding other students. Most universities have yet to devise a clear policy, however. In any case, the Bologna Process has prompted moves among individual institutions to seek solutions to this issue of compatibility. For example, other institutions have discussed introducing a "Master's qualifying year" or are only accepting four-year "Bachelor with honours" degrees (see Bell and Watkins 2006).

However, another scenario is also possible, which would actually entail convergence by American colleges and universities on the Bologna model. As a result of the current economic recession and the uncontrolled rise in tuition costs, there is much discussion about the introduction of three-year B.A. degrees (Strauss 2009). This would require that students know in advance exactly what they wish to study (which is infrequently the case with American college students), as well as a more intense workload. For example, Hartwick College in Oneonta, New York in February 2009 became the highest-profile school to offer a wide range of students the option of finishing a B.A. degree in three years (and to save an average of $42,000) (Pope 2009). In the smallest state, Rhode Island, legislators recently approved a bill that requires all state institutions of higher education to create three-year B.A. programs starting in fall 2010 (Strauss 2009). Such measures, which are driven essentially by financial woes but also legitimated by references to the European model, would essentially entail convergence on the Bologna model with the positive effect of immense cost savings and greater compatibility with international standards. At the same time they would alleviate the technical issue of recognition of Bologna-based degrees.

The Bologna Process is very likely to increase *problem pressure* on U.S. providers of higher education. Thanks to Bologna, a massive increase in communication among European policymakers has taken place. Bologna has proven to be more than just a voluntary declaration, but has also created a platform for policy exchange and the emulation of best practice. In addition to stronger media attention on higher education issues, it has helped various countries to overcome reform backlog and optimize higher education policies (see Niemann and Bieber, Chapters 4 and 5 in this volume; Dobbins and Knill 2009). In fact, European universities have made advancements in better addressing student demands and needs. In particular German universities have moved away from their self-understanding as purely research entities and now place greater emphasis on the career prospects of students, both within and outside scientific research. Adelman (2009) goes as far as to claim that the core features of the Bologna Process are likely to become the dominant global higher education model in the next two decades and laments the blindness of top U.S. policymakers towards Bologna.[7]

Therefore, the bundling of resources, ideas, talent, and concerted elaboration of ideas and best practices at the European level may have the effect that global leadership in higher education will shift to Europe (Gordon 2009). The attractiveness of the European Higher Education Area to prospective foreign students is enhanced not only by the significantly lower tuition fees than in the U.S.A, but also by greater transparency of degrees as a result of the Bologna Process. Referring to the reform endeavors and advancements undertaken in Europe, the Institute for Higher Education Policy (IHEP) in Washington, for example, has reached the conclusion that the Bologna Process has increased problem pressure on U.S. universities and shed doubt on their international competitiveness. Along these lines, the IHEP study "The Bologna Process for U.S. Eyes: Relearning Higher Education in the Age of Convergence" (Adelman 2009) contends that European countries are producing degrees which are just as good or better, but also more transparent, internationally compatible, and with better defined qualifications of graduates. As for the U.S.A., however, the report laments the severe lack of transparency in degrees awarded to graduates.

This has triggered an increased dialogue among U.S. policymakers over what can be learned from the Bologna Process. Although it is too early to draw definitive conclusions, the greater international presence and success of the European Higher Education Area is generating a greater sense of urgency among American policymakers with regard to attracting talent from abroad. For a while after the Cold War, the perception that education needed to be revamped in order to face challenges beyond American borders had temporarily subsided (Altbach and McGill Peterson 1998). Until the turn of the century, U.S. higher education remained a magnet for attracting and recruiting foreign talent. However, internationalization of higher education and the recruitment of foreign students were somewhat reframed as dangers to national security after the terrorist attacks of September 11, 2001, as the perpetrators were holders of student visas. This led to a more rigid practice with regard to the issue of student visas for American colleges, which has contributed to a significant drop in international applications to U.S. institutions since 2002. These realities, combined with the emergence of European universities as major contenders in the race to attract foreign talent, have raised the issue of a brain drain in the U.S.A. Hence, the hitherto global leader in higher education and center of science and scholarship is increasingly perceiving itself as a laggard with regard to attracting foreign talent—in an era in which economic prosperity increasingly depends on a nation's ability to survive in the knowledge economy (Sadat Hussain 2006).

While the Obama administration is acting on a promise to alleviate the funding burden on college students and thus expand access to higher education, the U.S.A. has not yet put forward a concerted overarching strategy for internationalization—unlike the Bologna participants who continually stress the internationalization of higher education as a policy. Thus, the emergence of Europe as a hotspot for higher education innovation and reform has contributed at the very least to increased problem pressure in the U.S.A. over the loss of academic talent from abroad and falling behind the rest of the world in this critical area.

However, the Bologna Process should not be interpreted merely as a process of "catch-up" with Anglo-American models. In one very significant aspect, it represents a momentous advancement beyond American practice and thus is bound to provoke action among U.S. policymakers: with regard to the documentation of skills and qualifications, the Bologna countries are clearly surpassing American institutions. At the heart of the Bologna Process are "qualifications frameworks" which are intended to be statements of what skills students must have acquired in order to earn a B.A., M.A., or doctoral degree. Ideally, this enables the reader to determine immediately differences between the three degree levels; the knowledge acquired by students; their ability to apply it, communicate it, and autonomously deal with it; and take sound judgments based on these skills and knowledge. This documentation of skills and qualifications is further pursued with regard to individual disciplines. The aim here is to devise common points of reference for writing statements on student outcomes and defining why, for example, a degree in sociology is distinct from others. Unlike the U.S. system where a degree is essentially composed of a mathematical formula of 120 credits, 40 completed in the major, and a particular grade point average (see Gordon 2009), the Bologna system aspires to define the distinct qualifications acquired by the student. According to Adelman (2009), the advantage lies in the "accountability loop" which the Bologna Process creates by developing detailed degree qualification framework qualifications, instead of "simply posting numbers on public dashboards—what U.S. higher education seems to think is sufficient to satisfy policy-makers" (ibid.: xi). This "accountability loop" is not only enhanced by newly implemented multilateral quality assurance measures, but also by the introduction of a "diploma supplement." This is a document attached to each diploma, aimed at facilitating academic and professional recognition of qualifications and designed to provide an overview of the content, level, and context of studies.

The perception that other systems have eventually caught up and perhaps surpassed the U.S.A. in offering attractive, transparent, market-related academic products by means of precisely such innovations is well reflected in the above-mentioned IHEP study. To overcome the lack of compatibility and, frequently, transparency of American degrees—which poses a problem even within the boundaries of individual states—the chief author of the study (ibid.: 4), Clifford Adelman, has proposed developing such Bologna-inspired qualification frameworks at least for state higher education systems and popular major courses of study which would involve the following:

- Revising the reference points and terms of the American credit system;
- Expanding dual-admissions "alliances" between community colleges and four-year institutions;
- Refining the definition and treatment of part-time students; and
- Developing a distinctive version of a diploma supplement that summarizes individual student achievement.

Hence, the main story line for U.S. policymakers who are bound to be intentionally or unintentionally familiarized with the Bologna Process is the necessity to provide students with a clear picture of what their path through higher education would look like, what knowledge and skills would qualify them for a degree, and what their degrees mean for them outside the university. According to Adelman and the IHEP (Adelman 2008: 24), these aspects are severely underdeveloped in the U.S.A., which has never significantly attempted to benchmark learning outcomes on a significant scale. Unlike preexisting policies which focus excessively on quantitative indicators such as credits and hours of studies, future policies should focus more on documenting the quality, depth, and potential application of knowledge based on more transparent thresholds of performance and backing up these qualifications with a "public warrantee" in the form of a diploma supplement (ibid.: 24).

Finally, U.S. policymakers, for the reasons addressed above, may gradually engage in the *emulation* of Bologna standards. In February 2009

President Obama announced before Congress his aim for the U.S.A. to be the country with the world's highest graduates by 2020. Besides an expansion of college grants and a stronger focus on education issues, this ambitious goal and the increased problem pressure outlined above have prompted some policymakers to start to learn from the experiences of other countries (Inside Indiana Business 2009). This is exactly the case for certain universities in the American Mid-West, who have begun to harmonize their catalogs of qualifications offered in degree programs. More specifically, dozens of universities in Utah, Indiana, and Minnesota have voluntarily begun to tap into the Bologna model with a project based on knowledge transfer between U.S. and European scientists (Wiarda 2009). Financed by the Lumina Foundation[8], this so-called "Tuning USA" project draws on the Bologna model and similar Bologna-inspired projects in 18 Latin American and Caribbean countries, Central Asia, and Africa. Tuning U.S. aims to foster a "shared understanding among higher education stakeholders of the subject-specific knowledge and transferable skills that students in six fields must demonstrate upon completion of a degree program" and is a chance to "experiment with a process beyond our borders that could help us advance our thinking about the quality of higher education" (Inside Indiana Business 2009). Like the Bologna Process, it focuses on clearer learning expectations, greater quality and relevance of degrees, a better alignment and credit transfer mechanisms between different higher education institutions, and a greater relevance of degrees in order to address the stagnating labor market. Depending on its success, the pilot project will potentially be emulated by other states and higher education providers. Thus like the proposed three-year B.A. degrees, "Tuning USA" is an additional example of how American higher education policymakers are increasingly looking abroad for innovations aimed at overcoming the current economic crisis and achieving the aims set by the present administration.

Conclusion

Our analysis of PISA in the U.S.A. has shown that a poor ranking in a highly reputable international comparison does not necessarily lead to broad media coverage and public debate, let alone far-reaching reform efforts. In fact, it is safe to say the policy change resulting from PISA was actually greater in New Zealand, a country whose schoolchildren ranked much higher than American children (see Dobbins, Chapter 7 in this volume). As for the U.S.A., the reason for the weak reaction, despite the disappointing results, is simply that the study did not produce any new or shocking information on the quality of secondary education, but rather merely stated the already obvious. The lack of groundbreaking revelations meant that the PISA Study thus had little impact on opinion formation in the U.S.A., allowing little leeway for the OECD to apply its mechanism of governance by opinion formation. Apparently, the objective misfit between the orientational framework as promoted by the OECD and the actual results did not provide the necessary impetus for national reforms in secondary education. Instead, the misfit perceived by the broader public and/or conveyed by the mass media is what counts.

Ironically, the Bologna Process, in which the U.S.A. does not participate because of its geographic distance, may have a greater impact on American education than the PISA Study. Although it is too early to draw definitive conclusions, there are indications that Bologna will compel U.S. higher education policymakers to embrace various practices which originated within the Bologna framework. Our analysis has shown that U.S. policymakers are beginning to understand that the Bologna Process entails much more than a concerted European effort to emulate U.S. traditions such as B.A. degrees, quality assurance, and market relevance. Instead, Bologna has also generated a series of policy innovations which go beyond standard U.S. higher education practices. Mechanisms such as qualifications frameworks and diploma supplements ensure transparency and compatibility, while enabling institutions to define and document the skills of graduates better and to align them with the labor market. Thus, besides an increasing fear of a global shift in higher education policy innovation to Europe, the Bologna Process has already prompted various U.S. states to emulate Bologna-style qualification frameworks and stimulated discussion about introducing diploma supplements. It remains to be seen whether the global appeal of the new European higher education model will increase with the tentative completion of the Bologna Process in 2010. In any case, a continent which just ten years ago perceived itself as a higher education laggard, is now unintentionally serving as a learning platform for other countries around the world wishing to fine tune their own domestic higher education policies.

Notes

1. Parts of this section draw on Martens and Niemann (2009). Research on PISA perceptions in the U.S.A. were conducted during a two-month stay

in Washington in summer 2008. Kerstin Martens would like to thank the American Institute for Contemporary German Studies (AICGS) and the German Academic Exchange Service (Deutscher Akademischer Austauschdienst—DAAD) for having enabled this stay with a generous grant.
2. The newspapers examined include: *New York Times, Newsweek, International Herald Tribune, Washington Post, USA Today, The Wall Street Journal,* and *Los Angeles Times.* The research was conducted with "factiva"; the keywords were "OECD" and "PISA."
3. For details how this act came about, see Kosar (2005: chapter 6).
4. The Act also requires that the schools distribute the name, home phone number, and address of every student to military recruiters unless the student specifically opts out.
5. The Tenth Amendment to the U.S. Constitution specifies that powers are not granted to the federal government; education powers are reserved for the individual states. However, NCLB is seen as the greatest increase in federal power over education since the Elementary and Secondary Education Act of 1965. See for example, McGuinn (2006). For the evolution of the federal role in school education, see McGuinn (2005).
6. For more details on the OECD's role in education, see Martens (2007).
7. http://globalhighered.wordpress.com/2009/04/28/tuning-usa-reforming-higher-education-in-the-us-europe-style/.
8. The Lumina Foundation for Education is an Indianapolis-based, private, independent foundation that strives to expand access to and success in education beyond high school.

References

Adelman, Clifford (2008) "Learning Accountability from Bologna: A Higher Education Policy Primer," IHEP Issue Brief 2008 (July).
Adelman, Clifford (2009) *The Bologna Process for US Eyes: Re-learning Higher Education in the Age of Convergence*, Report for the Institute for Higher Education Policy with the support of the Lumina Foundation, Washington DC: IHEP.
Altbach, Philip and Patti McGill Peterson (1998) "Internationalize American Higher Education? Not Exactly?" *International Higher Education* 1998 (11), 15–17.
Bell, Jeannine and Robert A. Watkins (2006) "Ground Work: Strategies in Dealing with the Bologna Process," *International Educator* 15 (5), 70–5.
Bologna Declaration (1999) *The Bologna Declaration of June 19, 1999—Joint Declaration of the European Ministers of Education* (Online: http://www.bologna-berlin2003.de/pdf/bologna_declaration.pdf, last access: December 15, 2009).
Dobbins, Michael and Christoph Knill (2009) "Higher Education Policies in Central and Eastern Europe: Convergence toward a Common Model?" *Governance* 22 (3), 397–430.
European Commission (2003) *The Role of Universities in the Europe of Knowledge* (Online: http://eur-lex.europa.eu/smartapi/cgi/sga_doc?smartapi!celexplus!prod!DocNumber&lg=en& type_doc=COMfinal&an_doc=2003&nu_doc=58, last access: June 20, 2009).
Gordon, Tia T. (2009) *There Has Been a Global Shift in Higher Education Leadership: Europe Is Heading It Up as the United States Starts to Follow*, Report for the Institute of Higher Education Policy, Washington DC: IHEP.

Gross, Ronald and Beatrice Gross, eds. (1985) *The Great School Debate,* New York: Touchstone.
Inside Indiana Business (2009) *Lumina Foundation Launches Tuning USA Project* (Online: http://www.insideindianabusiness.com/newsitem.asp?ID=34943, last access: April 8, 2009).
Kosar, Kevin R. (2005) *Failing Grades. The Federal Politics of Education Standards,* Boulder, CO and London: Lynne Rienner Publisher.
Martens, Kerstin (2007) "How to Become an Influential Actor—the 'Comparative Turn' in OECD Education Policy," in K. Martens, A. Rusconi, and K. Leuze, eds., *New Arenas of Education Governance—the Impact of International Organisations and Markets on Education Policy Making,* Houndmills: Palgrave Macmillan, 40–56.
Martens, Kerstin and Dennis Niemann (2009) "Governance by Comparison—How Ratings & Rankings Can Impact National Policy Making in Education," paper presented at the "International Studies Association," meeting, New York City, New York, February 15–18.
McGuinn, Patrick (2006) "Swing Issues and Policy Regimes: Federal Education Policy and the Politics of Policy Change," *Journal of Policy History* 18 (2), 205–40.
McGuinn, Patrick (2005) "The National Schoolmarm: No Child Left Behind and the New Educational Federalism," *Publius* 35 (1), 41–68.
Pope, Justin (2009) "Some Colleges Offering 3-Year Bachelor's Degrees," *USA Today,* February 24, 2009.
Sadat Hussain, Sakina (2006) "Schools Struggle to Combat Foreign Student Drop," *MSNBC Online* (Online: http://www.msnbc.msn.com/id/14034413, last access: June 20, 2009).
Strauss, Valerie (2009) "Colleges Consider 3-Year Degrees to Save Undergrads Time, Money," *Washington Post,* May 23, 2009.
Thompson, Timothy (2007) "Transatlantic Reflections on the Bologna Process," Paper presented at the *Balance Project Seminar,* Cambridge, July 5, 2007.
Vögtle, Eva-Maria, Christoph Knill, and Michael Dobbins (2009) To What Extent Does Transnational Communication Drive Cross-National Policy Convergence? The Impact of the Bologna-Process on Domestic Higher Education Policies, unpublished manuscript, Constance: University of Constance.
Wiarda, Jan-Martin (2009) "Die Bologna-Kopie," *Die Zeit,* April 8, 2009.

Part IV
Comparative Analyses

9
Comparing Education Policy Networks

Alexander-Kenneth Nagel

Having once been a traditional domain of the nation state, the political responsibility for education is now increasingly dispersed between regional, national, and international, as well as public and private, actors. It is the aim of this chapter to shed light on the territorial and modal dispersion of national education policy networks by means of a systematic network analytical description. The central research question therefore is how the interactions and coalitions between international and national, private and public, actors have changed (both qualitatively and quantitatively) within the last decade, thus to account for changes in national education policymaking. The descriptive enterprise refers to four case studies, that is, Germany, Switzerland, England, and New Zealand, which will subsequently be put in a synoptic and comparative perspective. Drawing from pair-comparisons, the explanatory aim of this chapter is to study the influence of international organizations on national education policymaking and the capacity of national veto players to cope with that interference as determinants of change in national education policymaking.

According to our theoretical sampling (for details see the introductory chapter of this volume) changes in education policymaking should be greatest in England—as the exposure to international organizations (IOs) is relatively strong while there are only a few national veto points or players—whereas it should be minimal in Switzerland, which is less exposed to IOs and characterized by a highly federal system of decisionmaking. As outlined in the introductory chapter we conceptualize change of national education policymaking in three dimensions: policies, polities, and politics. The dimension of *policies* refers to changes of political contents, that is, goals, instruments, and settings whereas changes in education *polities* reflect alterations in the institutional structure of decisionmaking. In contrast, the dimension of *politics* refers to the process of decisionmaking itself, that is, its modes and the actors involved. This is where the network perspective comes in. As policy network approaches generally set out to decompose complex processes of decisionmaking in so called "dyads"—distinct relationships between two actors—they seem to be especially suitable tools with which to identify change in the dimension of politics (Börzel 1998).

Comparative analysis of policy networks is still quite rare and so is the network analysis of structural dynamics or change. The first step in the comparative study of policy networks was to analyze and compare policy networks within a nation state. A cutting-edge piece of work in that respect was the study by Edward Laumann and David Knoke on the "Organizational State" (Laumann and Knoke 1987). Here, the authors compare the policy fields of health and energy and develop a concept of public-private decisionmaking which is both theoretically plausible and empirically manageable in terms of social network analysis. On this foundation Knoke and others embarked on a more comprehensive endeavor as they compared labor policy networks across Germany, Japan, and the U.S. (Knoke et al. 1996). It was a particular strength of these groundbreaking studies to combine conceptual assumptions as to the network structure of modern, pluralist decisionmaking with tangible network analytical empirics. Yet, from a perspective of internationalization it can be considered a desideratum that they did not touch issues of multilevel governance (Bache and Flinders 2004; Nagel 2010). Moreover, in recent years there has been a lively methodological debate on how to model structural change and network dynamics (Suitor, Wellmann, and Morgan 1997). Although the dynamic perspective has extensively been applied to interpersonal networks (e.g. Feld 1997; Wellmann et al. 1997) change in policy networks has been neglected so far. This is all the more surprising as interaction patterns in these networks can be held to be rather precarious because of the instrumental orientation of the corporative actors involved: "An iterative gaming strategy develops, in which organizations continually shuffle from coalition to coalition in opportunistic pursuit of advantage" (Laumann and Knoke 1987: 386).

For a structural analysis of the internationalization of education politics and its impact on national policy networks both the phenomenon of multilevel governance and the aspect of change need to be taken into account. In some countries, such as Germany or Switzerland, education policy has been a two-level game for quite some time as a result of their cultural federalism (Braun 2004; Wolf 2006; see also Niemann and Bieber, Chapters 4 and 5 in this volume). Former network approaches dealt with federalist systems in a pragmatic way as they included federal actors as one distinct type of interest group or state department among others (Knoke et al. 1996: 73; Laumann and Knoke 1987: 99). Thus it seems appropriate to treat international or European organizations likewise and to conceive them as a special type of interest group within national education policy networks. The advantage of such a virtual expansion of the network boundaries is that interactions and coalitions across the territorial axis can be covered at all. The price for such a broadening of scope, however, is the disguise of relational complexity within the international or subnational sphere. The extrapolation of network change, finally, is a methodical rather than a conceptual challenge and will be dealt with in the following section.

Methodical remarks and operationalization

To account for the impact of international and European actors in national policy networks we need relational data sensitive enough to reflect various relational contents, abstract enough to allow for cross-country comparisons, and sufficiently dynamic in order to consider structural changes. To compile such data I used a mixed-method design combining quantitative content analysis and network analysis (Nagel 2008; Seibel and Raab 2003). In a first step I explored hyperlink networks of actors likely to be involved in education policymaking for each country, drawing a snowball sample from the respective national ministries of education. In a second step a corpus of texts was compiled for each country, while the number of documents was weighed by the prevalence of actors in the hyperlink networks. In a third step a codebook was created for each country to operationalize our general comparative categories of actors with regard to the national policy network in question. In a fourth step a computer-based search was performed for all organizations in the codebook. The resulting retrievals were scanned manually for relational contents, such as "organization A does something to organization B" and interpreted according to a given scheme of political interaction in policy networks. Finally, this collection of dyads was compiled into actor-by-actor-matrices to apply quantitative means of network analysis.

Obviously, the categorization of actors and relations is a crucial step to operationalize our research question for a comparative network analysis. On the one hand, categories have to be abstract enough to cover the characteristics of all four countries; on the other hand they need to be sufficiently concrete as to allow substantial insights with regard to national decisionmaking and its changes. Generally, nodes within the network represent types of (corporate) actors whereas lines represent types of relations between them.

In the following I use a total of 16 categories of actors and six categories of relations,[1] which are derived from earlier studies and pretests (Nagel 2006; Nagel 2008). As multiple levels of policymaking are concerned, the categories of actors comprise international organizations (IOs), especially the Organisation for Economic Cooperation and Development (OECD), European and Bologna Process actors (e.g. the European Commission and the Bologna Follow-up Group), and state actors (national and federal ministries, parliaments and political parties), as well as public (universities, quality assurance agencies, and students) and private interest groups (business representatives, labor unions, and professional associations). In terms of operationalization, it is crucial from a network perspective that the usage of governance instruments is not restricted to IOs, but that national veto players or interest groups may also apply them to realize their interests in the process of decisionmaking. Such an operationalization of governance instruments is consistent with earlier network-analytical approaches, e.g. the distinction of "stick," "carrot," and "sermon" as ideal-typical strategies of intervention (Burth and Starzmann 2001: 54) or the differentiation of enforcement, incentive, and persuasion (Howlett and Ramesh 1993: 255). Here, relations of control resemble the option of stick or enforcement; relations of transaction resemble the option of carrot or incentive; and relations of symbolic affirmation resemble the option of sermon or persuasion. It should be obvious, however, that discursive intervention, such as relations of symbolic affirmation or lobbyism, is less demanding in terms of resources and competencies than manifest relations of transaction or control. Some types of relations reflect strategies of political intervention which can be conceptualized as governance instruments. Thus governance by opinion formation is operationalized by relations of symbolic affirmation reflecting affirmative speech acts and discursive empowerment. Governance by financial means can be measured by relations of transaction while governance by norm setting can be operationalized by relations of control reflecting binding prescription.

Partner or trespasser? International actors in national education politics

In this section I will present comparative network-analytical evidence with regard to the macro-, meso- and microstructure of the education policy networks in Germany, Switzerland, England, and New Zealand. On the *macro*level I will illustrate how national education politics have changed since international and European actors have entered the arena of education policymaking. Here, special emphasis will be given to variations across the four countries to account for a potential convergence or divergence of domestic education politics. On the *meso*- and *micro*levels in contrast, I will look more closely at IOs and national veto players, their interplay, and social environment.

Education politics: Changes of patterns and patterns of change

Political decisionmaking is a multiplex process which encompasses both formal and informal, manifest and discursive, relations. Changes in the distribution of these relations can account for variation in the modes of political interaction and thus for changes in the dimension of politics. Figure 9.1 illustrates the composition of the education policy networks in our four countries at two periods of time (1997–2003 and 2004–2007).[2]

At a very first glance there is quite a variation in countries, although variance across countries is more visible than within. To give the example of reading. In Germany education policymaking at first is mainly made up by relations of cooperation (about one-third), lobbyism (about one-quarter), and symbolic affirmation (about one-fifth). In contrast, relations of information, transaction, and control are less prevalent. In

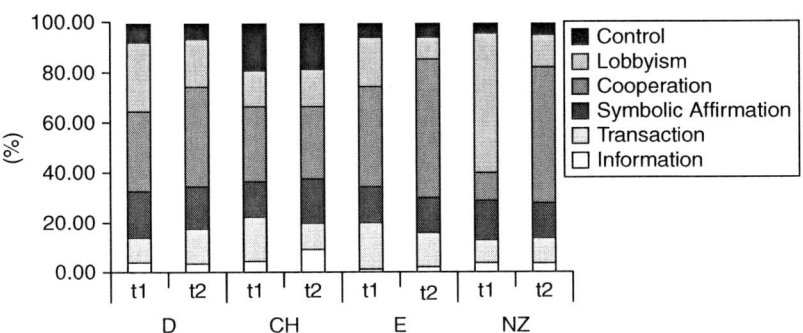

Figure 9.1 National education politics: Modes of political interaction

the second period of time, there is an expansion of cooperation and transaction and a reduction of lobbyism. Thus, the general mode of decisionmaking in education policy in Germany changes from political argument to collective action, which may be an expression of the policy cycle having advanced from program formulation to implementation.

Taking a look at similarities and differences between countries by means of pair comparison referring to the number of *veto players,* the education policy networks in England and New Zealand are characterized by a higher share of cooperation and a lower share of control and lobbyism than Germany and Switzerland. The latter represent political systems with a relatively high number of veto players in a federal arrangement, whereas decisionmaking in England and New Zealand is more centralized and there are only a few veto players. The number and power of veto players is also reflected in the patterns of political interaction: the more veto players, the more need to exert influence on other actors (lobbyism) and to regulate decisionmaking in a hierarchical manner (control). On the other hand, the fewer veto players, the greater the need for collective action on a more mutual yet less institutionalized level. Taking a closer look at the statistical evidence of this pair comparison, however, it becomes obvious that the impact of veto players on the modes of political interaction should not be overestimated as the respective differences in percentages are rather low. Regarding change, the disparities between the two pairs of countries tend to persist (and even increase) over time, which yields to a slight *sigma-divergence* (for details see the introductory chapter of this volume).

A second pair comparison refers to the degree of exposure to *international organizations*. In our theoretical framework we hypothesized that education politics in Germany and England would be more likely to change, for these countries are exposed both to the OECD and to the European Union (EU) as well as the Bologna Process. Switzerland and New Zealand in contrast, are members only of the OECD and should therefore be able to preserve national structures to a higher extent. With regard to the patterns of political interaction, however, there is not as visible a difference as with regard to veto players. In the first period (1997–2003) the policy networks in Germany and England show a lower share of lobbyism and slightly higher share of cooperation and control; in the second period (2004–2007) there is evidence for assimilation with regard to lobby relations, reversion with regard to cooperation, and continuity with regard to control. These ambiguous results indicate that the exposure of nation states to IOs (measured by the number of memberships) does not affect the general patterns of domestic decisionmaking in the area of education in our sample. Instead, the variation within the pairs of countries is considerably higher than between the pairs. In fact, Switzerland and New Zealand prove to be most dissimilar cases as to the composition of their respective policy networks: while the share of cooperation in New Zealand is almost twice as high as in Switzerland, the latter shows a significantly higher share of relations of control. Obviously, the impact of domestic structures of decisionmaking, such as a federal system and the prevalence of veto players, superposes the effect of a country being a member of one or more IOs.

The composition of education policy networks as to the modes and patterns of political interaction can provide some general evidence about changes or continuity of national education politics. A comparison of shares of several relational dimensions across countries and across time has shown that there has been only little change in national education politics within the last decade, that variation between countries is (and has been) bigger than within, and that the modes of political interaction depend on domestic structures of decisionmaking rather than membership in international organizations. Thus, the composition of national education policy networks can be characterized by *path-dependency and continuity* rather than change: political culture prevails over international impulses (see Weymann, Chapter 3 in this volume).

Aside from the modes of interaction, network analysis can account for other structural characteristics of education policy networks, such as the density and centralization of political interaction. Density is defined as the ratio of all factual to all possible relations (Jansen 2003: 108). Dense networks are more egalitarian in the sense that more actors have access to the resources of more other actors, which impedes a monopolization of power positions. In contrast, (degree-based) centralization refers to the structuration of network interaction around one prominent actor and thus reflects its hierarchical structure. Subsequently, a discordant change of density and centralization may indicate a more inclusive (more dense, but less centralized) or exclusive (less dense, but more centralized) character of a network. Table 9.1 provides an overview about these measures for all countries and relational dimensions and their variation over time.

In the columns of Table 9.1 are the four countries observed in two periods of time (1997–2003 and 2004–2007). The columns highlighted in grey represent countries less exposed to the influence of IOs while the framed columns represent countries with a high number of veto players as to our theoretical sampling. In all countries and in nearly all relational dimensions there is a concordant increase of density and centralization.

Table 9.1 Structural change, synopsis

Country	Measures	D		CH		E		NZ	
Time		t1	t2	t1	t2	t1	t2	t1	t2
Information	Density	0.08	0.1	0.07	0.1	0.02	0.06	0.04	0.09
	Centralization (od)	0.2	0.25	0.28	0.24	0.05	0.15	0.24	0.4
Transaction	Density	0.08	0.15	0.1	0.08	0.11	0.18	0.07	0.13
	Centralization (od)	0.28	0.41	0.32	0.27	0.24	0.45	0.42	0.64
Symbolic	Density	0.18	0.3	0.15	0.21	0.1	0.27	0.14	0.2
Affirmation	Centralization (od)	0.44	0.32	0.48	0.7	0.25	0.43	0.35	0.43
Cooperation	Density	0.36	0.41	0.23	0.21	0.28	0.53	0.34	0.4
	Centralization (d)	0.43	0.45	0.34	0.44	0.53	0.47	0.56	0.53
Lobbyism	Density	0.16	0.19	0.12	0.13	0.1	0.16	0.07	0.13
	Centralization (id)	0.18	0.51	0.3	0.28	0.39	0.47	0.36	0.57
Control	Density	0.03	0.06	0.06	0.09	0.05	0.06	0.03	0.06
	Centralization (od)	0.18	0.36	0.22	0.13	0.24	0.5	0.32	0.44

Notes: Legend: od = outdegree-based centralization; id = indegree-based centralization; d = degree-based centralization.

Thus, during the last decade the arena of national education politics has somewhat expanded, which reflects the increasing involvement of private and international actors. This expansion, however, does not lead to a more egalitarian setting, but fosters internal structuration.

A closer look at single relational dimensions reveals some similarities in the structural constitution of education policy networks across all countries: political interaction in the dimensions of symbolic affirmation, cooperation, and lobbyism appears to be more intense and comparably less hierarchical than relations of information, transaction, and control.[3] Obviously, the political arena consists of two different spheres: the first sphere is inclusive and characterized by elusive discursive interaction of persuasive (symbolic affirmation) or appellative shape (lobbyism) and unspecific cooperation. In contrast, the second sphere is exclusive and characterized by specific and more institutionalized relations, such as the transfer of money, information, and directions within a given chain of command. Thus, the inclusion of new actors and the general expansion of interaction in the field of education politics do not necessarily imply enhanced participation (and thus a boost of democratic quality). However, neither do they indicate a subversive shift of political authority from national states to interest groups of doubtful provenance. Instead, processes of internationalization and privatization of education politics seem to foster functional differentiation within the set of actors, an observation which will be of further interest in the following subsection.

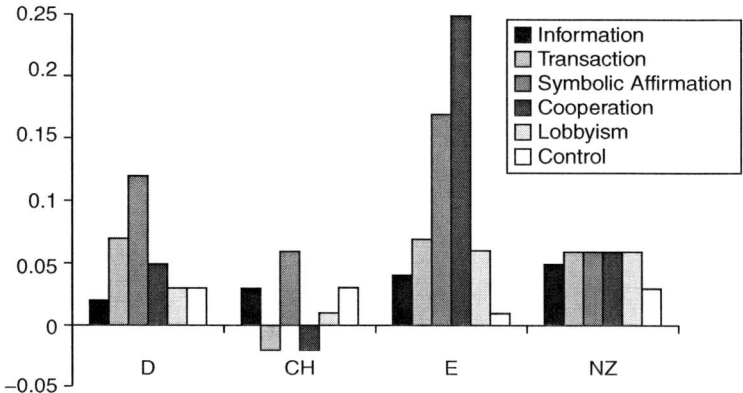

Figure 9.2 Change of density

Before turning to subgroup analysis, however, I want to take a closer look at the patterns of change across our countries with respect to density and centralization. Figure 9.2 illustrates the change of density in all countries and relational dimensions.

The bars in Figure 9.2 represent *changes* between the first and the second time period. Positive values indicate an increase of density, negative values point to a decrease. At first glance, the diagram underlines previous observations of an overall increase of density across all countries and relational dimensions. The degree of change, however, differs distinctly across countries. Most remarkable in this respect is the education policy network in England where intensity and thickness of political interaction have risen considerably between the two time periods, which goes along with an overall increase of attention for international initiatives of education. As pointed out in the country case studies, New Zealand and Germany exhibit moderate change whereas Switzerland shows only little and heterogeneous alteration. These results are perfectly in line with our theoretical assumptions as we expected the English education policy network to be most affected by processes of internationalization because of its high exposure to international organizations (OECD and EU) and its relatively small number of national veto players. On the other hand, we held that changes in education politics should be minimal in Switzerland as a result of its low exposure to IOs and the high number of veto players in its cantonal system. Finally, both Germany and New Zealand were expected to exhibit moderate change as they are more (Germany) or less (New Zealand) exposed to internationalization *and* national veto players. Obviously, the pattern of veto players and IOs makes a difference with regard to the intensity of political interaction: the membership of a country in IOs creates channels of interaction and legitimates interference. The prevalence of veto players, however, may be apt to counterbalance this effect, be it through actual exertion of power of veto or the result of the higher degree of competition in the process of decisionmaking in general.

The previous results from a comparative analysis of the density of national education policy networks underline the capacity of our theoretical framework to explain structural changes of national education *politics*. Figure 9.3 illustrates changes of centralization in these networks and thus points to internal structuration and hierarchy as other important structural dimensions.

Figure 9.3 shows changes in (degree-based) centralization between two periods of time for all countries and all relational dimensions. Positive values indicate an increase of internal structuration and hierarchy while negative values point to a decrease and thus a more egalitarian pattern of interaction. Even at a very first glance it becomes obvious that the internal structuration of political interaction in the field of education develops in a more heterogeneous way than its general vitality and intensity. If we construct an indicator of change by summing up the absolute values of relational dimensions and weigh it by their prevalence it shows that alterations in network centrality are more visible

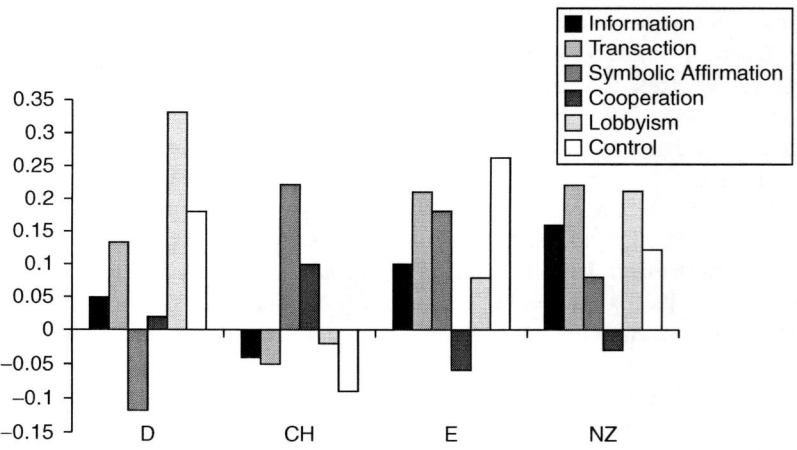

Figure 9.3 Change of centralization

in Germany and England than in Switzerland and New Zealand. This observation does not match our expectation that education politics would change most in England and least in Switzerland. Yet, a tentative explanation may be achieved by pair comparison. As to our theoretical framework Germany and England are similar in being more exposed to IOs than the other two countries. Thus, with regard to the internal structuration of national education policy networks IOs seem to cause more change than domestic veto players are able to impede. As pointed out earlier, the general direction of these changes clearly is a centralization of the decisionmaking process, that is, an increase of hierarchical interaction. Thus, increasing exposure of national education politics to international actors claiming legitimate interference fosters not only an expansion (see above), but also a closure of political interaction. From a macroperspective such evidence remains ambivalent: it may point to a "viral intrusion" and usurpation of national policy networks through IOs replacing domestic actors at their very center or to national actors closing ranks and forming a "laager" against the international level. Here, network analysis on the level of subgroups (mesoperspective) and single actors (microperspectives) promises further insights.

Setting the stage: How roles of international actors and veto players change

Having examined patterns of change of national education policymaking on the macrolevel, I now turn to changes of positions or roles of crucial actors in order to gain further insights into the participation of international actors and veto players beyond the surface of an overall intensification and hierarchization of political interaction. To do so, I make use of blockmodel analysis to identify positions of structural equivalence. In a blockmodel, actors are classified according to similar patterns of interaction (Jansen 2003: 212–13). Therefore, a block represents a set of actors who maintain similar relations to other actors in the network. Unlike a group or clique such a block does not represent a manifest social configuration, but rather a structural position, which accounts for a function or role within the network. Different to cliques or groups structural equivalence in a policy network does not necessarily indicate mutual understanding or collective action. Instead, it may point to competition and antagonism arising from the structural "exchangeability" of actors (Jansen 2003: 213). Table 9.2 illustrates these positional changes in an ideal-typical form focusing on international actors and veto players and their respective governance capacities.

Table 9.2 Positional change

Country	International Actors		Veto Players			Patterns of Change
	IO	EUB	NSA	FSA	P/L	
Network of Transaction						
D	P → R	S – S	S – S	P → S	0 → S_2	Growing competition; EUB consolidate their position, IOs marginalized
CH	0 – 0	0 – 0	S → S/P	R/P → S/P	R/P → S/P	National consolidation; laager of veto players
E	0 – 0	S – S	S – S	S – S	0 – 0	Continuous competition between EUB, NSA and FSA
NZ	0 → R	0 – 0	S – S	0 – 0	0 – 0	Continuous national centralism
Network of Symbolic Affirmation						
D	R → S/P	S/P → S_2	S/P – S/P	S/P – S/P	S/P – S/P	Emancipation of EUB/IO
CH	S → P	S → S/P	P/S → P	P/S → P	S → P	National incorporation of IO; emancipation of EUB
E	S → 0	P → 0	S → S/P	P → P/S	P → S/P	Active exclusion of IO/EUB: crowding out
NZ	0 → P/S	0 – 0	S/P → S	0 – 0	0 → S	National consolidation; emancipation of IO
Network of Control						
D	P → 0	P → 0	P_2 → S	P_2 → S	0 – 0	Recapture of national responsibility; skirmish for national/federal competence
CH	S → S/P	S → S/P	S → S/P	S → S/P	P → S/P	Ongoing competition
E	0 – 0	0 → S	P/S → S	S – S_2	0 → S	Growing competition; EUB consolidate their position,
NZ	0 → S	0 – 0	S/P – S/P	0 – 0	S/P → S	National consolidation; emancipation of IO

Notes: *Legend:* S = Sender; R = Receiver; P = Processor; 0 = no participation; S_2 or P_2 = second block.

The letters in the lines represent schematic roles which are attributed to an actor because of its position within the network. The letter "S" indicates a position of sending money, affirmative speech acts, or directions, while "R" marks a receiving position. The letter "P" represents a position of processing or brokerage, that is, self-referential interaction between the actors within a block. Finally, "0" describes a position which is neither sending and processing nor receiving. To give an example of reading: in the transaction network of Germany, European and Bologna actors as well as national actors used to be in a sending position while IOs and federal state actors used to be processors of funds, but the participation of parties and legislative actors remained unclear. In the second period of time both federal state actors and legislative actors changed to become senders of funds while IOs turned into receivers.

Altogether, the German *network of transaction* exhibits a growing competition between international actors and national as well as regional veto players in the field of governance by financial means. In the course of this contest European and Bologna actors manage to consolidate their position, for example, by means of education programs, such as ERASMUS or COMENIUS, while IOs play a more passive role. The result is neither a laager of veto players nor a viral intrusion by international actors, but the formation of a hybrid, pluralistic, and competitive sphere of governance by financial means. Taking a look at Switzerland, international and European organizations, along with some minor interest groups, are neither providers nor recipients of funds. In contrast, federal and national veto players manage to consolidate their position as active applicants of governance by financial means. Here, we have an ideal-typical example of veto players who close ranks against internationalization and thus deter international actors to gain ground. Relations of transaction in England are clustered quite similarly to Germany with European, national, and federal actors forming a block of providers, whereas IOs such as the OECD are not involved in governance by financial means. In contrast to both Germany and Switzerland there is a striking continuity of roles and positions. Obviously, the competition between European, national, and regional actors has been successfully institutionalized. Finally, in New Zealand there is but one actor in a steady position of sending money: national state actors. All other actors are either not involved or even become clients of the first. These results underline the centralistic setting of decisionmaking in New Zealand.

While there are both clear-cut positions and some continuity in the role structure of governance by financial means, governance by opinion formation seems to be more hybrid and fragmented in structural terms. In the German *network of symbolic affirmation* veto players appear to be both senders and processors of affirmative speech acts, whereas international and European actors are subject to positional change: while international actors advance to become active participants in the national contest for opinion formation, European actors manage to acquire a unique selling proposition reflected by them forming an autonomous block of senders. This development can be understood as a successful emancipation of international actors. Positional changes in Switzerland exhibit a trend toward integration or consolidation: while in the first period international and legislative actors had formed a clear-cut block of senders they are now merged with national and cantonal state actors into a self-referential unit. At the same time, European actors, just like in Germany, take a distinct, autonomous position of sending and processing affirmative speech acts. The pattern of change can therefore be characterized as national incorporation on the one hand and emancipation of European actors on the other hand. In England there was evidence for an antagonistic development of international actors and veto players: while both international and European organizations lost their status of active participation in opinion formation, veto players have consolidated their position, a pattern that could be labeled as crowding out or active exclusion. Finally, in New Zealand national veto players have reinforced their position as providers of legitimizing speech acts while at the same time IOs managed to establish their own position of discursive intervention. This pattern of change may be characterized as national consolidation combined with international emancipation.

In the *network of control* resembling governance by norm setting there was a surprising degree of positional change. In Germany two concurrent streams of change could be observed: international actors have lost their position as processors of directions (e.g. by giving mandates to quality assurance (QA) agencies by order of the national states), while at the same time national and federal veto players have changed from processors to issuers of directions. The recapture of national responsibility in the area of education therefore brings along increasing competition between national and federal state actors, a process which is very visible in the German *Föderalismusreform*; after all, renationalization is the cradle of national concupiscence. In contrast, relations of control in Switzerland are marked by a continuous structural similarity of international actors and veto players. Thus, there is an ongoing competition of international or European guidelines imposed on schools or universities and cantonal or national regulation in the classical sense. More change and differentiation can be seen in England. Here, European actors and national veto players compete for the allegiance of research institutions and QA agencies, while regional authorities administer distinct responsibilities and international organizations are not part of the game. Finally, the policy network of New Zealand exhibits minor changes with regard to governance by norm setting: national state actors can preserve their regulative position, but on their part become subject to mandates by legislative actors and IOs.

Altogether, positional analysis has revealed a significant change in the structural roles of both IOs and veto players in all countries, that is, the impact and interplay of international and domestic actors change during the course of internationalization of education politics. While IOs such as the OECD are strong in the field of opinion formation, unsurprisingly they play a less active role with regard to governance by financial means or norm setting (with the important exception of New Zealand). In contrast, European and Bologna actors become structurally similar to domestic actors, which is an expression of increasing competition. This positional assimilation of European actors is particularly visible in Germany and England, which is in line with our assumptions about the relevance of IO membership. At the same time there was evidence for a moderate yet visible impact of European and Bologna actors in Switzerland although it is not a member of the European Union. Obviously, geographical and cultural proximity as well as the Bologna Process as an intergovernmental "transmission belt" create an opportunity structure for European intervention. Finally, in the whole period of observation domestic veto players have kept their position as crucial providers and processors of funds, regulations, and political legitimacy. This holds true for the more decentralized and federalist systems such as Germany and Switzerland as well as for the more centralized systems of England and New Zealand. Therefore, there is quite a bit of positional change in the policy networks which is accompanied by an increasing participation of international actors. Yet, these actors by no means displace the domestic sphere of decisionmaking, but rather find themselves attached or incorporated.

The analysis of positions yields qualitative evidence as to the roles and social location of international actors and veto players, but it does not allow for a quantitative assessment of whether the actual impact of the international sphere has increased or not. In the following subsection

I will therefore address changes of prominence of international actors with regard to their respective governance instruments.

IO governance activity

In this last subsection I assess the factual activity of international actors on the microlevel. A basic index to characterize activity in a policy network is degree centrality, that is, the normalized number of out- and ingoing relations. The centrality of an actor reflects his or her chance to influence other actors in the policy network. Table 9.3 shows the standardized ranks of international and European actors weighted by the number of outgoing relations as an indicator for their factual exertion of governance by opinion formation, financial means, and norm setting.

The rank is a relative measure for the status of international and European actors compared to other actors. Subsequently, low values indicate relative centrality whereas high values indicate marginality.[4] An "x" indicates that there was no participation at all. At first glance two basic results are noticeable: there is evidence of IO governance in all national policy networks and there are considerable differences both within and between the countries.

In the *German* policy network we see an increase of IOs, such as the OECD, in the network of symbolic affirmation. As a result, the formation of symbolic alliances initialized by IOs as well as discursive benefits can be observed. To illustrate how such usage of opinion formation works in the actual process of decisionmaking it seems sensible to take a step back and draw upon the relational retrievals which form the basis of this network analysis. The following statement may serve to illustrate the noncommittal mode of discursive governance:

Table 9.3 Sending ranks of international actors

Country	Measures	D		CH		E		NZ	
Time		t1	t2	t1	t2	t1	t2	t1	t2
Symbolic Affirmation	IO	x	0.55	0.63	0.64	x	x	x	0.54
	EUB	0.33	0.45	0.88	1.00	0.33	0.67	x	0.77
Transaction	IO	0.88	x	x	x	x	x	x	0.33
	EUB	1.00	0.27	x	x	0.50	0.55	x	0.67
Control	IO	0.75	x	0.80	1.00	x	x	x	1.00
	EUB	x	x	0.80	0.57	x	1.00	x	x

"We [the OECD] fully agree with the statement of the largest teacher trade union GEW that 'teachers' professional identity is defined by quality" (OECD 2004: 44). Here, the OECD uses an affirmative speech act to create a discursive coalition with the Labor Union GEW. Decorated with the international seal of approval, the GEW can now act more self-confidently in political argument on quality assurance and professional identity. While IOs manage to enter the arena of symbolic interaction, they lose ground with regard to governance by transaction and norm setting, a trend which may be characterized as a discursive turn. At the same time, European actors strengthen their position in the network of transaction while withdrawing from the discursive arena, which most likely reflects the development of the Bologna Process from a period of agenda setting to implementation. Figure 9.4 shows the overall composition of the German education policy network and the participation of international actors. In addition to network-analytical coefficients the visualization of policy networks provides a more holistic *prima-facie* evidence as to the structuration of the decisionmaking process. The lines in Figure 9.4 indicate political interaction and the application of governance instruments such as governance by opinion formation, norm setting, or financial means. The thicker the line, the more dense or multiplex is the respective figuration of actors. The nodes, on the other hand, represent different types of actors in the network. The bigger a node, the more significant is the respective actor (e.g. as a powerful applicator of governance instruments).

In our case selection *Switzerland* constitutes a country with a high number of veto players and a low degree of exposure to IOs. Nevertheless, international and European actors are notably involved in governance by opinion formation and norm setting in the first period. Over time, however, there is a decrease of activity by international and European actors in all modes of governance, except for a constant level of influence of European actors in the network of control relations. Considering the autonomy and neutrality of Switzerland this evidence seems to be counterintuitive. In fact, the list of retrievals shows that these relations of control are related to the Swiss participation in the Bologna Process, as the following sample exemplifies: "Thus, the present Guidelines for the coordinated modernization of teaching at the Swiss Universities in the context of the Bologna Process [...] are obligatory for the contractual partners of the cooperation agreement, that is, the Federal Authorities and the University Cantons" (SUK 2003: 2, author's translation). By signing the Bologna declaration in 1999, the policy network in Switzerland has opened up channels of interaction for

216 *Transformation of Education Policy*

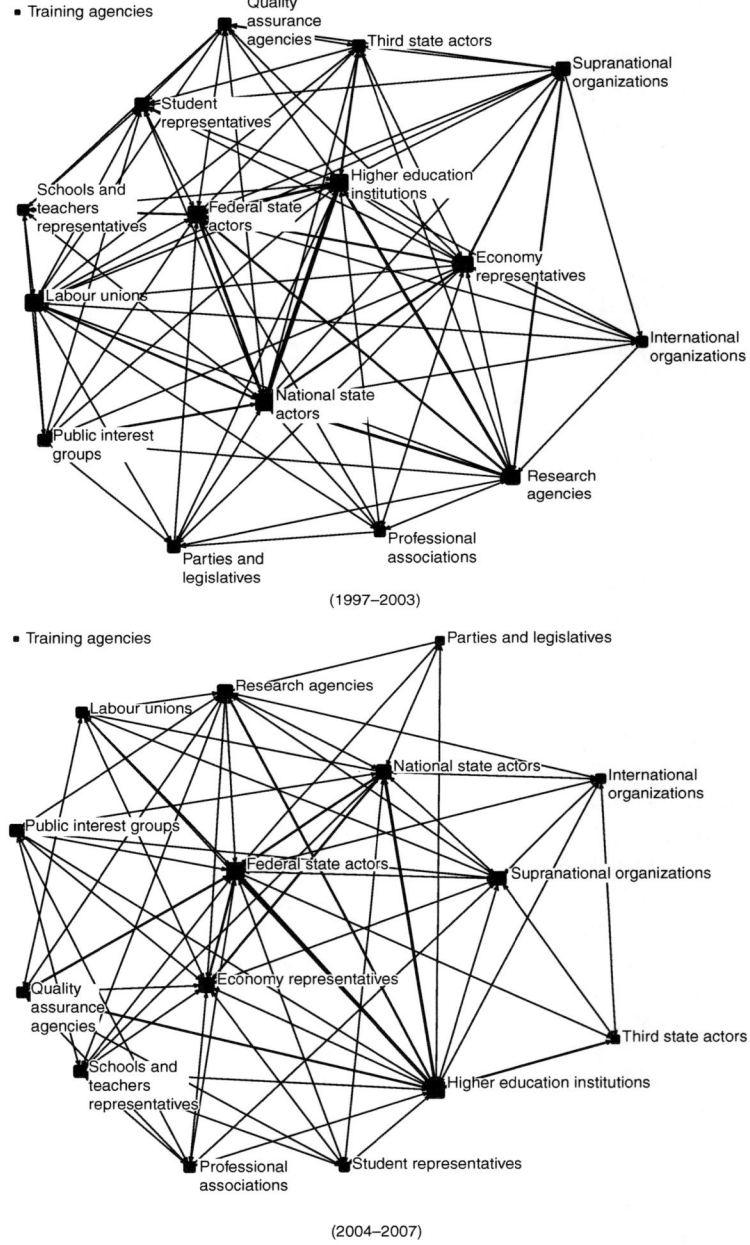

Figure 9.4 International actors in the German policy network

impulses from European actors, for example, the Bologna Guidelines of 2003 and the corresponding recommendations for accreditation of the Rectors' Conference of the Swiss Universities (CRUS). However, taking into account the results of positional analysis, international actors have not replaced the powerful veto players in Switzerland, but have successfully attached themselves to the federal structure of decisionmaking. Figure 9.5 reflects the overall composition of the Swiss education policy network and the participation of international actors.

Similar to Switzerland, European actors seem to be active members in the policy network of England. Over time they manage to sustain their influence in the network of transaction (e.g. funds of the sixth Framework Programme for Research and Technological Development and respective education programs, such as SOCRATES and LEONARDO, see Education Department 2003: 24) while they appear to gain some significance in the network of control relations, yet are less active in the realm of discursive governance. In contrast, IOs play a less important role in English education policymaking, exhibiting only a minor increase in governance by opinion formation. Regarding change, however, such evidence may point to IOs incrementally finding their way into the political discourse in England, as pointed out in the country case study. Altogether, there is a considerable degree of international interference within the British policy network marked by a clear dominance of the EU over IOs, such as the OECD. Figure 9.6 reflects the overall composition of the English education policy network and the participation of international actors.

Finally, an analysis of international actors in the policy network of *New Zealand* leads to a clear-cut, yet striking observation: while there was no evidence for international interference in the first period of time (1997–2003), there is strong participation by both IOs and European actors in the second period. This "boost" of international governance is not restricted to governance by opinion formation as in England, but refers to a broad scope of governance instruments. An analysis of the retrievals promises further insights: political communication refers to a broad set of international actors, from the OECD and UNESCO to the World Bank and the European Commission. Most of the retrievals are results of common projects, for example, a UNESCO-ASPAC conference in Wellington 2006, which aimed to improve the management of education systems as well as to promote a mutual recognition of degrees, diplomas, and certificates in the Asia Pacific Region. Funding from UNESCO "was provided to cover the Congress' infrastructural costs (venue, functions, interpretation, equipment, printing, communications, etc.), as well

218 *Transformation of Education Policy*

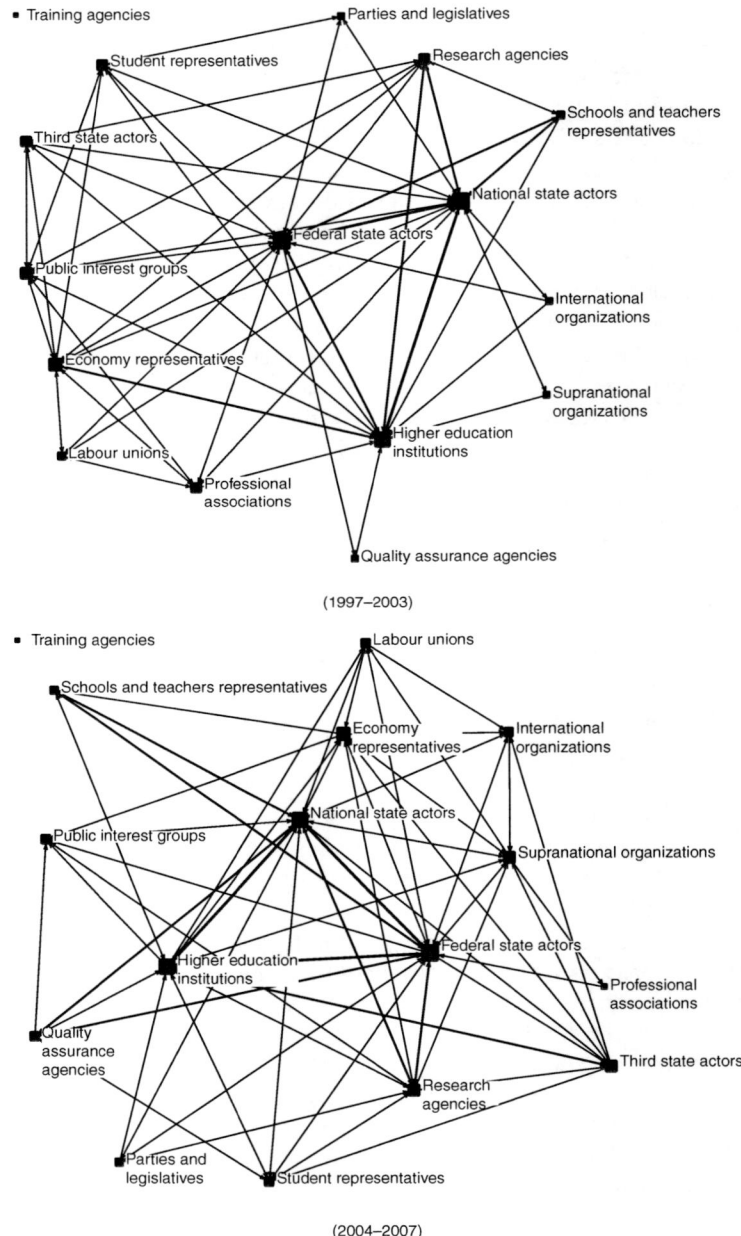

Figure 9.5 International actors in the Swiss policy network

Comparing Education Policy Networks 219

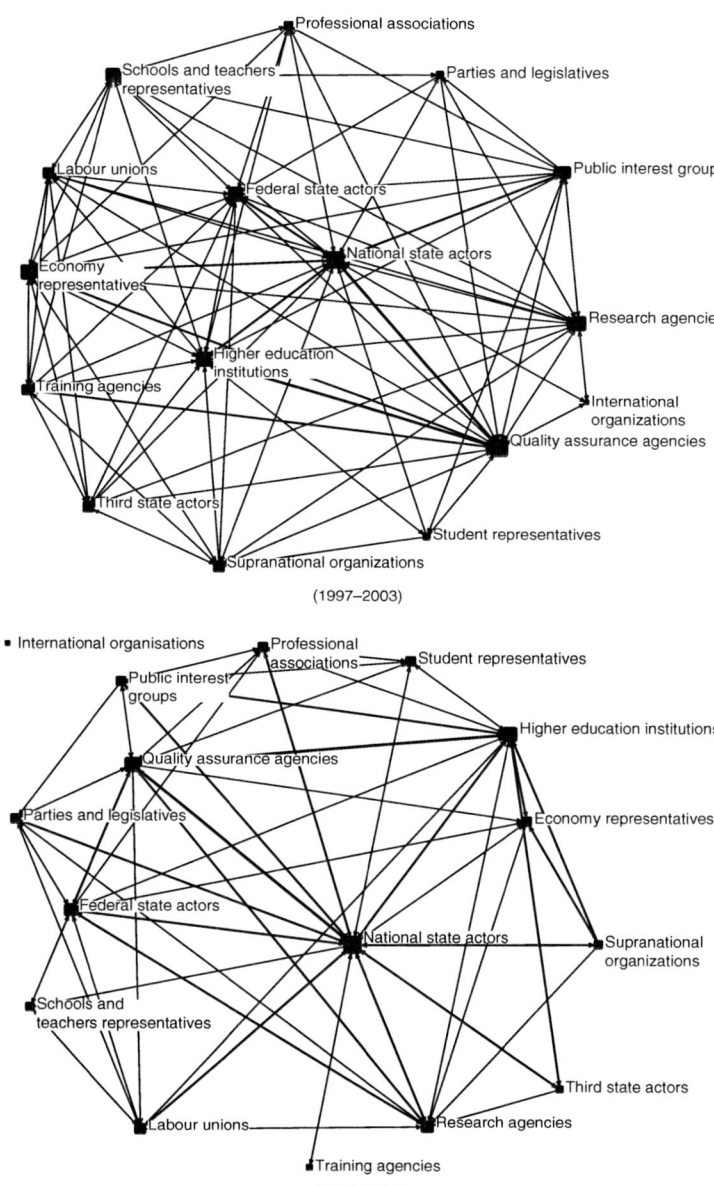

Figure 9.6 International actors in the English policy network

as international travel and accommodation for participants" (Ministry of Education 2007: 146). It is striking that European actors are also perceived to take part in education politics in New Zealand (for details see Dobbins, Chapter 7 in this volume), for example, by financial means of the LEONARDO program: "The programme will be jointly funded by Tertiary Education Commission (TEC) and the European Commission, with participating institutions also making a small contribution."[5] Maurice Maxwell, Head of the European Delegation in Wellington, comments the purpose of such programs as follows: "This pilot program will further strengthen the ties between the European Union and New Zealand and potentially serve as a model for the future cooperation in higher education."[6] Referring to our theoretical assumptions, the results for governance by European and Bologna actors are quite surprising, since we sampled New Zealand as a country which is a member of the OECD only. On the other hand, there is only a small number of veto players and thus a more centralized structure of decisionmaking. Along with a traditional openness to external impulses, the political system of New Zealand offers a fertile ground for governance by international and European actors. Figure 9.7 reflects the overall composition of the New Zealand education policy network and the participation of international actors.

The previous section aimed at exploring national variations in the participation of international actors in all four countries. To take a step from description to explanation and to examine potential interdependencies between our dependent (IO governance) and intermediate variable (national transformation capacities), these results are put in a pair-comparative perspective with regard to different *veto patterns*. As a reminder: In our theoretical sampling we assume strong veto patterns in the federal systems of Germany and Switzerland and weaker patterns in the more centralized systems of England and New Zealand. Network analytical evidence suggests that the activity of international actors decreases in federalist systems with decentralized structures of decisionmaking, an effect which is stronger for IOs such as the OECD than for European actors. This result is in line with the observation made above that strong veto players tend to superpose the role of international actors and thus the isomorphic power of IO governance. Drawing on the patterns of "viral intrusion" and "laager" there is evidence for domestic veto players shielding national decisionmaking against international intervention: former vertical channels of interaction between national and international actors trickle away and political interaction is recaptured as a national affair. In contrast, governance by

Comparing Education Policy Networks 221

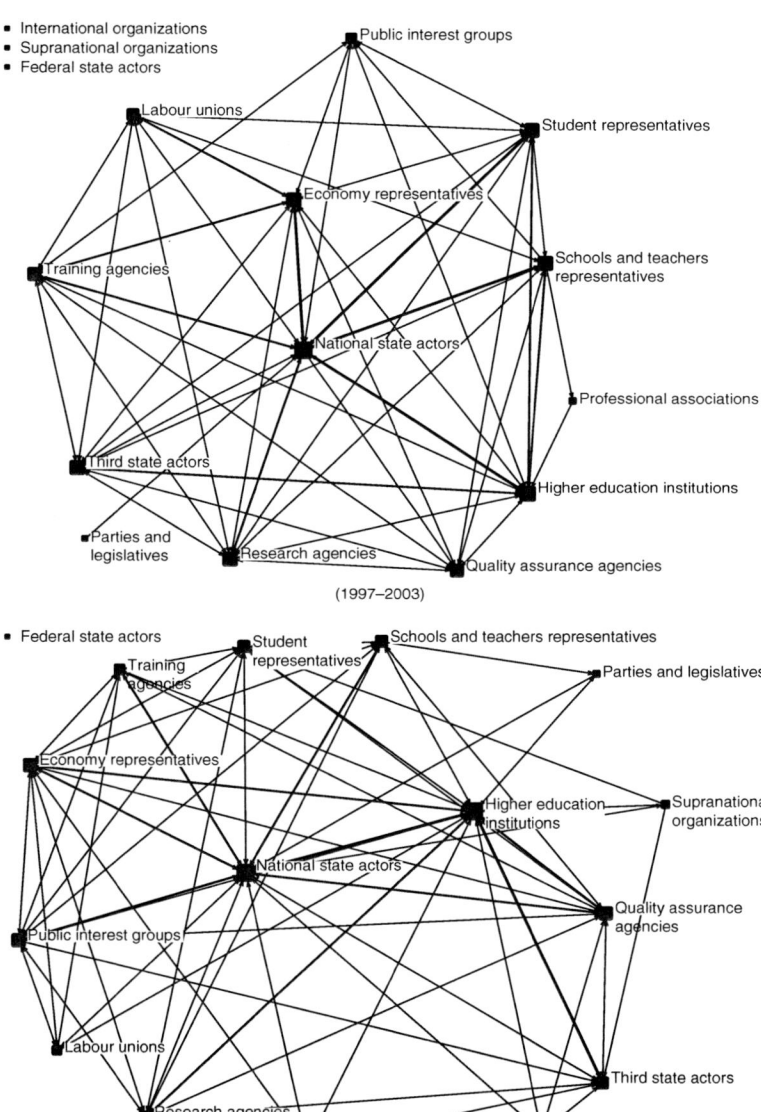

Figure 9.7 International actors in the New Zealand policy network

international actors in countries with a smaller number of veto players (English and New Zealand) is subject to more significant and heterogeneous changes. While European governance has switched from discursive modes to norm setting and transaction in the English policy network, the influence of international as well as European actors has increased significantly in New Zealand. Nevertheless, there is an overall tendency toward an increasing activity of governance by international and European actors. With regard to the lack of veto players in these countries this result shows the susceptibility of centralized decisionmaking structures to international impulses.

To put it in a nutshell, even though there is no evidence for an overall expansion of IO governance, there are remarkable changes in the activity and participation of international actors: IOs such as the OECD increasingly apply discursive strategies to influence national structures of decisionmaking, while they scarcely use financial means or norm setting. This emphasizes the character of the policy field of education as a highly sensitive domain of national policymaking, where sensible arguing is just as important as efficient bargaining. However, European and Bologna actors are in charge of a broader set of governance instruments, including funding and norm setting. Moreover, comparative network analysis suggests that strong veto-patterns in a policy network affect the activity of international actors as indicated by an overall decrease of IO governance in Germany and Switzerland. Despite processes of internationalization, domestic policy networks do not inevitably open up channels of interaction. On the other hand, a small number of veto players and a centralized decisionmaking structure appear to be a fertile ground for international impulses to bear fruit.

Conclusion

In this chapter I pursued a comparative analysis of education policy networks to study patterns and mechanisms of internationalization of education politics in Germany, Switzerland, England, and New Zealand. To this end, I examined political interaction between international and European organizations, national and regional veto players, and interest groups of various kinds on three different levels. On the macrolevel I focused on *structural change* in the patterns and modes of political interaction, whereas on the mesolevel I sought insights into *positional change*. On the microlevel, finally, I explored *governance activities* of international and European actors. As a result, I found considerable var-

Table 9.4 Degrees of change

	Germany	Switzerland	England	New Zealand
Change of education politics	0/+	0	+	0
Positional change of IOs and national veto players	0/+	+	0/+	0
Change in IO activity	+	0	0/+	+

Notes: *Legend*: 0 = little or no change; 0/+ = some change; + = noticeable change; ++ = much change.

iation across rather than within countries on all levels of observation. Table 9.4 schematically concludes the degrees of change within the single countries.

Table 9.4 is an attempt to rank changes in national education policy networks on different levels of observation. While there is little or no change in the dimension of politics in Switzerland and New Zealand there is quite a degree of change in England and Germany. By and large these results are in line with the theoretical assumptions underlying our case selection (for details see the introductory chapter of this volume): we expected changes of national education policymaking to be likely and extensive in countries with a high exposure to international governance and a weak veto patterns, such as England. In fact policy network analysis can account for considerable changes of actors and modes of political interaction in England as well as for moderate changes of roles and positions within the set of actors and with regard to the political activity of international actors. On the other hand we expected political change to be less likely and less extensive in countries with a lower exposure to international governance and a strong veto pattern, such as Switzerland. In accordance, network analysis points to a high level of continuity of political actors and processes in Switzerland as well as with regard to the interference of international actors. The moderate degree of positional change reflects processes of domestic closure as a reaction to increasing political competition between the national and international level.

But what about the intermediate cases, Germany and New Zealand? In Germany the degree of change in the dimension of education politics is considerably higher than in New Zealand regardless of the level of observation, a result which is also mirrored by the respective country case studies (see Niemann and Dobbins, Chapters 4 and 7 in this volume). Drawing from our selection of cases this difference can be attributed to the exposure to international interference which is supposed to be higher in Germany, which is a member of both OECD and EU, than in New Zealand, which is a member of the OECD only and geographically out of the scope of the Bologna Process. Such an interpretation underlines the function of international actors as important agents of change in national decisionmaking in the field of education. It would be premature, however, to infer from these results that the exposure to IO governance is a paramount determinant of change in domestic political actors and processes, while national veto patterns only play a marginal or catalytic role. On the contrary, one of the key findings in this chapter was that the effect of veto players superposes the effect of IO governance. In most countries an internationalization of education politics is taking place in the sense of an increasing participation of international actors who apply a more and more diversified portfolio of governance instruments. However, such intervention does not remain uncontested as domestic veto players are developing a rich set of strategies to cope, compete, or collaborate with international actors. It appears to be just like in Aesop's famous fable about the Hare and the Tortoise: the hare may be more agile than his competitor, but the tortoise always seems to be ahead making use of its look alike kinsfolk. In the last decade national education policy networks have become more inclusive to international actors, yet we are far from any sort of international hegemony or denationalization. The internationalization of education politics has taken place as a process of attachment rather than displacement. The ongoing prominence of national and regional veto players leads to path-dependency rather than convergence of actors and processes in national decisionmaking. At the same time international actors may use their new closeness to the national policy domain to launch changes in education policies.

Complementary to the country case studies, this chapter has mainly focused on changes in education politics which were conceptualized and analyzed as national policy networks in the domain of education. This perspective has proved significant for our overall endeavor to study the impact of IOs in national education policymaking as it sheds light on a piece of evidence which is almost unanimously reported in the country case studies: despite considerable changes in the dimension of education policies and a substantial degree of change in education polities there has been a striking continuity with regard to education politics. Thus, domestic political actors such as veto players may be convinced or find it in their own interest to promote policy initiatives from the international level—yet prove to be very conservative when it comes to their very domain, that is, the composition of the policy network and the modes of political interaction.

Notes

1. I distinguish types of relations by their content: *Information relations* are characterized by knowledge transfers in the policy network, *transaction relations* indicate exchange or transfer of material goods or services in a more or less monetary form, *relations of symbolic affirmation* are characterized by the transfer of institutional and symbolic capital, for example, by affirmative speech acts. *Cooperation relations* represent general collaboration between corporative actors, whereas *lobby relations* encompass purposeful and instrumental interventions of corporate actors in order to impose their will on others. Finally, *relations of control* apply to the exertion of formal authority (Nagel 2008: 18).
2. The first time period reflects a phase of *implementation* of international initiatives in education politics starting with the preparation of both the PISA (Programme for International Student Assessment) Study and the Bologna Process in the late 1990s and ending with the second PISA Study and the Berlin Conference in 2003 whereas the second period marks a phase of further *establishment* of these initiatives and encompasses the third wave of PISA in 2006 as well as the Bologna conference in Bergen 2005.
3. This observation refers to the *ratio* of the centralization index and the density.
4. Ranks can only be specified for actors who actually participate in a network. As a consequence the number of ranks varies over different networks. For comparative matters, ranks have been standardized as the quotient of the actual rank to all ranks counted. Hence, a standardized rank of "1" represents the last of all ranked actors, be it the fifth of five or the ninth of nine.
5. http://www.beehive.govt.nz/node/21396.
6. http://www.beehive.govt.nz/node/19176.

References

Bache, Ian and Matthew Flinders (2004) "Themes and Issues in Multi-level Governance," in I. Bache and M. Flinders, eds., *Multi-level Governance*, Oxford: Oxford University Press, 1–11.

Börzel, Tanja (1998) "Organising Babylon. On the Different Conceptions of Policy Networks," *Public Administration* 76 (2), 253–73.

Braun, Dietmar (2004) "Education, Science and Cultural Policy," in U. Klöti, Peter Knoepfel, and Hanspeter Kriesi , eds., *Handbook of Swiss Politics*, Zürich: NZZ, 743–76.

Burth, Hans-Peter and Petra Starzmann (2001) "Der Beitrag des Theoriemodells Strukturelle Kopplung zur instrumententheoretischen Dimension in der Policyanalyse," in H.-P. Burth and A. Görlitz, eds., *Politische Steuerung in Theorie und Praxis*, Baden-Baden: Nomos, 49–75.

Education Department (2003) *International Opportunities within Scottish Education and Training 2003* (Online: http://www.scotland.gov.uk/Resource/Doc/46951/0024019.pdf, last access: May 16, 2009).

Feld, Scott L. (1997) "Structural Embeddedness and Stability of Interpersonal Relations," *Social Networks* 19 (1), 91–5.
Howlett, Michael and M. Ramesh (1993) "Policy-Instrumente, Policy-Lernen und Privatisierung: Theoretische Erklärungen für den Wandel in der Instrumentenwahl," in A. Héritier, ed., *Policy-Analyse. Kritik und Neuorientierung*, Opladen: VS, 245–64.
Jansen, Dorothea (2003) *Einführung in die Netzwerkanalyse*, Opladen: Leske + Budrich.
Knoke, David, Franz U. Pappi, Jeffrey Broadbent, and Yutaka Tsujinaka (1996) *Comparing Policy Networks. Labor Politics in the U.S., Germany, and Japan*, Cambridge: Cambridge University Press.
Laumann, Edward O. and David Knoke (1987) *The Organizational State. Social Change in National Policy Domains*, Madison, WI: Wisconsin University Press.
Ministry of Education (2007) *"The Annual Report of the Ministry of Education Te Tāhuhu o Te Mātauranga for the year ended 30 June 2007,"* Wellington: Ministry of Education (Online: http://www.minedu.govt.nz/~/media/MinEdu/Files/TheMinistry/AnnualReport0833.pdf, last access: March 10, 2009).
Nagel, Alexander-Kenneth (2006) *Der Bologna-Prozess als Politiknetzwerk. Akteure, Beziehungen, Perspektiven*, Wiesbaden: DUV.
Nagel, Alexander-Kenneth (2008) "Analysing Change in International Politics. A Semiotic Method of Structural Connotation," TranState Working Paper No. 70.
Nagel, Alexander-Kenneth (2010) "International Networks in Education Politics," in A.P. Jakobi, K. Martens, and K.D. Wolf, eds., *Education in Political Science—Discovering a Neglected Field*, New York and London: Routledge, 156–74.
OECD (2004) *Attracting, Developing and Retaining Effective Teachers Country Note: Germany*, Paris: OECD (Online: http://www.oecd.org/dataoecd/32/48/33732207.pdf, last access: March 10, 2009).
Seibel, Wolfgang and Jörg Raab (2003) "Verfolgungsnetzwerke. Zur Messung von Arbeitsteilung und Machtdifferenzen in den Verfolgungsapparaten des Holocaust," *Kölner Zeitschrift für Soziologie und Sozialpsychologie* 55 (3), 197–230.
Suitor, Jill J., Barry Wellmann, and David L. Morgan (1997) "It's About Time: How, Why, and When Networks Change," *Social Networks* 19 (1), 1–7.
SUK (2003) *Kommentar zu den Bologna-Richtlinien zuhanden der Universitätskantone, des Kantons Luzern und des Bundes*, Bern: SUK (Online: http://www.diz.ethz.ch/projects/abgeschlossene_projekte/master4/dokumente/Kommentar_Richtlinien_SUK_2003.pdf, last access: March 10, 2009).
Wellmann, Barry, Renita Yuk-lin Wong, David Tindall, and Nancy Nazer (1997) "A Decade of Network Change: Turnover, Persistence and Stability in Personal Communities," *Social Networks* 19 (1), 27–50.
Wolf, Frieder (2006) "Bildungspolitik: Föderale Vielfalt und gesamtstaatliche Vermittlung," in M. Schmidt and R. Zohlnhöfer, eds., *Regieren in der Bundesrepublik Deutschland*, Wiesbaden: VS, 221–41.

10
The Internationalization of Education Policy in a Cross-National Perspective

Anja P. Jakobi, Janna Teltemann, and Michael Windzio

Education policymaking is influenced by various different factors on different levels. In order to be able to draw general conclusions on the influence of international organizations (IOs) on national policymaking in the field of education we take a quantitative approach. In this chapter we will assess the impact of international and national factors on education policy change by applying different quantitative methods.

The chapter is structured as follows. We will first shortly subsume the theoretical concepts outlined in this volume, highlighting several assumptions regarding the influence of national and international factors on education policy change. In a further section, we will present the data and methods for our research, building upon the methodology outlined elsewhere in this volume. In the third section, we will present evidence on cross-national convergence and divergence in secondary and higher education. In the fourth section, we will assess policy changes in secondary education in the context of the influence of IOs and national politics, carrying out regression analyses. The fifth part will present similar analyses for higher education. In the concluding section, we will compare our findings and outline their significance for research on policy convergence and social policies, as well as for the internationalization of education policy.

National and international sources of education policy change

The country case studies in this volume have already shown that states react very differently to the challenges of internationalized education policy. The Organisation for Economic Cooperation and Development (OECD) and the European Union (EU) have invested much effort in trying to trigger policy change within their member countries and beyond. The OECD in its Programme for International Student Assessments (PISA) promotes broader and more implicit targets, involving for example a fair chance for all students in the education system, increasingly autonomous institutions, and, most importantly, acceptable educational outcomes. In the case of the Bologna Process, countries were required to change their degree structure to a model of B.A. and M.A. or to introduce certificates like the diploma supplement. In addition to the Bologna Process, the EU has developed the Lisbon Strategy, aiming at making "...the European Union the leading knowledge-based economy in the world" (European Council 2000). Among other things, like "...facilitating the access of all to education and training systems" (Ertl 2006: 16), further training should be expanded, and further investments in education should be undertaken by the member states. In the implementation of the agenda, the Open Method of Coordination was applied in education, listing targets such as a higher rate of completed upper secondary education and reduced rates for early school leavers or pupils with low reading achievements (Lange and Alexiadou 2007: 324, 332).

As we have seen in the case of Germany, policies promoted by IOs can have a large impact on national education policy. More specifically, and as outlined in the theoretical chapter (also Leuze et al. 2008), we assume that IOs will have an influence on education policy and, even more, that (H1) *countries that have close ties to IOs are more likely to adopt international policies than countries which are less closely linked to these organizations*. Close ties might be defined as being a member or being involved in education policy review procedures in the case of the OECD, to name two examples. The latter results from consulting services provided by IOs (see the introductory chapter of this volume). Among other OECD services such as consulting on educational building and equipment (e.g. Posch 1998), these country-specific reviews on educational institutions reflect the rather "soft" governance instrument of consulting activities. By providing consulting services the OECD brings in substantial expertise. As regards the tertiary education system of Spain, for instance, the OECD explicitly makes policy recommendations based on an in-depth analysis of the Spanish situation (Santiago et al. 2009). Moreover, as outlined both in the introductory chapters and the case studies of this volume, even in times of internationalized policymaking, national politics and the established education system are still important factors in shaping education reforms. Veto players and the structure of political decisionmaking can enhance or restrict policy change. For example, a federal system might demonstrate a slower or uneven development, while centralized systems demonstrate a quicker adoption of favored policies. We thus assume that (H2) *countries that have many veto players in their political system are less likely to adopt international policies compared to countries that have fewer veto players.*

At the same time, the national welfare system constitutes an important point of reference for which education ideas are more or less likely to be adopted. In the theory of welfare regimes it is argued that contemporary welfare regulations result from historical processes of conflicting ideas and class coalitions. Basically, these ideas refer to equality and social rights on the one hand and naturally given inequality on the other hand. From a social democratic perspective, equality should be established by preventing actors from being exposed to market risks, called decommodification in Esping-Andersen's (1985; 1990) groundbreaking work. Since these basic guiding principles of equality and inequality not only result in different welfare policies, but also in more general goals of state intervention, we link guiding principles manifested in welfare regimes to the transformation of education policies. We therefore assume that (H3) *the welfare system of a country should impact on education policy change, and more specifically, conservatism in continental and southern European countries should result in higher inequality and a lower convergence to the ideal case in secondary education in the PISA Study, namely Finland.*

Moreover, from our perspective, the consequences of the national and international interplay in education policy are twofold. As one consequence, we can expect national policy change resulting from the activities of IOs. Activities like norm setting, opinion formation, financial means, coordinative activities, and consulting services might thus induce a shift in national policy preferences, leading to new ideas, aims, and policies. As a second consequence, we can assume that, because of an accumulation of these changes, countries converge towards internationally promoted policy goals—representing a horizontal perspective on cross-national policy change (see Jakobi 2009a).

However, we expect different countries to respond to IO impact in different ways. A welfare and education system that already embodies many of the internationally promoted policy goals might be more likely to adapt to new policy advice than a system that is more distant to such ideas. On the other hand, countries that are not yet close to international policies might be the ones that are particularly eager for policy change, a process which is commonly denoted as beta-convergence. Moreover, if they use the same set of political solutions to common problems we would expect sigma-convergence, meaning that countries become more similar with respect to education policies, but not in terms of approximating towards an ideal case. It is our aim to explore these different forms of education policy convergence across our sample in the third section of our paper.

In sum, we therefore assume different developments with regard to national policy change: On the one hand, given the potentially homogenizing influence of IOs, countries should converge with a view to the promoted policy goals. On the other hand, we can assume that national factors, such as national ideas, institutions, potential veto players, the welfare system, or other preconditions determine a strong path-dependency. The next section will elaborate on the methods for examining these changes.

Data, methods, and measurements

The generation and collection of data on education has faced considerable changes in recent decades, thereby creating severe challenges for longitudinal comparative analyses (Jakobi 2007; Jakobi and Teltemann 2009: 6). Since there is no existing database for our research question we had to draw on different sources (see also Nagel et al. 2009: 16). We have four sets of theoretical variables that need to be quantified, namely the independent factors of *IO governance*, *national transformation capacities*, and *alternative explanations* as well as our explanandum *change in education policies*.

In order to operationalize the independent factor *IO governance* we basically measure membership and its duration. Our sample consists of a maximum of 38 countries. Since nearly all of these countries have been OECD members since the 1990s variation with regard to membership and duration of OECD membership is low. As far as EU membership is concerned, we have some variation as a result of the enlargement of 2004. However, information on formal membership does not allow us to differentiate the influence of an IO for different countries. For a more accurate assessment of OECD impact, we therefore collected data on education policy reviews since 1996.[1]

To assess EU influence, we first take the years of membership in the Bologna Process as a proxy for the extent to which a country is linked to European education policy. We derived necessary information for generating these indicators from documentary or website analyses, for example, those provided by the Eurydice Information Network.[2] Additionally, we collected data on financial transfers from the EU to the member states since the 1990s and constructed a dummy variable on whether a country is a net spender of EU funds or not. We assume that net receivers are more closely linked to European policy goals than are net spenders, which are more autonomous in their policymaking.

With regard to our second independent variable *national transformation capacities* we distinguish between institutional factors (veto players) and ideational factors (guiding principles of education). For the institutional part, we measure if a country is more or less open to policy change depending on the number of veto options (see Chapter 2 in this volume). Aside from presidential and bicameral veto players we also relied on an indicator that already exists, namely the indicator PolCon V that is included in the Political Constraint Index Dataset by Henisz (2002).[3]

With regard to the ideational dimension outlined in the introductory chapter we could not refer to an existing typology of education *guiding principles* since none exists yet. Thus we had to rely on a proxy variable. Since welfare regimes have emerged from the interplay of class conflicts and class alliances in history and from the establishment of basic guiding principles by powerful social actors, we expect them also to be systematically related to education outcomes as well as to outputs of education policies. Based on previous studies of Castles and Obinger (2008), Esping-Andersen (1990), Inglot (2008), Keune (2009), Kuhnle (2007), Murai (2004), Schubert, Bazant, and Hegelich (2008), and Windzio, Sackmann, and Martens (2005) we derived a classification of welfare regimes (see Table 10.1). The liberal regime type is characterized by a restrained state and a dominance of market transactions, which is also reflected in welfare and education. In contrast, as an outcome of a strong labor movement throughout history, the state in the social democratic type protects individuals from market risks and allows them to exist comfortably without selling their labor force on markets—which is "decommodification" in Esping-Andersen's (1990) terminology. Likewise, partial decommodification is a characteristic of the conservative type as well, but only for selective groups and to the extent that they contribute to the social insurance system. Here, the guiding principle is the preservation of status differences in periods of not working and retirement. In this respect, the "southern" type is similar to the conservative type, but in the former, the welfare system is only weakly developed and many services are provided by the family. The "Minimal Bismarck" type consists of eastern European countries trying to overcome the legacy of socialism by painful processes of recommodification, attenuated by marginal welfare states based on rudimentary social insurance systems. Finally, in the "legacy of Confucianism" type there is a strong emphasis on family solidarity, diligence, self-reliance, entrepreneurial spirit, and on education as a valuable goal. Like many typologies of nations, our classification also suffers from some ambiguity and within-category variation. An overview of classifications that have been applied in the literature reveals that each of those classifications remains debatable (see Schubert, Bazant, Hegelich 2008: 16). On the other hand, in the literature cited above there is a high degree of agreement on the assignment of the majority of countries. Moreover, by adding three additional categories to the classical "Three Worlds" (Esping-Andersen 1990) we avoided an undifferentiated treatment and allowed for a separation of effects within the broad group of rather residual welfare systems. Nevertheless, our proceeding remains tentative and the application to the explanation of education outcomes and policies is rather explorative. Depending on availability of data, the multiple regression models presented below are based on countries listed in Table 10.1, whereas the analysis of convergence includes some additional countries.[4]

Table 10.1 Welfare regimes in countries of this study

Type of regime	Countries	Main characteristics
Liberal	Australia, Canada, Ireland, New Zealand, England, U.S.A.	Market based society, commodification
Social Democratic	Austria, Denmark, Finland, Iceland, Norway, Sweden	Decommodification, equality
Conservative	Belgium, France, Germany, Italy, Netherlands, Luxembourg, Switzerland	"Naturally" given order, preservation of social inequality
Southern	Greece, Mexico, Portugal, Spain, Turkey	"Naturally" given order, emphasis on strong family bonds, emphasis on male breadwinner (Keune 2009)
Minimal Bismarck	Czech Republic, Hungary, Poland, Slovakia	Overcoming socialism, "recommodification"
Legacy of Confusianism	Japan, South Korea	Confucian family solidarity, paternalism, emphasis on diligence, work ethic, self-reliance, entrepreneurial spirit, education (Kuhnle 2007)

In order to ensure that measured effects of national transformation capacities are not the result of other omitted variables (unobserved heterogeneity) we further control for several alternative explanations as a third independent set of factors. Thus we test factors such as the political majority in parliament and the level of productivity. Data for these indicators are mainly derived from the OECD online database[5] and from the "Quality of Government" Dataset.[6]

Finally, as regards our dependent variable, education policy change, we draw on several available indicators that measure policy outputs and policy outcomes. For secondary education we examine how the output structure, namely the autonomy of schools in three different dimensions (setting teachers' salaries, staffing, and defining course contents) as well as pupil-teacher ratios and instructional time, has changed and to what extent achievement and achievement differences have developed according to this structure. As outcome dimensions in secondary education, we have measured "performance" by the (inverse) rank position and the mean value of the average performance in math according to the PISA Study. In addition, inequality in math achievement is measured by the difference between the fifth and the ninety-fifth on percentile on the PISA test scale. With regard to tertiary education we focus on expenditure per student and the ratio of private expenditure (output dimension) and on the share of students and graduates in tertiary education (outcome dimension). We generated these indicators from data provided by the OECD which stem mainly from the three PISA cycles now available and the "Education at a Glance" Series. Additional data come from the World Development Indicators published by the World Bank and the International Data Base of the U.S. census bureau.[7] Since our research approach requires longitudinal data we only included indicators with at least three measurement points. We collected data for as many years as possible. However we still face problems of missing data and short time series. Since available data do not cover more than the last ten years, the period for which we might observe convergence is rather short (Heichel and Sommerer 2007: 113; Héritier 1993: 17–18).

Our approach is based on different quantitative methods. For the assessment of convergence and divergence we follow the approach outlined in Heichel and Sommerer (2007: 117–22; see also Jakobi and Teltemann 2009: 7–9). We assess three dimensions of convergence by using different methods. First, we examine the heterogeneity of policies across our sample by comparing the variation of our indicators over time, referring to statistical measures of dispersion, the range, or the standardized coefficient of variation to account for sigma-convergence. We further use Levene's robust test for the equality of variances to verify if the observed changes in our coefficients are significant (see Field 2007; Glaser 1983; Loh 1987).[8] As a second indicator of convergence we computed a pair-wise correlation (Pearson's R) between the value of the starting year and the subsequent growth rate. If we obtain strong negative (>|0.5|) correlations we assume beta-convergence, which is a necessary condition for sigma-convergence. Beta-convergence denotes a process of "catching up" and appears if countries with higher (lower) starting values show lower (higher) growth rates (see Jakobi and Teltemann 2009: 8).

A third concept of convergence is delta-convergence, which occurs if countries change toward a certain model or policy goal. Given the strong orientation toward successful policies in PISA, we therefore calculated a regression model of delta-convergence in secondary education, to show whether and why countries tend to implement policies that are similar to one of the "best practice" countries, namely Finland. For our estimation of the determinants of delta-convergence to this ideal case, we subtracted the value of each explanatory variable for the corresponding value of the Finish case. Subsequently we reversed the sign of each value by multiplying with −1 so that the final value of each x measures convergence: the higher the effect of x, the more similar is a country's policy to the ideal case Finland, which was the best performer in all three PISA cycles.

In order to examine determinants of policy change we also refer to regression modeling. At the level of secondary education pooled OLS regressions have been used in order to estimate effects on output and outcome variables. Since the number of countries is low, we used multiple observations per country if possible so that the minimum number of cases amounts to 44 country years. Nevertheless, we hold the number of explanatory variables as low as possible. Aside from the random and fixed effects models in Tables 10.6 and 10.7, where we investigate determinants of education policies at the tertiary level, we estimated pooled OLS regressions and corrected for dependence of observations within countries by using Huber-White standard errors (Greene 2008: 185).

In sum, drawing on this large set of data sources and a variety of methods, we can shed light on the diverse cross-national changes that have taken place in education over recent years as well as on their reasons.

Convergence and divergence in education policy

In this section, we analyze whether or not countries have become more similar or more different in education policy over time, irrespectively of reasons for this change. Early results have shown slight tendencies of convergence in secondary education (Jakobi and Teltemann 2009), but many indicators in secondary and tertiary education still have not yet been examined.

In our analyses we differentiate between indicators that represent relevant policy *output* structures in secondary and tertiary education and measures of policy *outcomes* on these two educational levels. In order to assess changes within the output structures of secondary education we draw on indicators that measure the degree of three different dimensions of autonomy in schools. We further examine the pupil-teacher ratio in secondary education and hours taught per year in public lower secondary education institutions, which are seen to play decisive roles in reaching adequate education outcomes (Baker 2004; Blatchford et al. 2007; OECD 2004: 259).

Our results (see Table 10.2) show that the overall degree of school autonomy increased between 2000 and 2006. We see an increase of 6 percent compared to 2000 for the autonomy of schools in staffing and 23 percent as regards the setting of teachers' salaries. At the same time, however, the heterogeneity across our sample as measured by the coefficient of variation decreased by about 6–20 percent, pointing at sigma-convergence. An exception is hours of instruction where the variation increased by 25 percent. With regard to the content and staffing dimension of autonomy we also find significant beta-convergence. This means that countries with lower autonomy in 2000 had a higher increase than countries that already had a high level in 2000. This finding might be a result of policy convergence towards goals that the OECD promoted after the first PISA study. As regards the pupil-teacher ratio in secondary education there is a trend towards fewer pupils and decreasing heterogeneity across countries, but no sign of significant beta-convergence. Further, we cannot assess any sign of convergence with regard to instructional time across our sample.

How do these changes in the output structure relate to a change in outcomes? We examine school achievement as measured in PISA by observing the changes in average achievement and in the density of the distribution, measured as the range on the achievement scale between the fifth and ninety-fifth percentiles, thereby reflecting one dimension of achievement inequality in a country. We observe only slight changes of <1 up to 3 percent for all measures, which are too weak to be interpreted as trends. However, our test for beta-convergence revealed that countries with a lower mean value in math in 2003 tend to perform better in 2006, whereas countries with a higher achievement in 2003 held or lowered their achievement level. The same holds for the inequality of the distributions in both mathematics and reading. A closer look at differences for selected indicators reveals differences between certain groups. Recent EU member countries (membership since 2004 or later) showed the highest degree of autonomy, nearly twice as high as the average degree of autonomy in the old EU. Furthermore, new EU countries perform better over time, whereas old EU countries and those OECD countries who are not members of the EU showed lower achievement. Thus, if one aggregates achievement scores for these three groups we observe a trend towards convergence which cannot be shown with an analysis that includes all countries without grouping them (as displayed in Table 10.2).

Table 10.2 Change of selected indicators of secondary and tertiary education

	Δ Mean (t_0=100)	Δ Coefficient of variation (t_0=100)	Δ Range (t_0=100)	Beta-convergence (Pearson's R)
Secondary Education				
Output Dimension				
Autonomy: Content	108.18	92.44	112.97	−0.68*
Autonomy: Salaries	123.93	80.69	123.34	−0.36
Autonomy: Staffing	106.04	94.31	89.54	−0.63*
Pupil-Teacher Ratio	93.06	92.26	75.22	−0.35
Hours of instruction	101.30	124.54	126.91	0.02
Outcome Dimension				
Math Achievement	100.14	99.86	83.53	−0.66*
Reading Achievement	99.00	101.01	117.74	−0.24
Math Distribution	97.67	102.39	75.57	−0.71*
Reading Distribution	103.33	96.78	70.62	−0.66*
Tertiary Education				
Output Dimension				
Expenditure per capita	139.91	84.08	157.32	−0.51*
Share of private expenditure	116.64	82.06	88.04	−0.49*
Outcome Dimension				
Share of students	124.08	73.30	98.80	−0.47*
Share of graduates	140.73	74.90	137.82	−0.44*

Notes: * $p < 0.05$; the figures indicate the level of change between the first and last year of measurement and can be interpreted as percentages. For example, the degree of autonomy in staffing increased by 8 percent between 2000 and 2006.

Figure 10.1 shows the development of PISA reading achievement in the OECD, EU, and Finland.

In order to assess policy change in tertiary education we draw on data on expenditure (*output*) and graduates (*outcomes*). More specifically, we examine the change in expenditure for tertiary education institutions per head of the working population (age 15–65) as well as the share of private expenditure in total expenditure. For the *outcomes* dimension we include the share of enrolled students in the working population and the share of graduates in the working population since the expansion of education systems is one of the core agreements of the education goals within the Lisbon Strategy of the EU (see Ertl 2006; European Council 2000).

Our results in Table 10.2 show rising values for all four indicators with the highest increase for the share of graduates in the working population. Further, all measures of dispersion show decreasing heterogeneity, indicating sigma-convergence. Our indicator of beta-convergence is also significant, albeit rather moderate, since the negative correlations are slightly below |0.5|. As regards the share of private expenditure, Levene's test further hints at significant sigma-convergence. A closer look at expenditure per head reveals that there are considerable differences between different groups of countries. The highest rates of expenditure per head are in countries that are members of the OECD, but not of the EU, followed by countries that were members of the EU before 2004. The new EU members show the lowest levels of expenditure. Figure 10.2 further illustrates the process of beta-convergence,

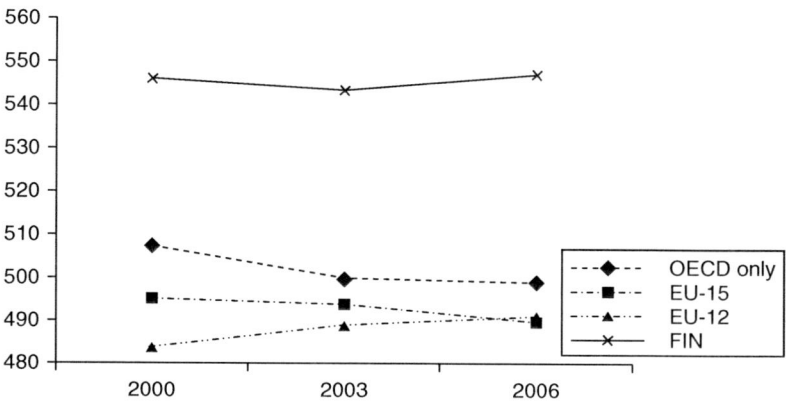

Figure 10.1 Pisa reading achievement

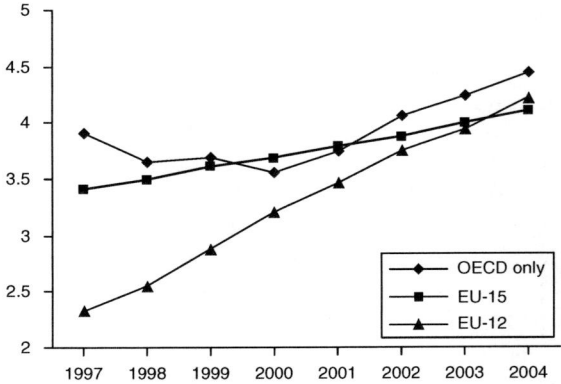

Figure 10.2 Share of students in the working population

since new EU countries, with low numbers of students at the beginning of the period of observation showed higher growth rates over time than countries with a higher level from the beginning.

Determinants of change in secondary education

Our next aim is to show how policy outputs at the level of secondary education are related to policy outcomes. In the first step of the multivariate analysis we estimate effects on achievement and inequality in performance in math. Our first dependent variable is the rank position in the distribution of math scores. Since rank distributions are not strictly continuous, we also estimate effects on average test scores on the math achievement scale in order to check for robustness. The same approach has been followed for ranks and test scores on the reading literacy scale, but results are not shown in tables here because of space limitations. In the second step we examine indices of policy outcomes as dependent variables and show how these outcomes correspond with political and institutional characteristics, but also with welfare regimes. Finally, we investigate determinants of delta-convergence towards the ideal case, Finland.

Table 10.3 shows determinants of a country's rank position in average math achievement scores. Rank scores have been reversed in order so that the high values represent top performers whereas lower values indicate low educational performance. For each dependent variable, the first model "0" includes the cumulative number of OECD reviews which is our indicator of IO impact on secondary education. Here, the effect is not significant. Model "math rank 1" shows two positive effects on the rank position: the higher the GDP per capita, the higher the rank on the mathematics scale. Moreover, countries with school autonomy in defining the contents of their courses perform better in relative terms. In model "math rank 2" we predict the math rank by our typology of welfare regimes. Compared with the reference group of the "minimal Bismarck" type, which consists of eastern European countries, welfare systems based on liberal and social democratic guiding principles have significantly higher ranks, whereas countries of the "southern" welfare type rank on average seven positions lower than the reference group. By far the best performing type is "legacy of Confucianism," consisting of Japan and South Korea. The overall tendency of the effects of welfare regimes remains stable in the full model "math rank 3." Based on 44 observations only, the full model should be interpreted with caution. Nevertheless, school autonomy apparently does not have only desirable effects. Model "math inequality 1" shows that higher proportions of students attending schools that are responsible for setting teachers' salaries increase the inequality in achievement in math.

Except for the effect on inequality of autonomy in setting teachers' salaries, we get the same result if we consider effects on mean test scores in math. Thus, school autonomy in defining course contents has a positive effect on performance. Regarding the impact of OECD reviews on mean math scores, we find positive effects in the models "math mean 0" and "math mean 3." Moreover, guiding principles corresponding with welfare regimes have a considerable impact on performance: the conservative southern and the eastern European "minimal Bismarck" states perform worst, whereas liberal and social democratic countries perform much better, although not as well as the Asian countries Japan and South Korea. We get similar results (not shown here) when we estimate effects on reading literacy ranks and mean reading literacy. But in contrast to the math scores, there is no significant effect of "autonomy in teacher salaries" on inequality in average reading literacy achievement. In contrast, the effect of autonomy in setting teachers' salaries on the mean value and the rank position in reading literacy tends to be negative.

Interestingly, when also controlling for the pupil-teacher ratio in secondary education (models not shown here), we did not find any significant effect. The same holds for average teaching hours per year, which does not increase performance, in either the math or reading literacy dimensions. Thus, just increasing the number of teachers or teaching hours does not raise the performance of the education system. Since we did not want to overcharge our regression models with insignificant explanatory variables and did not want to lose more observations, we left pupil-teacher ratio and teaching hours out. What seems to matter more is the decision about the course content, which should be adequate for the specific student population in each school. In Table 10.3 the effect of school autonomy in staffing has a positive sign on performance and a negative sign on inequality, but neither of these effects is significant.

In the next step, we are interested in institutional and political determinants that create relevant output structures. Model "content 1" in Table 10.4 shows that countries with presidential veto players have a higher share of students in schools which are responsible for the content—and this turned out to enhance performance of secondary education systems, as we have seen in Table 10.3. School autonomy in defining course content is highest in the "legacy of Confucianism" regime and lowest in the "southern" type, which corresponds with the large difference between these two types in terms of performance. In contrast, political and institutional characteristics do not have any impact on school autonomy in staffing. In model "teach. sel. 2," the reference group of countries of the eastern European "minimal Bismarck" type has the highest autonomy in staffing, but this does not seem to have a significantly positive effect on performance, as we have seen in Table 10.3. Controlling for institutional factors as well as for regime types in model "teach. sel. 3" in Table 10.4, we find that GDP per capita and presidential veto players increase school autonomy in this dimension. However, the implausible effect of slightly more than 100 percentage points difference between the "legacy of Confucianism" regime and the "minimal Bismarck" type reveals some multicollinearity. For this reason, the latter model, based on 48 observations only, should be interpreted with caution.

In model "salary 0" in Table 10.4 the cumulative number of OECD reviews significantly increases school autonomy in setting teachers' salaries, but this effect is not significant any more if we control for further explanatory variables. Having a left-of-center government increased school autonomy in teacher salaries. Even if we control for regime types in model "salary 3," the effect of left-of-center governments remains significant at 10 percent. Again, the eastern European "minimal Bismarck" type, which is the reference group, shows the highest school autonomy in setting teachers' salaries. We found a similar result with respect to staffing. We also found in the preceding analysis that the "minimal Bismarck" type performs comparatively poorly in math and reading literacy achievement—only the "southern" type performed even less well.

In the public debate, the pupil-teacher ratio is considered as an important target for policy to focus on (see Blatchford et al. 2007). However, we noted that it turned out to have no impact on education performance, although it is a rather costly policy output in economic terms. Thus, we are interested in determinants of such disinvestment. In model "pt-ratio 1" in Table 10A.1 (Appendix), countries which have presidential veto players also have an increased pupil-teacher ratio, meaning that the average number of pupils a teacher has to deal with is higher. In model "pt-ratio 3," where we also control for regime types, GDP per capita decreases the pupil-teacher ratio, that is, the richer a country, the lower the average number of pupils per teacher. Strikingly, liberal states, in particular, and those with a "legacy of Confucianism" have high pupil-teacher ratios compared with the reference group of the eastern European "minimal Bismarck" type, but these two regimes also had the highest rank positions in the math and reading literacy tests according to model "math rank 2."

The model "teaching hours 1" in Table 10A.1 (Appendix) results in a positive effect of presidential veto players on average teaching hours. Thus, the average yearly number of teaching hours is higher in countries with presidential veto players. From the pupils' point of view this means either that they learn in larger classes or that one teacher, who has a rather high work load, works with many classes. It is in the liberal regime type in model "teaching hours 3" where we find the highest average teaching load for teachers. As we know from previous analyses, countries of the liberal regime type perform quite well in math. However, the best-performing type is "legacy of Confucianism"—countries which have the lowest average teaching load.

To sum up, outcomes of education institutions differ strongly according to welfare regimes. Countries of the liberal, social democratic, and especially the "legacy of Confucianism" regime rank high in student math and reading literacy performance, whereas countries of the "southern" welfare type perform comparatively poorly. Furthermore, effects of regime types on student performance are confounded with effects of school autonomy. Autonomy in defining the course content leads to better performance, whereas autonomy in other dimensions does not. However, school autonomy in setting teachers' salaries even increases the inequality of mathematics achievement. Results remain rather similar if we analyze reading achievement. As regards these results, education policies do indeed have an impact on student performance in secondary education, but not all of these impacts are desirable from the policymakers point of view, especially if they do not enhance performance, but increase inequality. The same holds true for the pupil-teacher ratio and for teaching hours which are costly policy outputs but do not increase performance. Characterized by high autonomy of teacher selection and payment, countries of the eastern European "minimal Bismarck" type maintain education policies which do not correspond with good student performance.

Interestingly, veto players and veto points do not have a decelerating or inhibiting effect, contrary to our second hypothesis (H2). Rather, the opposite is true since effects of presidential veto players tended to be significantly positive on school autonomy with respect to deciding on course content and staffing. This result is not in line with our hypothesis formulated in the theoretical section of this chapter. At this point, it is important to note that we used Henisz' (2002) more sophisticated Index of Political Contraints (PolCon V) in order to check for robustness, which also led to the finding that political constraints do not impede or retard change in education policies.

However, simply estimating effects of institutional and political determinants on education policies does not tell us much about factors of convergence or divergence. Although different types of convergence are conceptually meaningful in exploratory and descriptive analysis, it does not make sense to estimate causes of sigma-convergence in a regression framework. The reason is that an effect of characteristic x in country i on sigma-convergence also depends on the change of x in all other countries during the respective year. In other words, the mean value of a variable in one year depends on the development of all other countries as well and so does the deviation of country i from this mean. Hence, we investigated effects on delta-convergence in secondary education and chose the PISA 2000 best performer, Finland, as an ideal case. Each dependent variable in Table 10.5 has been measured as the absolute difference between the value of country i in year t and the corresponding value of Finland, multiplied by −1. Consequently, we actually measure convergence, meaning that a positive effect of an explanatory variable indicates increasing similarity to Finland. Finland itself has been excluded from the models. In Table 10.5, none of these models shows significant effects of GDP per capita, bicameral veto players, and the cumulative number of OECD reviews.

As the only significant effect on convergence with respect to autonomy in defining course contents, model "conv. content 1" reveals that countries which have presidential veto players show higher similarity with Finland. These countries are 13 percentage points closer to the ideal case than countries without presidential veto players. Here, veto players do not seem to block the transformation of the educating state (see Chapter 3 in this volume). More interestingly, in model "conv. content 2" countries of the "conservative" and the "southern" type are most different from the Finish ideal case, whereas "legacy of Confucianism" countries are 8 percentage points closer to the ideal case than the reference group of the "minimal Bismarck" type. Concerning signs and significance, this result remains stable in the full model "conv. content 3." Even though the number of observations is very low, the absolute strength of the effects increases. In this model, right-of-center as well as left-of-center governments seem to increase convergence to the best performer Finland, whereas presidential veto players do not have a significant effect.

Moreover, regarding delta-convergence with respect to school autonomy in staffing, we find a very similar picture: delta-convergence is highest in the "legacy of Confucianism" regime and lowest in the reference group of the "minimal Bismarck" type in model "conv. teach. sel. 2." In addition, convergence is also high in the "southern" regimes. Institutional factors have only a minor and inconsistent effect. Again, having veto players leads to ambiguous results and they should not be regarded as an impediment to change in education policy. We have to keep in mind that in contrast to countries of the southern regime type, which are least autonomous in teacher selection, schools in the "minimal Bismarck" regime are most autonomous. Regarding school autonomy in setting teachers' salaries in model "conv. salary 1," left-of-center governments have a negative impact on delta-convergence, but this effect disappears in model "conv. salary 3." In this model, as well as in model "conv. salary 2" countries of the "southern" regime type show the highest convergence to the Finnish ideal case. As we have seen above, school autonomy in this dimension does not increase performance but it increases inequality in performance in math. The same is true for autonomy in teacher selection. Hence, the "southern" regime type shows convergence only in dimensions which do not matter for student performance. At the same time, there is rather strong divergence in dimensions which have a considerable impact on student performance, especially school autonomy in defining the course content. Thus, we can conclude that "southern" and "minimal Bismarck" states are indeed experiencing some convergence to the Finnish ideal case, but only in dimensions that do not increase student performance.

Table 10.3 Outcomes of secondary education policy—math achievement and inequality, OLS regressions[a]

	Rank position in average math achievement				Mean score in average math achievement				Inequality in math achievement			
	math rank 0	math rank 1	math rank 2	math rank 3	math mean 0	math mean 1	math mean 2	math mean 3	math inequ. 0	math inequ. 1	math inequ. 2	math inequ. 3
GDP per capita	–	0.29+	–	–0.17	–	1.45*	–	0.41	–	0.07	–	0.05
Cum. num. OECD reviews	0.82	0.06	–	0.50	3.97*	0.82	–	2.13+	–1.90+	–0.13	–	1.02
% resp. for course content	–	0.25**	–	0.10	–	0.96**	–	0.45	–	–0.33	–	–0.25
% resp. for teacher selection	–	0.02	–	0.06	–	0.16	–	0.09	–	–0.10	–	–0.14
% resp. for teacher salary	–	–0.09	–	–0.07	–	–0.42	–	–0.39	–	0.38+	–	0.29
Minimal Bismarck	–	–	reference	reference	–	–	reference	reference	–	–	reference	reference
Liberal	–	–	8.82*	9.20+	–	–	29.36**	2.81	–	–	–9.79	–7.52
Social Democratic	–	–	8.44**	9.83+	–	–	28.74**	–1.34	–	–	–13.95+	–18.62
Conservative	–	–	5.90	11.46+	–	–	17.67	4.15	–	–	9.66	3.96
Southern	–	–	–7.37**	–4.37	–	–	–41.23*	–57.09	–	–	–5.68	–20.25
Legacy of Confucianism	–	–	18.22***	18.99*	–	–	57.38***	26.21	–	–	–8.01	–10.42
Constant	17.25***	–1.36	14.94***	7.75	485.55***	402.14***	484.35***	466.52***	308.26***	321.25***	306.95***	328.29***
N	92	44	92	44	92	44	92	44	92	44	92	44
R^2	0.03	0.44	0.51	0.66	0.06	0.46	0.55	0.69	0.04	0.16	0.17	0.32

Notes: [a] Huber-White Standard Errors +p≤.10; *p≤.05; **p≤.01; ***p≤.001.

Table 10.4 Output of secondary education policy—school autonomy indicators, OLS regressions[a]

	School autonomy in course content				School autonomy in teacher selection				School autonomy in teachers' salaries			
	content 0	content 1	content 2	content 3	teach. sel. 0	teach. sel. 1	teach. sel. 2	teach. sel. 3	salary 0	salary 1	salary 2	salary 3
GDP per capita	–	0.12	–	-0.75	–	0.45	–	1.47+	–	-0.16	–	0.5
Cum. num. OECD reviews	1.99+	-0.05	–	-0.22	0.15	-2.24	–	-3.33	3.46*	2.63	–	2.61
Left-of-center government	–	-1.61	–	8.93	–	26.46	–	8.73	–	21.36*	–	16.25+
Right-of-center government	–	-1.92	–	12.08	–	6.75	–	4.83	–	7.86	–	9.03
Presidential veto player	–	13.81+	–	4.97	–	10.48	–	23.60*	–	15.22	–	16.21
Bicameral veto player	–	13.26*	–	3.87	–	21.07	–	18.31	–	4.51	–	-0.44
Minimal Bismarck	–	reference	reference	reference	–	reference	reference	reference	–	reference	reference	reference
Liberal	–	–	2.68	17.82	–	–	-17.92*	-37.9	–	–	-18.89	-29.43+
Social Democratic	–	–	-6.19	12.08	–	–	-33.82*	-57.18*	–	–	-30.51+	-41.29+
Conservative	–	–	-14.49	-4.97	–	–	-35.50*	-58.64+	–	–	-28.32+	-37.09
Southern	–	–	-35.27***	-21.77*	–	–	-71.56***	-65.14***	–	–	-42.73**	-38.58*
Legacy of Confucianism	–	–	16.21***	33.47*	–	–	-67.47***	-100.5***	–	–	-32.84*	-36.62+
Constant	67.74***	58.45***	81.72***	70.90***	63.62***	25.29	99.04***	66.58**	17.83**	4.28	54.07***	28.32
N	77	47	77	47	78	48	78	48	77	47	77	47
R^2	0.04	0.10	0.43	0.49	0.00	0.18	0.44	0.54	0.07	0.19	0.19	0.36

Notes: [a] Huber-White Standard Errors +$p \leq .10$; *$p \leq .05$; **$p \leq .01$; ***$p \leq .001$.

Table 10.5 Determinants of delta-convergence—Finland's education policy as an ideal-type, OLS regressions[a]

	School autonomy in course content			School autonomy in teacher selection			School autonomy in teachers' salaries		
	conv. content 1	conv. content 2	conv. content 3	conv. teach. sel. 1	conv. teach. sel. 2	conv. teach. sel. 3	conv. salary 1	conv. salary 2	conv. salary 3
GDP per capita	0.07	–	–0.65	–0.17	–	–0.66	0.12	–	–0.45
Cum. num. of OECD reviews	–0.56	–	–0.98	2.03	–	2.67	–2.84	–	–2.58
Left-of-center government	3.5	–	13.12*	–23.90+	–	–6.99	–20.14+	–	–15.88
Right-of-center government	3.99	–	18.01**	–4.59	–	–0.31	–5.12	–	–7.32
Presidential veto player	13.45+	–	6.57	1.14	–	–14.14*	–14.04	–	–15.76
Bicameral veto player	9.66	–	2.11	–12.79	–	–11.73	–5.6	–	0.26
Minimal Bismarck	reference	reference	reference	reference	reference	reference	reference	reference	reference
Liberal	–	2.86	16.35+	–	17.92*	23.71	–	18.89	27.93+
Social-democratic	–	–7.73	6.27	–	24.53*	27.71	–	26.48	36.17
Conservative	–	–15.21+	–6.98	–	25.41*	29.40+	–	28.25+	35.52
Southern	–	–33.37***	–22.43*	–	51.97***	44.75***	–	42.57**	37.15*
Legacy of Confucianism	–	8.35*	22.97*	–	66.22***	79.19***	–	32.84*	34.91
Constant	–36.34***	–13.24***	–25.06**	–21.35+	–70.84***	–51.14***	–3.68	–52.67***	–27.44
N	45	74	45	46	75	46	45	74	45
R^2	0.1	0.44	0.51	0.23	0.51	0.66	0.2	0.19	0.35

Notes: [a] Huber-White Standard Errors +p≤.10; *p≤.05; **p≤.01; ***p≤.001.

Moreover, in Table 10A.1 (Appendix) the pupil-teacher ratio is also rather low in both regimes (few students, many teachers), indicating, in a sense, that they pursue unprofitable investment strategies in their secondary education policies.

Determinants of change in higher education

At the level of higher education we examine the institutional and political determinants of the percentage of students, expenditure on tertiary education per capita and finally the share of private expenditure on tertiary educational institutions. Compared with our analysis of secondary education the number of observations is much larger. Thus, we use fixed and random effects regression models (Greene 2008; Halaby 2004). In Table 10.6, for each dependent variable we first estimate a fixed effects (FE) model in order to capture the net effects of change in x on change in y within countries, and to control for unobserved heterogeneity at the country level. Here, all explanatory variables change over time. By estimating random effects (RE) models we also control for time-invariant characteristics as the regime type.

According to the FE specification in model "students 1" we find positive effects of GDP per capita, years of Bologna membership, and EU membership, whereas left- and right-of-center governments as well as political constraints decelerate the overall process of increasing the number of students in tertiary education. Again, the initiatives of the EU, more precisely the Bologna Process and the Lisbon Strategy, seem to have a strong impact on the change in the outcomes of tertiary education.[9] Effects of regime types on the percentage of students enrolled remain stable in the RE model "students 2" and do not substantially differ from results in model "students 3." Compared with countries of the eastern European "minimal Bismarck" type, "liberal" and "legacy of Confucianism" countries have a higher share of students in the working population. It is worth noting that the effects of welfare regimes are not confounded with political and institutional determinants.

In the following models the dependent variable is expenditure on tertiary educational institutions per capita. Model "exp. 1" in Table 10.6 shows that education expenditure increases with rising GDP per capita. This result remains stable in the RE specification. Moreover, becoming member of the EU increased the per capita expenditure on tertiary education considerably. Since our period of observation ends with the year 2004, this effect is a result of the accession of the EU 12 in 2004, consisting of eastern European countries and Cyprus and Malta. For

Table 10.6 Institutional and political determinants of tertiary education policies—fixed and random effects models

	Share of students in the working population				Expend. on tertiary education per capita in U.S.$				Share of private expend. on tertiary education			
	students 0 FE	students 1 FE	students 2 RE	students 3 RE	exp. 0 FE	exp. 1 FE	exp. 2 RE	exp. 3 RE	share pr. 0 FE	share pr. 1 FE	share pr. 2 RE	share pr. 3 RE
GDP per capita	–	0.044+	0.009	–	–	29.312***	20.559***	–	–	–0.007+	–0.006*	–
Years of Bologna memb.	0.130***	0.100***	0.120***	–	17.41***	2.117	6.251	–	0.003*	0.004	0.003	–
Member of EU	0.419*	0.489**	0.402*	–	148.82***	181.28***	144.71***	–	0.017	0.015	0.007	–
Left-of-center government	–	–0.230+	–0.219+	–	–	–12.847	–40.479	–	–	0.015	0.02	–
Right-of-center government	–	–0.279*	–0.275*	–	–	28.581	0.314	–	–	0.045*	0.053**	–
Political constraints	–	–1.286*	–1.170*	–	–	64.327	68.12	–	–	0.161*	0.152*	–
Minimal Bismarck	–	–	reference	reference	–	–	reference	reference	–	–	reference	reference
Liberal	–	–	1.336+	1.271*	–	–	–311.450+	104.731	–	–	0.309***	0.211***
Social-democratic	–	–	0.519	0.85	–	–	–478.088*	101.067	–	–	–0.022	–0.137*
Conservative	–	–	–1.078	–0.448	–	–	–552.098**	–55.993	–	–	0.05	–0.05
Southern	–	–	0.015	0.229	–	–	–371.492*	–213.738	–	–	–0.01	–0.044
Legacy of Confucianism	–	–	1.808+	1.615+	–	–	–364.227+	13.114	–	–	0.611***	0.501***
Constant	3.126***	3.411***	3.748***	3.141***	204.94***	–412.988*	162.569	330.440**	0.218***	0.210*	0.073	0.193***
N	221	221	221	227	173	173	173	179	198	173	173	205
R^2	0.428	0.469	–	–	0.267	0.349	–	–	0.047	0.155	–	–

Notes: FE: fixed effects, RE: random effects +p≤.10; *p≤.05; **p≤.01; ***p≤.001.

Table 10.7 Institutional and political determinants of tertiary education policies – random effects models, EU countries

	Share of students in the working population			Expend. on tertiary education per capita in U.S.$			Share of private expend. on tertiary education		
	students 0 EU RE	students 1 EU RE	students 2 EU RE	exp. 0 EU RE	exp. 1 EU RE	exp. 2 EU RE	share pr. 0 EU RE	share pr. 1 EU RE	share pr. 2 EU RE
GDP per capita	–	−0.005	−0.008	–	10.072*	12.600**	–	−0.009***	−0.019***
Net contributor to EU	−0.180*	−0.083	−0.079	−31.142*	10.949	12.708	0.022+	0.024**	0.017+
Years of Bologna membership	–	0.092***	0.094***	–	11.152***	9.808**	–	0.005*	0.010***
Left-of-center government	–	−0.246+	−0.245+	–	−16.181	−17.945	–	0.006	0.011
Right-of-center government	–	−0.333*	−0.337*	–	−8.89	−8.178	–	0.023	0.02
Political constraints	–	−1.554***	−1.522***	–	19.777	15.853	–	0.118*	0.129**
Minimal Bismarck	–	–	reference	–	–	reference	–	–	reference
Liberal	–	–	0.405	–	–	−436.304	–	–	0.459***
Social-democratic	–	–	0.674	–	–	−318.713	–	–	0.263*
Conservative	–	–	−0.791	–	–	−453.041+	–	–	0.296**
Southern	–	–	0.614	–	–	−422.272+	–	–	0.105
Constant	3.683***	4.765***	4.711***	354.211***	103.708	374.109*	0.146***	0.186**	0.141*
N	114	114	114	94	94	94	111	94	94

Notes: +p≤.10; *p≤.05; **p≤.01; ***p≤.001.

these countries the result is clear: becoming member of the EU has a strong impact on tertiary education policies. In the RE model "exp. 2" conservative and social democratic countries turn out to have the lowest relative expenditure. However, in model "exp. 3," including only regime types as explanatory variables, we do not find any differences.

Finally, models "share priv. 1" and "share priv. 2" test determinants of increasing private expenditures in tertiary education. In the FE model "share priv. 1" private expenditure decreases with increasing GDP per capita. In contrast, both right-of-center governments and political constraints increase the share of private expenditures. Controlling for regime types in the RE model "share priv. 2" did not change the results substantively. As we expected, liberal states have a significantly higher share of private expenditure than states in the "minimal Bismarck" reference group, and privatization is lowest in social democratic countries. We find the highest level of privatization within countries of the "legacy of Confucianism" type. This means that Asian countries rely even more heavily on private founding sources than the Anglo-Saxon countries, confirming the results of Windzio, Sackmann, and Martens (2005), which were based on a different methodological approach.

In Table 10.7 we estimate the effects of being a net payer to the EU in changing tertiary education policies. The sample consists of EU member states only. In the models "students 0 EU" and "exp. 0 EU" we find negative gross effects which become insignificant after controlling for additional covariates. Hence, from these models we cannot conclude with certainty that net payer countries are more reluctant to change education policies. However, models "share pr. EU 0" to "share pr. EU" show positive effects of being net payer on the share of expenditure on private education institutions. In other words, countries that are deeply interwoven in financing the EU tend to rely more on private financing than other countries. As a result, financial transfers to the EU do have an impact on education policy change, but not always in a way which we expected.

Conclusion

At the beginning of this chapter we gave reasons for our expectation of an impact of IO activities on national education policies. The two IOs of interest, the OECD and the EU, were supposed to initiate changes in national education policies. While the Bologna Declaration explicitly set normative standards on the structure of tertiary education, the OECD conducted the PISA Study as a benchmark of performance for secondary education systems and applied thus the rather soft instrument of opinion formation. Moreover, by preparing country-specific reports within the framework of its consulting services, the OECD was able to bring in its substantial expertise, enabling nation states to draw on external legitimacy when implementing unpopular reforms. Finally, institutions of the EU comprise regulations of large-scale financial redistribution. Although we do not argue that member states respond to direct financial assistance from the EU to their education systems, we expected financial means to affect change in national education policies indirectly. Net payers to the EU, according to our argument, might be more reluctant to adopt reforms initiated by the EU. However, not all nation states are susceptible to the impact of IOs to the same degree. Depending on IO membership, its duration, and the degree of involvement into the OECD review system, and finally on national transformation capacities, dynamics of change in education policies should differ between countries. Therefore, we tested our hypotheses using data from different sources on the basis of regression analysis.

To begin with, we have provided a descriptive overview of convergence in secondary and tertiary education. At the level of secondary education we noticed an overall trend toward sigma-convergence with regard to increasing autonomy of schools. Thus, in the output dimension of secondary education there actually is a tendency toward convergence, indicating that countries become more similar. However, we could not yet identify a clear trend with respect to the outcome dimensions of secondary education, that is achievement and inequality of achievement. While national education policies do indeed respond to the impact of the OECD through its opinion formation and consulting services, outcomes of these policies are not yet observable.

Concerning tertiary education indicators we found a clear trend toward both sigma- and delta-convergence within the output structure of secondary education. For new member countries of the EU, especially, which had tended to lag behind some internationally promoted goals at the beginning of our observation period at the end of the 1990s, we observed a process of catching up, corresponding with sigma-convergence and signifying decreasing heterogeneity across the sample. Consequently, corresponding with this catching up we also observed clear beta-convergence, meaning that countries lagging behind the internationally promoted goals increasingly compensated for their initial disadvantages. But a definite attribution of cause and effect remains complicated since new member countries possibly tried to reform their education system in order to meet the requirements for EU membership. Nonetheless, the dynamic change processes in the group of new EU members should be regarded as an effect of the EU because "anticipatory obedience" in governing national education policies is just as much a response to the process of European integration.

Regarding our hypotheses formulated in the conceptual section (see the introductory chapter of this volume), evidence of empirical results is rather mixed. Participation in the review system corresponds with higher scores in average math achievement and slightly reduced inequality, but it does not significantly change education policy outputs like school autonomy. Moreover, the more often a country takes part in the review system, the more it tends to pay comparatively high salaries to teachers. At the same time, we have seen that high teacher salaries do not have a positive effect on the performance level of students in secondary education. Consequently, IO consulting services do have an impact, but not always in the desired way.

According to our first hypothesis, we expected countries to be more reluctant to adapt to EU policy goals if they are net payers to the EU. At least the bivariate results are in line with our hypothesis because net-contributing countries show a lower share of students and a lower per capita expenditure on educational institutions, which is not in line with the goals of the Lisbon Strategy. In the full models controlling for additional covariates, however, only the effect on privatization remains significant. Rather than an indicator of reluctance to change, being a net payer might also correspond with a high commitment to the EU, the process of integration, and the goals of the Bologna Process and the Lisbon Strategy. Therefore, our results are ambiguous in this respect.

Furthermore, we referred to norm setting of IOs in the Bologna Process and in the Lisbon Strategy. Here, duration of membership in the Bologna Process was expected to increase the policy change towards the goals of the EU. Results of our analysis are clear: becoming a member of the EU corresponds with a considerable increase in the share of students in the working population and in per capita expenditure on education. In addition, duration of Bologna membership increased the share of students in the working population as well as per capita expenditure on education—even though the latter effect disappeared after we controlled for additional covariates. Once again, the attribution of cause and effect remains debatable, but the "anticipatory obedience" of upcoming members of the EU is an obvious effect of the IO on national education policies.

Perhaps, our rather ambiguous results regarding the "soft governance" of the OECD via opinion formation and consulting services, and the clear effects of the EU reflect differences in the degree of institutionalization of governance capacities. It matters, in other words, whether an IO is able to set norms as a formally institutionalized organization or whether an IO can only spread information and is condemned to hope that nation states make the right use of it.

Moreover, our analysis clearly demonstrated that there is a correspondence of welfare regime types carrying historical ideas of powerful collective actors with outcomes of education systems. By far the best performing countries in math are Japan and South Korea, which form the "legacy of Confucianism" regime, while the southern countries perform worst. In the light of the basic guiding principles the former result makes sense since the emphasis on entrepreneurial spirit and self-reliance goes in line with a high appreciation of education. On the other hand, why does this argument not fit the "southern" type, which is also based on strong family bonds? Further research should figure out more precisely the differences between these regimes. In any case, the extremely high appreciation of education, wisdom, and perfection in style is unique to the Confucian ideology (Weber 1972: 610), whereas the emphasis on male breadwinners and family support in the "southern" type probably does not encourage educational performance.

As regards transformation capacities, we did not observe impeding or decelerating effects of veto structures and veto players. This is a very interesting result which hints at a completely different view on transformation capacities, especially because we even identified some positive effects on change in education policies. Yet, the reasons why this is the case are somewhat speculative. It could be that especially in countries with "inert" political structures, actors prepare political concepts and legislative proposals more carefully in a collaborative setting, allowing them to consider and include elements of alternative drafts of their political opponents. At least, this interpretation is in line with results of the qualitative case studies of Niemann and Bieber (Chapters 4 and 5 in this volume).

Finally, we analyzed determinants of delta-convergence in secondary education and found out that with respect to school autonomy in deciding on course content, countries of the "legacy of Confucianism" regime are most similar to the ideal case, Finland. Autonomy in deciding on course content, in turn, had a positive effect on performance. In contrast, countries of the "southern" type converged best with regard to autonomy in staffing and had the largest divergence in autonomy in deciding on course content. This pattern was similar in the "minimal Bismarck" regime type. Thus, although "southern" and "minimal Bismarck" states do show convergence to the Finnish ideal-type, they do so only in dimensions which do not increase student performance. Since the pupil-teacher ratio is comparatively high in both regimes, we conclude that these countries pursue unprofitable investment strategies in their secondary education policies.

In sum, our analyses revealed an apparent change in education policies. In general, this change confirms our expectation of an internationalization of education policies. In addition, results corroborate our theoretical model in that IO governance instruments do indeed have an impact on change of national education policies and their outcomes. Aside from that, countries' responses toward the internationalization of education policies are moderated by their specific transformation capacities. Nevertheless, the critical acclaim of our theoretical model requires some qualifications. First, not all governance instruments turned out to be effective, as was the case with the effect of OECD education reviews on school autonomy. Certainly, school autonomy is just one topic among many others highlighted in the reviews, but it is an important policy indicator which has both desired and undesired effects on educational outcomes. Secondly, some intervening factors were significant, but not always in the direction we expected. Moreover, in some cases causality is not unambiguous. The effect of being an EU net financial contributor on the share of private expenditure on tertiary educational institutions might indicate that there simply is a correspondence between being a net payer to the EU and having a privatized educational system. Further research is needed in order to test alternative measurements of changing education policy, including differences of policy agendas and implementation, as well as a distinction between member and nonmember countries (see e.g. Jakobi 2009b). Moreover, future research on change in the outcome dimension of education policies should focus on the microlevel using individual or household panel data, since individual level data is much better suited to measuring effects of education policy change on outcomes and to avoiding an ecological fallacy.

Appendix: Additional Models

Table 10A.1 Output of secondary education policy—school autonomy indicators and level of teachers' input, OLS regressions[a]

	PT-Ratio 0	PT-Ratio 1	PT-Ratio 2	PT-Ratio 3	Teaching hours 0	Teaching hours 1	Teaching hours 2	Teaching hours 3
GDP per capita	0.03	0.03	–	-0.18**	–	2.97	–	-4.23+
Cum. num. OECD reviews	0.03	-0.06	–	-0.09	-2.94	-4.95	–	2.41
Left-of-center government		-1.18	–	-0.08		171.51	–	96.73*
Right-of-center government		-1.55	–	0.91		161.93	–	89.25**
Presidential veto player		4.95**	–	2.57*		261.37**	–	338.84***
Bicameral veto player		0.6	–	1.32+		34.89	–	64.70+
Minimal Bismarck			reference	reference			reference	reference
Liberal		–	4.15***	8.28***		–	287.67**	307.11***
Social-democratic		–	-1.26**	3.26*		–	30.29	124.87+
Conservative		–	-0.56	3.37*		–	93.50+	182.41**
Southern		–	1.14	1.7		–	129.43	76.14*
Legacy of Confucianism		–	6.38**	8.55***		–	-45.38	-278.15***
Constant	12.44***	12.52***	11.76***	11.38***	717.1***	449.8***	601.7***	474.81***
N	235	87	156	87	134	80	134	80
R²	0	0.38	0.52	0.82	0	0.38	0.41	0.84

Notes: [a] Huber-White Standard Errors +p≤.10; *p≤.05; **p≤.01; ***p≤.001.

Notes

1. Data access was difficult and was conducted through the OECD website and its publication and document section. There is no data on reviews available for 1995 or earlier.
2. http://eacea.ec.europa.eu/education/eurydice/index_en.php.
3. The indicator is an index that measures the feasibility of policy change by aggregating the number of independent government branches with veto power, legislative fractionalization, the extent of alignment, and also judiciary and sub-federal entities. The index theoretically ranges from 0–1, while higher scores indicate less feasibility of change. The indicator was provided by the Quality of Government Institute (http://www.qog.pol.gu.se).
4. These additional countries are Bulgaria, Cyprus, Estonia, Latvia, Lithuania, Malta, Romania, and Slovenia.
5. http://stats.oecd.org/.
6. See Jan Teorell, Nicholas Charron, Marcus Samanni, Sören Holmberg and Bo Rothstein (2009). The Quality of Government Dataset, version 17 June 09. University of Gothenburg: The Quality of Government Institute, http://www.qog.pol.gu.se.
7. http://www.census.gov/ipc/www/idb/.
8. Our data were structured in long format in order to use the variable "year" as a grouping variable. We computed Levene's robust test statistic, referring to the mean value to measure the dispersion within groups. Since all years have been included in the analyses, the test reports significant results if there is a significant difference between any two years of the period, not only between the first and last year (see Jakobi and Teltemann 2009: 8).
9. It is possible to use the share of the working population as a dependent variable because the fixed effect model captures all unobserved differences in the demographic composition of the countries, and there are no sharp breaks in the demographic development within countries during the observed period. But in the random effects specification, these effects may by blurred by systematic differences in the demographic composition of the regime types.

References

Baker, David P., Rodrigo Fabrega, Claudia Galindo, and Jacob Mishook (2004) "Instructional Time and National Achievement: Cross-National Evidence," *Prospects* 34 (3), 311–34.

Blatchford, Peter, Anthony Russell, Paul Bassett, Penelope Brown, and Clare Martin (2007) "The Effect of Class Size on the Teaching of Pupils Aged 7–11 Years," *School Effectiveness and School Improvement* 18 (2), 147–72.

Castles, Francis G. and Herbert Obinger (2008) "Worlds, Families, Regimes: Country Clusters in European and OECD Area Public Policy," *West European Politics* 31 (1/2), 321–44.

Ertl, Hubert (2006) "European Union Policies in Education and Training: The Lisbon Agenda as a Turning Point," *Comparative Education* 42 (1), 5–27.

Esping-Andersen, Gøsta (1985) "Power and Distributional Regimes," *Politics & Society* 14–(2), 223–56.

Esping-Andersen, Gøsta (1990) *The Three Worlds of Welfare Capitalism*, Cambridge: Polity Press.
European Council (2000) *Presidency Conclusions* (Online: http://www.europarl.europa.eu/summits/lis1_en.htm, last access: August 12, 2009).
Field, Andy P. (2007) "Homogeneity of Variance," in N.J. Salkind, ed., *Encyclopedia of Measurement and Statistics*, Vol. 2, Thousand Oaks, CA: Sage, 442–43.
Glaser, R.E. (1983) "Levene's Robust Test of Homogeneity of Variances," in S. Kotz, N. Lloyd Johnson, and C.B. Read, eds., *Encyclopedia of Statistical Sciences*, Volume 4, New York: Wiley, 608–10.
Greene, William H., ed. (2008) *Econometric Analysis*, Volume 6, Upper Saddle River, NJ: Pearson Prentice Hall.
Halaby, Charles N. (2004): "Panel Models in Sociological Research: Theory into Practice," in *Annual Review of Sociology*, Vol. 30, 507–44.
Heichel, Stephan and Thomas Sommerer (2007) "Unterschiedliche Pfade, ein Ziel? Spezifikationen im Forschungsdesign und Vergleichbarkeit der Ergebnisse bei der Suche nach der Konvergenz nationalstaatlicher Politiken," in Holzinger, Katharina, Helge Jörgens, and Christoph Knill, eds., *PVS Sonderband 'Transfer, Diffusion und Konvergenz von Politiken'*, Wiesbaden: VS-Verlag, 107–30.
Henisz, Witold J. (2002) "The Institutional Environment for Infrastructure Investment," *Industrial and Corporate Change* 11 (2), 355–89.
Héritier, Adrienne (1993) "Policy-Analyse. Elemente der Kritik und Perspektiven der Neuorientierung," in Héritier, Adrienne, ed., *Policy Analyse. Kritik und Neuorientierung*, PVS-Sonderheft 23/1993, Opladen: Westdeutscher Verlag, 9–36.
Inglot, Tomasz (2008) *Welfare States in East Central Europe, 1914–2004*, New York: Cambridge University Press.
Jakobi, Anja P. (2007) *The Comparative Analysis of Political Programs. Large-N Analyses with Data from International Organizations*, TranState Working Paper No. 69, Bremen: CRC 597.
Jakobi, Anja P. (2009a) *Global Education Policy in the Making: International Organizations and Lifelong Learning*, Manuscript, University of Bremen.
Jakobi, Anja P. (2009b) *International Organizations and Lifelong Learning. From Agenda Setting to Policy Diffusion*, Houndmills: Palgrave.
Jakobi, Anja P. and Teltemann, Janna (2009) *Convergence and Divergence in Welfare State Development: An Assessment of Education Policy in OECD Countries*, TranState Working Paper No. 93, Bremen: CRC 597.
Keune, Maarten (2009) "Mittel- und osteuropäische Wohlfahrtsstaaten im Vergleich: Typen und Leistungsfähigkeit," in C. Klenner and S. Leiber, eds., *Wohlfahrtsstaaten und Geschlechterungleichheit in Mittel- und Osteuropa Kontinuität und postsozialistische Transformation in den EU-Mitgliedsstaaten*, Wiesbaden: VS Verlag für Sozialwissenschaften, 59–84.
Kuhnle, Stein (2007) "Which Way Forward for Korea's Welfare State. Is the Nation Ready to Face Higher Taxes Necessary to Finance More State Support," *The Korea Harald*, July 18, 2007, 7.
Lange, Bettina and Nafsika Alexiadou (2007) "New Forms of European Union Governance in the Education Sector? A Preliminary Analysis of the Open Method of Coordination," *European Educational Research Journal* 6 (4), 321–34.
Leuze, Kathrin, Tillmann Brandt, Anja P. Jakobi, Kerstin Martens, Alexander Nagel, Alessandra Rusconi, and Ansgar Weymann (2008) *Analyzing the Two-Level Game.*

International and National Determinants of Change in Education Policy Making. TranState Working Paper No. 72, Bremen: CRC 597.

Loh, W.Y. (1987) "Some Modifications of Levene's Test of Variance Homogeneity," *Journal of Statistical Computation and Simulation* 28 (3), 213–26.

Murai, Tomoko (2004) "The Foundation of the Mexican Welfare State and Social Security Reform in the 1990s," *The Developing Economies* 42 (2), 262–87.

Nagel, Alexander, Tonia Bieber, Anja P. Jakobi, Philipp Knodel, Dennis Niemann, and Janna Teltemann (2009) *Measuring Transformation: A Mixed-Method-Approach to the Internationalization of Education Politics*, TranState Working Paper No. 83, Bremen: CRC 597.

OECD (2004) *Learning for Tomorrow's World. First Results from PISA 2003*, Paris: OECD.

Posch, Peter (1998) "The Ecologisation of Schools in Austria," *PEB Exchange. The Journal of the OECD Programme on Educational Building* 34 (June), 12–15.

Santiago, Paulo, José Joaquín Brunner, Guy Haug, Salvador Malo, and Paola Di Pietrogiacomo (2009) *OECD Reviews of Tertiary Education: Spain*, Paris: OECD.

Schubert, Klaus, Ursula Bazant, and Simon Hegelich, eds. (2008) *Europäische Wohlfahrtssysteme. Ein Handbuch*, Wiesbaden: VS Verlag für Sozialwissenschaften.

Weber, Max (1972) *Wirtschaft und Gesellschaft. Grundriß der verstehenden Soziologie*, Tübingen: Mohr.

Windzio, Michael, Reinhold Sackmann, and Kerstin Martens (2005) *Types of Governance in Education—a Quantitative Analysis*, Transtate Working Paper No. 25, Bremen: CRC 597.

Conclusion

though # 11
Education Policy, Globalization, and the Changing Nation State—Accelerating and Retarding Conditions

Michael Windzio, Kerstin Martens, and Alexander-Kenneth Nagel

In many countries educational policy today is under transformation. New demands of the labor market, the necessity of lifelong learning, technological progress of education delivery, and last but not least international comparative surveys, such as the PISA Study (Programme for International Student Assessment) and the Bologna Process for a common European Higher Education Area bring about challenges for national policymaking in the field of education.

According to the theoretical arguments outlined in the introductory chapter of this volume we expected nation states to change their educational systems in response to these international activities and to orientational frameworks promoted by international organizations (IOs). However, IOs make use of different governance instruments. In addition, idiosyncratic national institutional structures and actors moderate such impulses of IO governance in specific ways. Therefore, the question of how IOs initiate changes in national education policymaking is neither simple nor capable of yielding straightforward answers. This holds true especially in a policy field like education, which in some federal countries is dominated by a dense network of powerful national and subnational actors.

In order to explain these phenomena, we argued in our theoretical framework that IOs stimulate change in domestic education policies by making use of five governance instruments, namely norm setting, opinion formation, financial means, coordinative activities, and consulting services. Since these instruments differ in their capacity to affect national policies, it is reasonable to assume that the degree of change in national policies also depends on available governance instruments. This may especially be the case in the field of education, which was a neglected policy field for a long time (Jakobi, Martens, and Wolf 2010).

The issue of education is now on the agenda of several IOs, such as the United Nations Educational, Scientific and Cultural Organization (UNESCO), the World Health Organization (WHO), and the World Bank. In this volume, we mainly focused on two international initiatives in education policy related to IOs, which are both well established, but with greatly differing governance instruments. At the level of secondary education, the Organisation for Economic Cooperation and Development (OECD) conducts the PISA Study in order to obtain performance benchmarks for national educational institutions, whereas the Bologna Process, in the context of the European Union (EU), aims at a harmonization of tertiary educational systems and degrees within the European region. In addition, the EU proclaimed in its Lisbon Strategy its aim "[...] to become the most competitive and dynamic knowledge-based economy in the world" (European Council 2000; see also Ertl 2006), and the expansion of tertiary education is considered a significant step in pursuit of this goal.

Starting from an idealistic perspective and under the assumption of clear and unequivocal policy models proposed by the IOs, one could argue that if nation states actually followed these models, educational institutions would have to converge toward one common model as proposed by the IO. However, empirical reality does not always fit into idealistic frameworks. Decisionmaking on new policies is a complex process in any case, but it becomes even more challenging if the actors' attitudes toward political subjects depend on ideology and historically inherited national guiding principles which could imply path-dependencies. Moreover, in many countries domestic institutions are supposed to impede or to retard, but probably also to accelerate convergence toward policy outcomes proposed by the IO. Having a complex veto structure, including many veto players and points could be obstructive to change since such characteristics diminish national transformation capacities (see the introductory chapter of this volume). It is thus questionable whether countries adapt smoothly to the proposed models, and even if they do so, it is not yet clear how quickly and to what extent national policy outcomes change.

Moreover, in the preceding literature it remained an open question if countries with institutions that were already well adapted *before* the process of internationalization began, change more quickly and, in the end, fit better to the policy models proposed by the IOs. In contrast, if the necessity of change to an international model of education becomes collectively accepted, in a sense that refusal to move to convergence would result in exclusion from the upcoming transnational and cosmopolitan world culture, then countries most dissimilar to the proposed model might try to catch up with the better-adapted countries in order to compensate for their "misfit" (Börzel and Risse 2000). In this regard, our theoretical framework outlined in the introduction to this volume turned out to be flexible and sophisticated enough to derive clear hypotheses, but also to leave room for alternative explanations for some unexpected findings.

In the following section of this chapter we summarize the main results of the empirical studies and try to identify common patterns of IO-driven change of educational policies in different countries. We relate this synopsis to our theoretical framework and reflect on possible explanations for unexpected results. Then, we give a critical assessment of our theoretical framework and our case selection, regarding their strengths and weaknesses. Finally, we outline further research on the outcomes of changing education policies, which should focus on individual data on outcomes in secondary and tertiary education.

Transformation of educating states

The interplay of social change and the transformation of the educating state is not a new phenomenon. Historically, the question of educating a sufficient number of persons necessary to rule a bureaucratic state already existed in the ancient civilizations of Egypt, China, and Rome (Weber 1972: 834). However, up to the Middle Ages access to literacy and proficiency in Latin, as well as higher education, were restricted to small elites, whereas the vast majority of the population maintained its traditional way of life, based on agriculture, with a majority of the population being illiterate. It was not until the formation of the nation state and the dissemination of Enlightenment thought during the transition to modernity in Europe that education for the masses became a matter of public concern. In the wake of the "enclosures" in the seventeenth century in England, for instance, which led to a redistribution and privatization of land and resulted in mass migration into the rapidly growing cities (Marx 1968: 753), the emerging urban underclass was perceived as a threat to the stability and integration of the nation state. As Weymann argues in Chapter 3 of this volume, the state began to undertake the challenging task of reintegrating the deracinated agrarian population by providing basic, but compulsory education. By including an increasing number of persons into educational institutions and human capital formation, the expansion of the educating state (see Weymann in this volume), in turn, led to transformations of state and society.

Up to the nineteenth century changes in national educational institutions can be regarded as adaptations to domestic functional requirements. The post-Second World War period saw for the first time an international configuration of competing superpowers, the U.S.A. and the Soviet Union, stimulating an expansion of higher education. Claiming to have implemented a superior way of organizing economic and social life, the Soviet Union invested vast amounts of capital into its cosmonaut program and was successful in launching the first satellite into the orbit. In many western countries this event has been interpreted as an indicator of technical superiority of socialist countries and induced the so called "Sputnik Shock." Consequently, the U.S. administration led by Dwight D. Eisenhower expanded educational institutions, especially in technical and scientific fields. However, even though this development was triggered by configurations of power in the world system, changes in domestic education policies were prepared and implemented by national actors and not by IOs.

At the present time we witness new agendas and new arenas of policymaking (Martens, Rusconi, and Leuze 2007). In the field of education, transnational actors appeared on the agenda and developed their own ideas of how to structure educational institutions. According to the analysis of Niemann (Chapter 4 in this volume) these new actors definitely account for recent changes in *German* education policies. Before the OECD published its PISA Study and revealed the painful result of Germany's secondary students' mediocrity, and before the Bologna Process set clear norms for the transformation of tertiary educational institutions, no noteworthy reforms in education policy took place. From the 1970s onward there even was a stalemate in education policymaking. After PISA and Bologna, both secondary and tertiary educational institutions underwent changes which were fundamental and comprehensive. This is all the more striking because Germany is a federal system with a bicameral veto structure and a "cultural sovereignty" for its federal states.

In fact, with respect to the implementation of the new degree program Germany proved itself to be an eager proponent of the Bologna Process. In 1998 German policymakers had already appended a tentative introduction of B.A./M.A. study programs to the "Framework Act for Higher Education." Just one year later, basic principles for accrediting

B.A./M.A. programs were developed. At the first sight, Germany's complex polity and power distribution was supposed to impede or to retard the reform process. However, as Niemann convincingly argues, the decentralization of power and the corresponding detriment of transformation capacities were compensated by "The Standing Conference of the Ministers of Education and Cultural Affairs of the Länder" (KMK). The KMK had a coordinating function since 1948 and it emerged as the central national political actor in coordinating education policy and prepared the transformation to the B.A./M.A. program. Thus, veto players and points do not necessarily impede or retard change in education policy initiated by an IO; if there is a specific institution that can be used to coordinate different actors and to circumvent inert polity structures, such veto players and points are not obstacles.

At the level of secondary education, the response towards the results of the PISA Study came instantaneously. In 2002 there was a consensus in the KMK on educational standards, as well as upon monitoring and evaluation of outcomes of secondary education. As the German example demonstrated, even if institutional modes of decisionmaking are complex and prevailing national guiding principles do not fit the proposed models, a smooth and quick transformation of educational institutions remains feasible if there is a high degree of consensus among political actors. Niemann pointed out that such consensus and consistency could circumvent veto points in advance. From the perspective of an empirical analysis on the functioning of political institutions this result could stimulate a radically new view on polity structures. Further research should investigate more systematically the conditions under which veto players and points are undermined by political actors, and also which institutions could serve as a functional equivalent in a particular policy field if no powerful centralized authority exists there.

Strikingly, in her chapter on the harmonization of education policy in Switzerland, Bieber comes to a similar result (Chapter 5 in this volume). Switzerland is characterized by reform-obstructing institutions like direct democracy, federalism, and consociationalism in its multilingual and multiethnic setting. Similar to the Länder in the German case, cantons in Switzerland are important actors in education policy-making. Moreover, similarly to the case in the U.S.A., communities also act powerfully in this field, resulting in a fragmented and disintegrated institutional structure at first sight. In line with a rather pessimistic view on Swiss transformation capacities there was a backlog of education reforms in the 1980s. However, despite of the 26 different cantonal education systems, actors in the field of education have proved themselves capable of acting as a result of intercantonal agreements. The goals of the Bologna Declaration have been quickly realized, so that Switzerland even became the "poster child" of the reform. The implementation of the Bologna goals in tertiary education is almost complete, and the last substantial reform of higher education polity structure took place in 2006, when the people and the cantons approved a revision of the constitution in a referendum. According to this revision, Federation and cantons enhanced their cooperation in governing higher education institutions.

Regarding secondary education, some political actors regarded the PISA Study as a "deliverance" from the backlog of necessary reforms. As a response to the moderate outcome of the PISA test in the field of literacy, quality assurance standards were widely accepted and the reform project "HarmoS" implemented with the aim of harmonizing the fragmented landscape in secondary education. The "HarmoS" reforms increased the minimum number of years of schooling from nine years to 11 and prescribed one foreign language in addition to the local standard language. Again, as in Germany, there was a powerful institution, the "Swiss Conference of Cantonal Ministers of Education" (EDK) that was used to circumvent the complex veto structure in Switzerland. Additionally, the passive behavior of potential veto players in Switzerland could be an indicator of a high consensus on the necessity of a reform. Overall, conditions for a quick and successful adaptation are similar in Germany and Switzerland, and this change actually took place despite federalism, veto players, and a misfit of guiding principles.

In contrast, the case of England outlined by Knodel and Walkenhorst (Chapter 6 in this volume) shows that many reforms had already been implemented in the early 1990s, including a policy shift towards marketization. These reforms happened before the PISA and Bologna initiatives were begun. Following our theoretical framework, there is no well-developed veto structure in England. Change in education policy—if desired—could have happened smoothly and quickly. Since there was already a comprehensive overlap between tertiary education in England and the model prescribed in the Bologna Declaration, the majority of political actors did not consider a substantive transformation necessary. However, in the meantime it became clear that the English system, especially the four-year Bachelor's (B.A.) and the one-year Master's (M.A.), does not perfectly fit into the globally converging tertiary education system. All other countries seem to do slightly differently and also a bit better than England. Therefore, IOs initiated at least a political discourse which is still going on in England and the result of which is not clear yet. According to our theoretical model, in the near future we expect a quick adaptation in England because of the absence of veto players and points as soon as a consensus on the necessity of transformation has emerged.

Interestingly, despite the moderate PISA test results for England, there was no public "PISA shock" like in Germany. This calmness almost certainly has to do with the fact that using testing systems was already very common in England. Nevertheless, as a result of the PISA Study political actors became sensitized to education policies in other countries and were able to compare English students with students in the rest of the OECD world. Not surprisingly, they drew their attention to countries that ranked higher, like Finland, for instance.

New Zealand is in many respects similar to the English case and has been analyzed by Dobbins in Chapter 7 of this volume. The author showed that the smooth introduction of several new modifications was facilitated by factors which we describe in our theoretical framework. Due to its unicameralism and near-absence of veto players New Zealand's transformation capacity is comparatively high. Once a consensus on policies has emerged, obstacles impeding the implementation of reforms rarely exist. In addition, political actors show a high degree of consensus over education policy goals and an overall commitment to economization and internationalization of education. This corresponds to the fact that New Zealand's system of tertiary education already fitted quite well to the model proposed in the Bologna Declaration. At the level of secondary education the OECD did not trigger groundbreaking changes. New Zealand's PISA results even reinforced existing policies. Nevertheless, New Zealand's tertiary education underwent some "small scale policy adjustment" processes, but these changes were implemented in an uncomplicated way.

As a contrasting case of weak response to international initiatives in education policy, Dobbins and Martens investigated the impact of the Bologna Process and the PISA Study on education policies in the U.S.A. (Chapter 8 in this volume). For a long time, secondary education in the U.S.A. has been subject to evaluation, but only within the domestic sphere and not in an internationally comparative design. Benchmarking is deeply rooted in the American society, so parents refer to rankings and ratings in order to choose an appropriate school for their children. However, the bad outcome in the international comparison revealed by the PISA Study did not trigger any noteworthy public debate. This is astonishing on the one hand, since it was the U.S. administration that gave the first initiative for conducting an international literacy assessment for outcomes of secondary education (Martens, Rusconi, and Leuze 2007). On the other hand, owing to the domestic evaluation programs the public was already aware of the situation and it is commonplace that "shocks" only occur when an event involves a "big surprise."

Ironically, the effects of the Bologna Process are more strongly felt in the U.S.A., although it does not belong to the European region—neither geographically nor politically. Recently, however, political actors began to look beyond their own noses and the progress in harmonizing tertiary education in Europe (and beyond) stimulated a debate on the introduction of three-year Bachelor degrees, which would enhance compatibility with most other industrialized countries. So at least with regard to the ongoing public debate, the Bologna Process has indeed had an impact on the U.S.A. Yet, it is not clear whether this debate will result in a concrete policy output in the field of education.

Who responds to IO governance and why? Accelerating and decelerating conditions

When we compare our four case studies and the contrasting case of the U.S.A., results can be interpreted from our theoretical perspective. First, we found strong evidence of the fit-misfit argument outlined in our theoretical framework. Even though neither New Zealand and England has significant veto players nor points, they show only slight changes in education policy as a response to IO governance. From their points of view the trend toward convergence of tertiary education systems in the wake of the Bologna Process—which applies not only to EU member states—is a dissemination of their own institutions into the wider world. Consequently, no change is necessary since the EU defines their model as an ideal type for other countries to converge toward. However, a closer look reveals that four-year Bachelor degrees still imply some obstacles to the international compatibility and the free movement of students. That is why English policymakers debate extensively on the introduction of a three-year program and on enhancing the Masters to a two-year program. In any case, the guiding principles of a market-based society and education as human capital formation, as well as the traditional English two-cycle degree structure fit much better to the Bologna model than does Humboldt's idea of self-fulfillment and pluralism, which was the guiding principle of higher education in Germany for a long time. After all, there is no substantial change in education policy ascribable to IOs in England and New Zealand. Many reforms had been already implemented during the 1980s and early 1990s. On the basis of these initial conditions, England and New Zealand got into the new global world order after 1990, and when the IOs made their debut as international policy makers in the field of education, there simply was no necessity to implement radical modifications any more. On the other hand, Germany and Switzerland had a backlog of reforms up to the 1990s. Because of an apparent misfit of tertiary degrees to the orientational framework elaborated in the Bologna Declaration as well as the bad performance in secondary education, Germany and Switzerland changed quickly and smoothly in response to the IO impact. In the Swiss case, the PISA Study was even considered to be a salvation from the backlog of reforms. Simply by publishing their results, the OECD provided the basis for naming and shaming on the global scale and triggered rapid and substantial reforms.

What do we learn from these results with regard to our theoretical model? In line with our theoretical arguments outlined in the introductory chapter to this volume, opinion formation by benchmarking and evaluation turned out to be a very efficient IO governance instrument. But this instrument only works effectively as an accelerator of change under specific conditions. First, the IO must refer to an unanimously accepted normative yardstick, which clearly is the case regarding standardized test outcomes in secondary education. Second, national policymakers will initiate debates on reforms only if they identify a misfit of domestic institutions and policy goals promoted by the IO. Third, as our contrasting case of the U.S.A. has shown, widely accepted normative yardsticks and a clear indication of misfit are far from being sufficient conditions for change in education policies. The absence of a public discourse on PISA in the U.S.A. is a result of prior awareness of poor performance in secondary education. It is, in other words, not an objectively measured but a subjectively perceived misfit which triggers transformations in education policy. Finally, responses to opinion formation can be substantial and instantaneous when national policymakers are eager to change educational institutions, but have suffered from inflexible institutions and a backlog of reforms for long time. On the other hand, if one of these conditions is not met, there will probably be no substantial change in the educating state.

At first sight it seems to be obvious that norm setting by IOs is very effective in transforming domestic education policies. We have seen in our quantitative analyses (Chapter 10 in this volume), for instance, that becoming a member of the EU does indeed have an impact on change in tertiary education policies. Since the EU set clear and rather unambiguous norms in the Bologna Declaration and in the Lisbon Strategy, the catching-up processes we observed in the group of new EU members could be interpreted as clear evidence of a causal effect of IO norm setting. Strictly speaking, this conclusion must be qualified as the estimation of causal effects of becoming an EU member on policy outcomes might suffer from selection processes. In econometrics such kind of selectivity means that observations get systematically into the "treatment," meaning here the explanatory variable (Cameron and Trivedi 2005: 546). Applied to our case, only those countries which already have the capacity to adapt quickly might either be selected by the EU to become members, or have selected themselves into the group of EU member candidates. But in any case the effect is ascribable to the EU impact at least to some extent since most countries have made great efforts to qualify for EU membership.

Concerning IO governance by consulting services we find rather mixed evidence of effectiveness. As an interviewee in Bieber's case study on Switzerland stated, the OECD has been regarded as a consultancy who provides external legitimacy of decisions made anyhow by internal actors, but which are difficult to implement. First and foremost, consulting services provided such legitimacy for decisions on policy reforms in the Swiss case. This leads to the question of why the OECD could play the role of an external source of legitimacy at all. Certainly, by conducting the PISA Study and by giving consulting services based on in-depth knowledge and expertise on determinants of student performance as well as on institution building in the field of education, the OECD became an authority whose statements and recommendations could not be rejected by politicians simply because the politicians were not able to hold a candle to the OECD experts. From a broader perspective, our quantitative results in Chapter 10 give only weak evidence of an impact of consulting services—measured here as the cumulative number of OECD reviews—on education policy outputs and their outcomes. Regardless of this weak evidence, we still assume an impact of such reviews since they are well elaborated and based on in-depth expertise. Further research should also try to investigate their effect with regard to the content of the review and also by applying qualitative methods.

Generally, by coordinating the evaluation of the national system and comparing it to other countries, the OECD created immense informal pressure on German policymakers to improve secondary education. By highlighting the shortcomings of German secondary education and giving examples of best practice from other countries at the same time, the OECD successfully promoted its orientational framework in secondary education through opinion formation as well as coordinative activities. Thereby, opinion formation and coordinative activities worked hand in hand. Since the OECD cannot govern by rules or financial means, other aspects like information exchange, knowledge creation, mutual learning, or resource pooling were at the center of its activities. Even though the EU Commission is a full member in the Bologna Process, its role can generally be interpreted as that of a coordinating institution which also provides financial incentives (for example within the EU "Framework Programme for Research and Technological Development").

However, coordinative activities and financial means as governance instruments do not play a major role in the English case. It seems that IOs treat England, via the UK government, with kid gloves since we mainly found evidence for rather soft governance, as for example opinion formation.

Transformation capacities: Being trapped in structures vs. using functional equivalents

As regards our four case studies veto players and points obviously do not play a decisive role if there is a consensus between political actors or if there is a powerful institution which can be used to bypass complex veto structures. In the cases of Germany and Switzerland such institutions exist: The KMK and the EDK had been established long before the internationalization of education policy began and they coordinate the fragmented decisionmaking processes in the field of education. Particularly when there are complex veto structures, actors might anticipate demanding decisionmaking processes and transfer decisionmaking to these superordinate institutions. This is an important insight which is also relevant for general social theory building: Although structure constraints agencies in the process of decisionmaking, actors are able to establish new institutions or to make use of already existing structures, which are functionally equivalent but more easily to handle, in order to circumvent joint-decision traps. This argument provides a preliminary explanation of why we encounter a high degree of change in countries with many political constraints. Obviously, these constraints do indeed have a mediating impact on IO governance, but, it turns out, not in the way we expected. Provided that there is a consensus among actors, they can be flexible and creative enough to find effective institutional arrangements that facilitate policymaking in the field of education. As we have seen in the case of Switzerland, opinion formation on the part of the IOs can be an impetus toward such kind of collective action, which takes place if all other conditions, such as, for example, the subjective perception of a misfit, are met.

These considerations are supported empirically by the quantitative analysis on a much higher number of countries presented by Jakobi, Teltemann, and Windzio in Chapter 10 of this volume. Overall, veto players and points did not retard change in the output of education policymaking. In some cases, they even showed accelerating effects. Moreover, the analysis of convergence in secondary education policy output and outcomes revealed that new EU members compensated for their initial misfit by catching up and taking off quickly, which resulted in a clear beta-convergence. It became obvious in the fixed effects regression models that becoming a member of the EU in 2004 had a strong effect on increasing the share of students in the working population and also on increasing the per capita expenditure on tertiary education, which is in accordance with the Lisbon Strategy. Having set clear and explicit norms, the EU thus had a considerable impact on institutions of tertiary education in new member countries. Probably, successful reforms took place in the new member countries in preparation for membership, but this would indicate an effect of the EU nonetheless. This confirms our argument that the transformation of the educating state is especially quick and fundamental when most significant actors reach a consensus on subjectively perceived misfit of domestic educational institutions. Given this condition, in some cases these actors find functional equivalents to inefficient institutions, allowing them to circumvent joint-decision traps.

Moreover, in the quantitative analyses in Chapter 10, welfare types have been used as indicators of normative guiding principles established and handed down in history by powerful collective actors. According to quantitative results predicting average math performance in secondary education, by far the best performing regime is the "legacy of Confucianism" type. The main guiding principles in this regime are emphasis on entrepreneurial spirit and self-reliance, which are in line with a high appreciation of education. But social-democratic and liberal regimes also performed comparatively well, whereas southern countries had the Lowest-ranked positions. Thus, with regard to educational outcomes, it seems that the guiding principles of self-reliance and entrepreneurial spirit in conjunction with a high value for education are most consistent with the requirements of a globalized knowledge society. However, since there is a strong indication of beta-convergence both in secondary and tertiary education policies, this does not necessarily mean that countries with "well-fitting" guiding principles respond most quickly to IO governance. Rather the opposite is true, as has been argued above.

A critical assessment of the research design

In this volume we have investigated the impact of IOs on domestic education policymaking. We have shown that even "soft" governance instruments such as opinion formation and consulting services can initiate considerable changes and at the same time, veto players and points do not necessarily hinder or decelerate change. This is what we could show on the basis of our research design. Each single study in this volume provides a great deal of new insight into governance of education policy at the national level as well as on multilevel policymaking. Certainly, research should not overstrain the capacity of its design and should be aware of what insights it can yield. At a closer look, our research design is not appropriate to a comparison of the effectiveness and efficiency of each IO governance instrument. This is because we analyze the impact of two different IOs with regard to their respective governance instruments on the one hand, and two different subfields of education policy on the other hand—secondary and tertiary education. Between these two subfields there is one important difference with respect to our research question: whereas internationalization and harmonization of programs in tertiary education have been necessary because of the high mobility of students even before the Bologna Process was initiated, there is no urgent need to harmonize secondary education systems, because mobility of students in secondary education is rather an exception. If the need for quick harmonization is low, we would not expect IOs to impose strict regulations. Moreover, the OECD has no legal authority and is thus unable to control national education policies directly. IO governance through norm setting is effective if it relates to members of an organization which has decision-making authorities with regard to the policy field of interest. Although the EU is not able to impose norms on domestic education policies, because of the commitment to EU integration in general and the harmonization of degree structures in tertiary education in particular, the Bologna Process is close to what we described as norm setting in the introductory chapter of this volume. Yet, a comparative evaluation of each instrument was never the aim of our project. Our results indicate that each IO makes use of its specific instruments and is indeed effective in doing so. Astonishingly, without any legal authority but only by opinion formation and coordinative activities, the OECD has triggered dramatic changes in Germany and Switzerland. In contrast, by establishing and consolidating standards, which became similar to norms, and further, by promoting the Bologna Process, the EU became increasingly involved in the process of transforming national education policies. Today, the Bologna Process affects nearly all EU countries and even countries outside of the EU. Moreover, overall, these changes occurred regardless of veto players and points.

Without doubt, our design is an appropriate one to shed light on these processes; nevertheless, some questions remain unanswered. First, our case selection in the qualitative part was driven by the need for variance in veto points. In parallel with the institutional structures we got different guiding principles, but in a way which made it difficult to distinguish between effects of institutional structures and national guiding principles. To solve this problem, we made use of a typology of six welfare regimes as indicators of guiding principles in our quantitative analysis. It has been shown, for instance, that liberal and social-democratic ideas fit comparatively well, but that countries of the "legacy of Confucianism" regime had by far the best outcome in terms of average PISA math and reading literacy scores. Consequently, we could draw on our "large-N" regression models in order to compensate for shortcomings in our case selection in the quantitative part. But again, there is a problem here as well, which is not merely one of technical nature: the most appropriate proceeding was the application of fixed effects panel regression which estimates effects of change in x on change on y (Halaby 2004). Since our research topic is the transformation of the educating state, change should have been modeled in any of our regression analyses. However, we assumed guiding principles to be constant over time, at least over the period we observed in our data. Hence, when we regard welfare regimes as indicators of guiding principles and model them as explanatory variables, we simply could not use fixed effects regression because it does not permit time-constant predictors for simple algebraic reasons (ibid.: 522). In future research we will therefore enhance our data set with as many additional measurement points as possible and try to estimate fixed effects models including welfare-regime-time interaction effects on the basis of sufficient data. In addition, we will also try to measure changes in national guiding principles.

Outlook to further research

So far the basic arrangement of our project has a clear focus on institutions. We tried to explain change in national education policy as a response to IO governance. Even if we produced some results on outcomes of education policies in the quantitative part of our project, further research should focus more on the outcome dimension at the individual level. It is still unclear if policy change induced by the IOs actually has an impact on individual behavior and achievements. Just to mention one example: the Bologna Process corresponds with an ongoing trend towards globalization. European policymakers thus developed concepts of harmonization of degree structures in tertiary education, but it remains open whether students really show a tendency towards increasing mobility. There are some hints for the German case that even indicate a decline in international student migration as a result of the workload and the rigid schedule of many B.A. programs (Heublein and Hutzsch 2009). Furthermore, even if student migration increases in the future, the question becomes whether social background systematically affects the propensity to go abroad.

Moreover, future research should focus on country-specific effects of social class and migration background on students' literacy outcomes, controlling for other explanatory variables. These analyses should simultaneously address factors at the student and school levels as well as country-specific policies and polity structures. Again, we will have to use all available streams of the PISA Study to investigate these questions in a multilevel framework (Windzio 2008).

Finally, in open democratic societies any change in policies is debatable. This is especially true regarding important issues such as education which stand at the crosslines of ideological debate. What has happened in Europe since the late 1990s is a fundamental change in institutions of tertiary education. Orientational frameworks as promoted by the Bologna Declaration were, among others, marketization, internationalization, and the formation of human capital and a new wealth of nations. Change in education policies took place, but has been in sharp contrast to what some political parties wanted. In addition, the orientational frameworks of the IOs do not fit various historically inherited national guiding principles. Moreover, the transformation of tertiary education institutions might evoke reactions of protest if basic goals like the facilitation of international student migration are not accomplished and rigid schedules and curricula turn out to be obstacles to the internationalization process. Thus, future research should also focus on a thorough analysis of the reactions of those groups which are directly affected by the more or less successful transformation of the education state.

References

Börzel, Tanja A. and Thomas Risse (2000) "When Europe Hits Home: Europeanization and Domestic Change," *European Integration Online Papers* 4(11).

Cameron, Adrian C. and Pravin K. Trivedi (2005) *Microeconometrics. Methods and Applications*, Cambridge: Cambridge University Press.

Ertl, Hubert (2006) "Educational Standards and the Changing Discourses on Education: The Reception and Consequences of the PISA Study in Germany," *Oxford Review of Education* 32(5), 619–34.

European Council (2000) *Presidency Conclusions* (Online: http://www.europarl.europa.eu/summits/lis1_en.htm, last access: August 12, 2009).

Halaby, Charles N. (2004) "Panel Models in Sociological Research: Theory into Practice," *Annual Review of Sociology* 30, 507–44.

Heublein, Ulrich and Christopher Hutzsch (2009) *Wiederholungsuntersuchung zu studienbezogenen Aufenthalten deutscher Studierender in anderen Ländern*. HIS Projektbericht, 3. Fachkonferenz zur Auslandmobilität, Hannover.

Jakobi, Anja P., Kerstin Martens, and Klaus Dieter Wolf, eds. (2010) *Education in Political Science—Discovering a Neglected Field*, London and New York: Routledge.

Martens, Kerstin (2007) "How to Become an Influential Actor—The 'Comparative Turn' in OECD Education Policy," in K. Martens, A. Rusconi, and K. Leuze, eds., *New Arenas of Education Governance—the Impact of International Organizations and Markets on Educational Policy Making*, Houndmills, Basingstoke: Palgrave Macmillan, 40–56.

Martens, Kerstin, Alessandra Rusconi, and Kathrin Leuze, eds. (2007) *New Arenas of Education Governance—the Impact of International Organizations and Markets on Educational Policy Making*, Houndmills, Basingstoke: Palgrave Macmillan.

Marx, Karl (1968) *Das Kapital*, Volume 1, Karl Marx—Friedrich Engels—Werke, No. 23, Dietz Verlag: Berlin.

Weber, Max (1972) *Wirtschaft und Gesellschaft. Grundriss der verstehenden Soziologie*, Tübingen: Mohr.

Windzio, Michael (2008) "Social Structures and Actors: The Application of Multilevel Analysis in Migration Research," *Romanian Journal of Population Research* 2 (1), 113–38.

Index

Adelman, Clifford, 189–91
Archer, Margaret Scotford, 53
ASPAC (Asia Pacific Network of Science and Technology Centres), 217

B.A. (Bachelor's degree), 4, 85, 87, 88, 95, 96, 112, 116, 123, 135, 138, 147, 186–8, 190, 192, 193, 228, 264–8, 275
Bachelor's degree, *see* B.A.
Bavaria, 79, 90, 93, *see also* Germany
Bavarian Act on Higher Education, 90
BBC, 69
BBT (Federal Office for Professional Education and Technology) (Switzerland), 108
Benn, Ernest, 67
BFUG (Bologna Follow-up Group), 122, 202
BMBF (Bundesministerium für Bildung und Forschung/Federal Ministry of Education and Research), 80
Bologna Declaration, *see* Bologna Process
Bologna Follow-up Group, *see* BFUG
Bologna Process, 4, 6, 262, 275
bulk-funding, 159, 165
Bundesrat (Germany), *see* federal council (Germany)
Butler Act (1944, England), 136

Callaghan, James, 137
capitalism, 56, 62, 63, 182
Center of Accreditation and Quality Assurance of the Swiss Universities, *see* OAQ
closure, *see* Weber, Max: closure
Collins, Randall, 53–4
COMENIUS, 211
Comte, August, 56

Concordance Treaty on School Coordination (Switzerland), 110
Conference of Prime Ministers (Germany), *see* MPK (Germany)
country case studies, 5, 20–1, 274
credential meritocracy, *see* credentials
credentialism, *see* credentials
credentials, 54, 59, 61–3, 69, 187
CRUS (Rectors' Conference of the Swiss Universities), 117, 215
cultural accounts, *see* national transformation capacities: guiding principles

DCSF (Department for Children, Schools and Families) (England), 134, 145
Dearing Report, 134, 141–2
Department for Children, Schools and Families (England), *see* DCSF
Department for Innovation, Universities and Skills (England), *see* DIUS
DIUS (Department for Innovation, Universities and Skills) (England), 134
document analysis, 20, 30, 33–7, 45, 79, 106
Durkheim, Émile, 56
Düsseldorf Agreement, 82

economic view on education, 9, 55–6, 61, 63, 67, 69, 94, 96–7, 111, 122, 139, 156, *compare* Smith, Adam
ECTS (European Credit Transfer and Accumulation System), 88, 95, 112, 116, 118, 123, 147
EDI (Federal Department of Home Affairs) (Switzerland), 108
EDK (Swiss Conference of Cantonal Ministers of Education), 107, 109–10, 115, 118, 121, 266, 271

educating state
  institutional development, 56–9
  political economy, 59–61
  role in nation building, 63–4
  world views, 55–6
Education Act (1877, New Zealand), 155
Education Act (1914, New Zealand), 155
Education Act (1986, England), 139
Education Act (1992, England), 140
Education Amendment Act (New Zealand), 156, 160
Education Reform Act (England), 139–40
Education Review Office (New Zealand), *see* ERO
Education Standards Act (2001, New Zealand), 167
educational credentials, *see* credentials
employability, 4, 11, 98, 122, *see also* labor market
England, 132–49
  Bologna Process, 132, 138, 145–9, 266
  education system, 132, 134–7
  educational reforms, 133, 138–43
  exposure to IO governance, 20–1
  governance instruments, 132, 144
  guiding principles, *see* England: national transformation capacities
  national transformation capacities, 21, 133, 135–7, 142, 148–9
  PISA Study, 132, 137–8, 142–5, 149, 267
  policy network, 217, 219
  veto players, *see* England: national transformation capacities
ERASMUS (European Region Action Scheme for the Mobility of University Students), 211
ERO (Education Review Office) (New Zealand), 161, 167
Esping-Andersen, Gøsta, 229, 231
ETHs (Swiss Federal Institutes of Technology), 107–9
EU (European Union)
  Commission: Directorate of Education, 96; Directorate-General for Education and Culture, 106
EUA (European University Association), 43, 146
Europe Unit (England), 147–8
European Credit Transfer and Accumulation System, *see* ECTS
European Economic Area, 115
European Higher Education Area, *see* Bologna Process
European Region Action Scheme for the Mobility of University Students, *see* ERASMUS
European Standards and Guidelines of Quality Assurance, 123, 125
European Union, *see* EU
European University Association, *see* EUA
Eurydice Information Network, 43, 122, 231
EVD (Federal Department of Economic Affairs) (Switzerland), 108
Every Child Matters Scheme (England), 140
excellence initiative (Germany), 87
expert, definition of, 35
expert interviews, 20, 30, 31, 32, 33–7, 38, 41, 45, 46, 47, 79, 106, *compare* expert, definition of

FAZ (Frankfurter Allgemeine Zeitung), 65–8
Federal Act on Universities of Applied Sciences, 116
Federal-Aid-to-Education-Program (U.S.A.), 182
federal council (Germany), 80
Federal Department of Economic Affairs (Switzerland), *see* EVD
Federal Department of Home Affairs (Switzerland), *see* EDI
Federal Law on Promotion and Coordination of Higher Education Institutions (Switzerland), *see* HFKG
Federal Ministry of Education and Research, *see* BMBF (Germany)

Federal Ministry of Education and
  Science (Germany), 83
Federal Republic of Germany,
  see Germany
Federalism Reform (Germany), 87,
  88, 91, 92, 98, 212
FHs (Fachhochschulen/Universities
  of Applied Science), 81, 107–9,
  113, 115–19, 125
Föderalismusreform (Germany),
  see Federalism Reform
Framework Act for Higher Education,
  see HRG
Framework Programme for Research
  and Technological Development,
  217, 271
Frankfurter Allgemeine Zeitung,
  see FAZ
front page coverage of education
  policy, 64–9
Funding Councils (England), 141
Further and Higher Education
  Reform Act (1992,
  England), 141

GATS (General Agreement on Trade
  and Services), 153
GCSE (General Certificate of
  Secondary Education), 139
General Agreement on Trade and
  Services, *see* GATS
General Certificate of Secondary
  Education, *see* GCSE
*German Education Catastrophe,
  The*, 82
Germany, 21, 77–100
  Bologna Process, 77, 84–5, 87–8,
    95–9, 264–5
  delta-convergence, 78, 100
  education system, 79–83
  educational reforms, 77–9, 82–3,
    85–92, 99, *see also* Germany:
    Bologna Process, PISA Study
  exposure to IO governance, 20
  governance instruments, 78, 95,
    98, 99–100
  guiding principles, *see* Germany:
    national transformation
    capacities

national transformation capacities,
  21, 78, 82, 83, 93, 96, 98–100
PISA Study, 77, 84, 86, 92–5, 98–9,
  264–5
policy network, 214–15
veto players, *see* Germany:
  national transformation
  capacities
GEW (Gewerkschaft Erziehung
  und Wissenschaft/Union
  for Education and Science)
  (Germany), 214–15
Gewerkschaft Erziehung und
  Wissenschaft (Germany),
  see GEW
globalization, 54, 63–4, 105
Goldstein, Judith, 14, *compare*
  ideational factors
governance instruments, 7, 10, 12,
  30, 34, 38, 42, 202, 211–17,
  222–4, 228–9, 251–4, 261–2,
  269–74
Green Paper (1997, New Zealand), 163

Hamburg Agreements, 82
HarmoS (Swiss Reform Project for
  the Harmonization of Obligatory
  School), 112–15, 118, 119,
  120–1, 124, 126, 266, *see also*
  Switzerland: educational reforms
Hawke Report (1988, New Zealand),
  160, 163
HDI (Human Development
  Index), 59
HEPI (Higher Education Policy
  Institute) (England), 147–8
Herder, Johann Gottfried, 55
HFKG (Federal Law on Promotion
  and Coordination of Higher
  Education Institutions)
  (Switzerland), 118
Higher Education Policy Institute
  (England), *see* HEPI
HRG (Hochschulrahmengesetz/
  Framework Act for Higher
  Education), 82–3, 87–8, 89, 264
Human Development Index, *see* HDI
Humboldt, Wilhelm von, 55–6, 83,
  111, 122–4, 173

Humboldtism, 156
Hume, David, 55

ideational factors, 14–15
  causal beliefs, 15, 144
  principled beliefs, 15, *compare* guiding principles
  world views, 14–15, 54–6: European understanding of education, 55; French nation state focused concept, 56, *compare* Comte, August, Durkheim, Émile; idealistic concept of education, 55–6, 83, *compare* Humboldt, Wilhelm von; utilitarian concept of education *see* economic view on education; western rationality, 56, *compare* Weber, Max
IHEP (Institute for Higher Education Policy, Washington), 189, 191
illiteracy rates, 59
Improving America's Schools Act, 184
INES (International Indicators of Educational Systems), 185
Institut für Qualitätsentwicklung im Bildungswesen, *see* IQB
Institute for Educational Progress, *see* IQB
Institute for Higher Education Policy (Washington), *see* IHEP
International Education Framework (2004, New Zealand), 157
International Indicators of Educational Systems, *see* INES
international initiatives, 3
international organizations, *see* IOs
interpretation frameworks, *see* national transformation capacities: guiding principles
IOs (international organizations)
  exposure to IO governance, 18–19, 20–1, 78, 133, 199, 204–9, 215, 223–4, 228, 251–2
  governance, 4
  governance instruments, *see* governance instruments
  institutional dynamics of, 6

IQB (Institut für Qualitätsentwicklung im Bildungswesen/Institute for Educational Progress), 87, 94

Joint Science Conference (Germany), 89

Keohane, Robert, 14, *compare* ideational factors
Key Stage National Curriculum Test, *see* SATS
Keynes, John Maynard, 67
Keynesianism, 62
KFH, (Rectors' Conference of the Swiss Universities of Applied Sciences), 117, 119
KMK (Standing Conference of the Ministers of Education and Cultural Affairs of the Länder in the Federal Republic of Germany/Kultusministerkonferenz), 13, 80, 82, 86, 88, 94, 265, 271
  scientific advisory body, 86, 94
Konstanz Agreement, 84
Kultusministerkonferenz (Germany), *see* KMK (Germany)

labor market, 5, 54, 62, 122–6, 160, 169, 171, 186, 192, 193
Leitideen, *see* national transformation capacities: guiding principles
LEONARDO, 217, 220
lifelong learning, 4, 261
Lisbon Qualification Recognition Convention, 172
Lisbon Strategy, 4, 6, 96, 138, 228, 237, 247, 252, 262, 270, 272
Locke, John, 55

M.A. (Master's degree), 4, 85, 87, 88, 95, 96, 112, 116, 123, 135, 138, 146–7, 186, 188, 190, 228, 264–5, 266, 268
Maori education strategy (New Zealand), 168–9
Master's degree, *see* M.A.

Index 281

misfit, 18, 19, 93, 94, 99, 120, 124, 127, 179, 193, 263, 266, 268–9, 272
mixed-method-approach, 19, 28–48, *see also* research design
 challenges of, 47
 definition of, 29
 degree of functional differentiation, 29
 dimensions: dimension of methods, 31–2; dimension of phenomena, 32; dimension of status, 32
 ideal-types of, 29
 implementation interdependence, 31, 32
 implementation timing, 31, 32, 45, 47
 methods applied, *see* document analysis, expert interviews, network analysis, quantitative regression analysis
 temporal logic, 29–30, 48
mixed-method-design, *see* mixed-method-approach
mobility, 4, 11, 81, 110–11, 113, 119–23, 126, 126, 186, 273, 275
MPK (Ministerpräsidentenkonferenz/ Conference of Prime Ministers) (Germany), 80

Nation at Risk, A (U.S.A.), 182, 185
National Assessment of Educational Progress (U.S.A.), 67
National Committee of Inquiry into Higher Education (England), 134
National Education Association (U.S.A.), 66
National Qualifications Framework (New Zealand), 159, 161
national transformation capacities, 4, 7, 12, 17, 19, 30, 34, 39, 42, 220, 230–2, 251, 262
 guiding principles, 12, 14–17, 229, 230, 239, 253, 265, 268, 272–3, 275, *see also* economic view on education: human capital, 15, 16, 156, 174; wealth of nations, 15, 16; self-fulfillment, 15, 16, 111; social right, 15, 16, 156, 174;

social duty, 15, 16, veto players, *compare* federalism, 12–14, 18, 199, 207–9, 211–12, 222–4, 229, 240–3, 253, 265, 268, 271–3
NCLB (No Child Left Behind Act) (U.S.A.), 183–4
network analysis, 19, 21, 37–41, 46, 199–224, *see also* political interaction, patterns of
 blockmodel analysis, 40, 209–11
 centrality, 40, 46, 208, 214
 clique analysis, 40
 density, 40, 205–8
 operationalization, 201–2
 positional change, 210–13, 217, 222–3
 structural change, 200, 203–6, 208, 222–3
network of methods, *see* mixed-method-approach
New York Times, The, 65–8
New Zealand, 21, 153–75
 Bologna Process, 154, 170–1, 267
 delta-convergence, 154
 education system, 153, 155–7, 174
 educational reforms, 157–69, 174–5
 exposure to IO governance, 20
 governance instruments, 154
 national transformation capacities, 154–5, 162–3, 173, 174
 PISA Study, 167–70, 267
 policy network, 217, 220–2
 veto players, 21
New Zealand Business Roundtable, *see* NZBRT
New Zealand Herald, 168
New Zealand Qualifications Authority, *see* NZQA
New Zealand Union of Students' Associations, *see* NZUSA
New Zealand Vice-Chancellors' Committee, *see* NZVCC
Newman, John Henry, 136
New-Math-Program (U.S.A.), 182
No Child Left Behind Act (U.S.A.), *see* NCLB
North Rhine-Westphalia, *see* NRW
NRW (North Rhine-Westphalia), 79, 90, 93, *see also* Germany

NZBRT (New Zealand Business Roundtable), 161
NZQA (New Zealand Qualifications Authority), 159, 161, 169, 172
NZUSA (New Zealand Union of Students' Associations), 161
NZVCC (New Zealand Vice-Chancellors' Committee), 161, 164, 172, 173

OAQ (Center of Accreditation and Quality Assurance of the Swiss Universities), 117, 119
OECD Centre for Educational Research and Innovation, 120
OFFA (Office for Fair Access) (England), 142
Office for Fair Access (England), see OFFA
OMC (Open Method of Coordination), 42, 228
Open Method of Coordination, see OMC
orientational frameworks, 13, 14, 19, 78–9, 94–6, 98–100, 120, 122, 125, 127, 133, 144, 149, 179, 193, 261, 269, 271, 275

path dependency, 53, 54, 62, 69, 205, 224, 230
PBRF (Performance Based Research Fund) (New Zealand), 164–5
Performance Based Research Fund (New Zealand), see PBRF
Ph.D. (Doctor of Philosophy), 4
Picot Report (New Zealand), 158, 162
PISA Study, 4, 5–6, 262
PolCon V (Political Constraints Index), 231, 242
policy convergence, 235–8, 268
  beta-convergence, 9, 230, 234–7, 251, 272–3
  delta-convergence, 9, 17, 18, 78, 100, 230, 234, 238, 242–3, 246, 251, 253
  sigma-convergence, 9, 230, 234–7, 242
political interaction, patterns of, 202–24

Programme for International Student Assessment, see PISA Study
PT-Ratio, 233, 235, 236, 239, 241, 247, 254
pupil-teacher ratios, see PT-Ratio

QA (quality assurance), 4, 8, 9, 11, 85, 86, 88, 91, 95, 98, 114, 117, 119, 122, 123, 125, 126, 138, 139, 142, 159, 161, 163–6, 171–2, 180, 186, 191, 193, 202, 212, 215, 216, 218–21, 266
quality assurance, see QA
Quality of Government Institute, 43
Quango (Quasi Nongovernmental Organization), 135, 157, 159, 162, 172
quantitative regression analysis, 19, 22, 41–5, 47, 227–55
  data collection, 230–1
  FE (fixed effect) models, 44, 234, 247, 248, 250, 272, 274
  operationalization, 230–3
  policy output and policy outcomes, 235–47, 272
  RE (random effect) models, 247–50

RAE (Research Assessment Exercise) (England), 141, 164
Rectors' Conference (Germany), 88
Rectors' Conference of the Swiss Universities, see CRUS
Rectors' Conference of the Swiss Universities of Applied Sciences, see KFH
Reform of Education Act (1989, New Zealand), 158
Research Assessment Exercise (England), see RAE
Research Councils (England), 141
research design, 19, 20, 273–4
  see also mixed-method-approach; validity, dealing with new analytical problems, 28
Robbins Report (1963, England), 136
Rousseau, Jean-Jacques, 55

SATS (Key Stage National Curriculum Test), 139–40

SBF (State Secretariat for Education and Research) (Switzerland), 107
Schließung, *see* Weber, Max: closure
school autonomy, 162, 235, 239–43, 245–6, 252–5
Schools Plus Strategy (New Zealand), 168–9
Schulkonkordat (Switzerland), *see* Concordance Treaty on School Coordination
self-transformation process, 6
Smith, Adam, 55–6
SOCRATES, 217
Sorbonne Declaration, *see* Bologna Process
Sputnik Shock, 181–2, 264
Standing Conference of the Ministers of Education and Cultural Affairs of the Länder in the Federal Republic of Germany, *see* KMK (Germany)
State Secretariat for Education and Research (Switzerland), *see* SBF
State's Ministry for Education and Cultural Affairs (Germany), 80
State's Ministry for Science and Research (Germany), 80
Structural Guidelines by the KMK (Germany), 88
SUK (Swiss University Conference), 117
Swiss Conference of Cantonal Ministers of Education, *see* EDK
Swiss Higher Education Landscape, 113, 118
Swiss University Conference, *see* SUK
Switzerland, 21, 105–27
  Bologna-Process, 106, 112, 116–19, 122–6, 215, 266
  education system, 107–12, 120
  educational reforms, 106, 113–19, 126, *see also* HarmoS, Switzerland: Bologna Process, PISA Study
  exposure to IO governance, 20–1
  governance instruments, 106, 119, 120–6
  guiding principles, *see* Switzerland: national transformation capacities

  national transformation capacities, 21, 106–7, 111, 113, 119, 121–7
  PISA Study, 105, 112, 114, 119–21, 124–6, 266, 269–70
  policy network, 215, 217–18
  veto players, *see* Switzerland: national transformation capacities

teaching hours, 239–42, 255
TEC (Tertiary Education Commission) (New Zealand), 164, 166, 220
Tertiary Education Commission (New Zealand), *see* TEC
Tertiary Education Strategy (New Zealand), *see* TES
TES (Tertiary Education Strategy) (New Zealand), 160, 166, 170
Third International Mathematics and Science Study, *see* TIMSS
Thomas Report (New Zealand), 155
time series cross-section regression models, *see* quantitative regression analysis
Times, The, 65–8
TIMSS (Third International Mathematics and Science Study), 84, 185
Tomorrow's Schools initiative (New Zealand), 158, 159, 161, 166
Trends-Reports (Bologna-Process), 11
TSCS (time series cross-section regression models), *see* quantitative regression analysis
Tsebelis, George, 13, 39, 172, 173
tuition fees, 9, 135, 142, 160–1, 175, 189
Tuning U.S.A. project, 192

UGC (University Grants Commission) (New Zealand), 160–1
UNESCO (United Nations Educational, Scientific and Cultural Organization), 43, 217, 262
UNESCO International Bureau of Education, 43

Union for Education and Science (Germany), *see* GEW
United Nations Educational, Scientific and Cultural Organization, *see* UNESCO
United States of America, *see* U.S.A.
Universities Act of 1961 (New Zealand), 155
University Academic Audit Unit (New Zealand), 161
university attendance in Europe, 60
University Grants Commission (New Zealand), *see* UGC
U.S.A. (United States of America), 21, 58, 179–93, 267–8
  Bologna Process, 181, 186–93, 268
  education system, 180–4
  PISA Study, 181, 185, 192–3, 267–9

validity, 28, 29, 36, 45, 47

Walls, Ernest, 67
Wealth of Nations, 55
Weber, Max, 28, 54, 56
  closure, 54
  western rationality, 54, 56
welfare, *see* welfare state
welfare regimes, 229, 231–2, 239–41, 243, 247, 253–4, 272, 274
welfare state, 5, 56, 62, 111, 136, 158, 232
western rationality, *see* Weber, Max: western rationality
White Paper (1998, New Zealand), 163
WHO (World Health Organization), 262
World Bank, 43, 217, 233, 262
World Health Organization, *see* WHO